China's Energy Security

THE DOMESTIC DISCUSSION

China's Energy Security

THE DOMESTIC DISCUSSION

PRACHI AGGARWAL

KNOWLEDGE WORLD
KW Publishers Pvt Ltd
New Delhi

ISBN 978-93-83649-53-2

Published in India by Kalpana Shukla

KNOWLEDGE WORLD
KW Publishers Pvt Ltd
4676/21, First Floor, Ansari Road, Daryaganj, New Delhi 110002
Phone: +91 11 23263498/43528107
Email: knowledgeworld@vsnl.net • www.kwpub.com

2011 FPBA BEST PUBLISHERS AWARD (ENGLISH)

Printed and Bound in India

To My Dearest Mummy

Dr. Renu Jain

Contents

List of Tables and Figures

Acknowledgements

This acknowledgement is not just an expression of gratitude but also a feeling of deep respect and honour for all those people who helped me to execute this work and complete it successfully. This work would not have seen the light of day had the support of various people not been involved in various stages of this work.

A special thanks to Dr. Srikanth Kondapalli for giving me valuable inputs throughout the period of work. This work, right from the title to the contents, has been nourished by valuable inputs and positive criticisms from him helping me from establishing a basic framework to settling the final details.

Another person who has been a reason for my resilience and perseverance throughout this work has been my mother, a source of constant support and inspiration. She mentored me in various forms, sometimes by helping with material, nursing me when I was sick or scolding me when I was lazy.

I would also like to take this opportunity of thanking my siblings especially my sister Shatakshi whose impromptu assistance sailed me through various troubled waters of technical snags, sudden mishaps and last-minute rushes. I also extend deep gratitude to the JNU library, for providing resource material and buying the CNKI database. This move helped me to access the rare Chinese sources which are available only in China.

This can be claimed to be my own work due to my good fortune of considering the above-mentioned people as my own family, teachers or friends. I thank God for being with me throughout this work in their disguises.

Abbreviations

APCO	Association of Public Safety Communications Officials
BP	British Petroleum
CAS	China's Academy of Sciences
CASS	Central Academy of Social Sciences
CBM	Coal Bed Methane
CCP	Chinese Communist Party
CCS	carbon capture and sequestration
CDM	Clean Development Mechanism
CDB	China Development Bank
CDT	China Datang Corporation Power Limited
CECIC	China Energy Conservation Investment Corporation
CEO	Chief Executive Officer
cfb	circulating fluidised bed
CGC	China Guodian Corporation
CGE	Computable General Equilibrium
CHD	China Huadian Corporation
ChinaCoal	China National Coal Group Corporation
CHNG	China Huaneng Group
CIC	China Investment Corporation
COFCO	China National Cereals, Oils and Foodstuffs Corporation
CNCIEC	China National Chemicals Import and Export Corporation
cng	compressed natural gas
CNLCMDC	China National Local Coal Mine Development Corporation
CNNC	China National Nuclear Corporation
CNOOC	China National Offshore Oil Corporation
CNPC	China National Petroleum Corporation
COD	Consumed Oxygen Demand
COSTIND	State Commission of Science Technology and Industry for National Defence
CPC	Communist Party of China
CPI	China Power Investment Corporation
CPPC	Chinese People Political Consultative Conferences
CREIA	China Renewable Energy Industries Association
CSEP	Communication Standardisation and Evaluation Programme
CSR	Corporate Social Responsibility
CSRC	China Securities Regulatory Commission
dme	dimethyl ether
DRC	Development Research Centre of State Council

DSM	Demand Side Management
EBT	Earnings Before Tax
EE	Energy Efficiency
ERI	Energy Research Institute
E's	Economy Ecology Equity
ESCO	Energy Saving Corporation
EU	European Union
Exim	China Export Import Bank
FDI	Foreign Direct Investment
GDP	Gross Domestic Product
GE	General Electric
GEF	Global Environment Facility
GHG	Green House Gases
Gj/tonne	Giga Joules per Tonne
GNP	Gross National Product
GPCR	Great Proletarian Cultural Revolution
GLF	Great Leap Forward
GW	Gigawatt
GWH	Gigawatt Hours
htgr	heightened gas cooled reactors
HSBC	Hongkong and Shanghai Banking Corporation Limited
IEA	International Energy Agency
ICBC	Industrial and Commercial Bank of China
IFC	International Financial Corporation
igcc	integrated coal gasification and combined cycle
IPO	Initial Public Offering
IRP	Integrated Resource Planning
JV	Joint Ventures
Km	Kilometre
kWh	Kilowatt hour
Ktpa	Kilo Tonnes per Annum
LNG	Liquefied Natural Gas
LPG	Liquefied Petroleum Gas
LSG	Leading Small Group
M&A	Mergers and Acquisitions
Mj/kWh	Mega Joules per Kilowatt hour
MLR	Ministry of Land and Resources
MOA	Ministry of Agriculture
MofCom	Ministry of Finance and Commerce
MOST	Ministry of Science and Technology
MW	Megawatt
MWR	Ministry of Water Resources
NDRC	National Development and Reform Commission
NEA	National Energy Administration
NEC	National Energy Commission
NELG	National Energy Leading Group
NIMUCIC	Northwest Inner Mongolia United Coal Industry Corporation

NOC	National Oil Corporations
NPC	National People's Congress
PBSC	Politbureau Standing Committee
PRC	People's Republic of China
PREEST	Population Resources Economy Environment Science and Technology
PV	Photovoltaic
pwr	pressurised water reactors
R&D	Research and Development
R's	Reduce Reuse Recycle
S&T	Science and Technology
SASAC	State Owned Assets Supervision and Administration Commission of the State Council
SDPC	State Development Planning Commission
SECIDC	State Energy Conservation Information Dissemination Centre
SEIC	State Energy Investment Corporation
SEI	Strategic Emerging Industries
SEPA	State Environment Protection Administration
SERC	State Electricity Regulatory Commission
SETC	State Economic and Trade Commission
Shenhua	China Shenhua Energy Company Limited
SINOPEC	China Petroleum and Chemical Corporation
SO2	Sulphur dioxide
SOE	State Owned Enterprises
SPC	State Power Corporation
SPR	Strategic Petroleum Reserves
CSQBTS	China State Bureau of Quality and Technical Supervision
SSTC	State Science and Technology Commission
SUV	Special Utility Vehicle
tce	Total carbon emissions
TWh	Terawatt Hours
uhv	Ultra high voltage
UNDP	United Nations Development Programme
US	United States
VAT	Value Added Tax
WTO	World Trade Organisation

1. Introduction

China has become synonymous with its economic pre-eminence and financial might. This not only cast China as the future superpower but also turned world attention to an Asian rise. Clearly, with China leading the growth entourage it would inevitably lead to questions of the tenacity and sustainability of its growth miracle. With voices of a slowing and sagging economy already simmering over the horizon it would be justified to explore the source of this growth miracle. That an economy thrives on energy sources is not an emphatic statement but a hard-felt realisation experienced by many governments of the world. Energy has been one of the core national interests of China since the day of its liberation. This has been proved as China established its Ministry of Petroleum Industry right after its liberation in the year 1949 itself (*Dangdai Zhongguo De Shiye Gongye*, 1988:629). It cannot be doubted that energy is the cradle of socio-economic development, and various forms of energy resources have played a unique but important role in the advent and progress of human civilisation. It has held different meanings not just in different civilisations but also in different perspectives. Hence, energy to be channelised in an effective manner requires a policy. A policy is defined as a plan or a course, as of a government, political party, or business intended to influence and determine decisions, actions and other matters (FreeDictionary.com. n.a). Energy policy is the way in which a given entity (usually governments of a nation) deals with issues of energy in production, consumption, methods of production and consumption, distribution, development, etc as defined in Wikipaedia. The attributes are usually mentioned through guidelines, work reports, government plans, etc. Basically energy policies are needed to fulfill the four basic tenets of

- Energy security
- Sustainable utilisation of energy
- Energy saving and energy efficiency
- Coordination between energy use and environmental protection.

Energy laws carry forward the basic principles of energy policies and their provisions are a blend of practical applications of various targets of the energy policies. A country's policies are often a reflection of the direction of the country's development, speed and achievement. The importance of energy in the growth (or even the existence) of a nation has been a ceaseless rhetoric since the oil shocks of the 1970s rocked the world. China—despite having defied many a contemporary praxis—is no exception. Energy dynamics of a nation are determined in two spheres: domestic and global resources of energy. The question of energy security in the domestic sphere is not just limited to exploring new sources of energy but also encompasses questions of energy efficiency, advanced technology and energy optimisation. This work tries to encompass energy issue not in its isolation but in the totality of the impact of economic growth and environmental deterioration.

When energy is in question the issue of "sustainable development" cannot be far behind. For most Chinese, sustainable development is another adage for "coordinated development." In attempting to quantify the coordination between energy economy and environment many definitions have been drawn about it. Hu Angang says, in one of his latest published books (*China: Innovating Green Development*) that he has drawn inspiration from ancient Chinese philosophy of coordination with nature, natural dialecticism in Mao Zedong's thought and from sustainable development (Correspondent Report in An Interview with Hu Angang, 2012:16). He believes that development with scientific concept constitutes green development and innovation (Ibid). The theory of sustainable development divided development into three aspects: namely, economic sustainability, environment sustainability and social sustainability. Wang Gehua (2005) in his book, *Energy and Sustainable Development*, highlighted the importance of synchronisation between energy and development (Zhao, 2008:16). High pollution rates has not only tarnished China's skyline or its international image but has also exponentially added on to its economic costs. Woetzel (2003:104) blames China's local producers and small-scale power plants who he says have taken tremendous advantage of supply bottlenecks and have contributed the maximum to "energy waste" and "environmental bottlenecks."

The study undertaken for this book was done with a view to finding plausible arguments or even some rudimentary solutions for the various questions which have been plaguing China's domestic energy sector for quite some time. The most common question about China's energy today is about its potential in the energy market and how much of energy it needs to sustain itself before delving into what it should do. However analysing this basic question requires a whole background of various other questions which need to be answered first. It involves a scrutiny of the current context of domestic energy conditions of China and how energy became an important factor in the road to China's development. What has been the course of energy policies and why are the priorities shifting with ensuing plans? What are the impacts of energy policies on China's political, economic and environmental conditions and the extent of influence and impact of the domestic determinants (both actors and factors) in the making of China's energy policies? It has been felt that there exists a divergence of interests of different determinants in the domestic decision-making, so can we assume that the domestic actors in China's energy sector are at variance with each other? Or maybe there is an inconsistency in the priorities of China's energy policies. But, if it is true, then why have these inconsistencies crept in a political stable country, or is it just a baseless rumour? Why has China been so obsessed with achieving self-sufficiency in energy and how can it do so now? More than self-sufficiency what needs to be probed is that if China's energy policies are directed at self-sufficiency of energy resources can they be achieved by optimum utilisation and acquisition?

Varied Viewpoints

There have been many debates regarding the approach to energy optimisation in China. The biggest contenders of this debate apart from all others in China are the *economic nationalists* versus the *economic liberalists.* These two archetypes reflect the dilemma which most states face in dealing with the question of energy security. Erica Downs in her dissertation on *Energy Security* writes explicitly about the two schools of thought.

The Liberalists

Economic liberalists (like Song Guoqing, etc.) believe that states should not interfere in energy markets. Free markets, by the liberalists, have always been vouched for as harbingers of efficiency most beneficial to the consumers and that states should produce energy based on the principle of comparative advantage. According to the liberalists efficiency should be aimed over self-sufficiency. Investment over scarce resources to promote self-sufficiency would do no help except to undermine economic sufficiency of a country. The nationality of energy companies is of no relevance to them. They believe that states should not involve themselves in promotion of their domestic companies. One of the foremost ways suggested by them to improve energy efficiency is in getting the prices "right."“Right” prices means to cover the cost of supply including the environment damages as a minimum. Fuel diversification (only if it makes economic sense) is another way suggested by them to reduce risk of energy starvation due to supply disruption (The above section is based on Downs, 2004).

Economic Nationalists

It is clearly evident that the current energy system of China is completely wary of the liberalists' theorem. In fact its approach corresponds more towards the *economic nationalists* especially through the strong voice of Hu Angang. The nationalists view regarding energy issues are starkly different from the liberalists. They believe that states' economics is determined by their politics and no state should risk the supply of important commodities, like energy resources, on comparative advantages. Thus, according to them, not only efficiency but self-sufficiency is also very important.

Self-sufficiency is achieved not by bringing in "low cost imports" say the economic nationalists but by subsidising "high cost" domestic products. This can be achieved only by state intervention. However, many analysts with nationalist leanings believe that "energy independence" is clearly a utopia and excessive subsidisation of domestic energy could undermine the economy and in turn the security of the nation. Since domestic energy companies are the nation's assets, control over ownership gives an assurance of undisrupted supply, capital and technology. Like the liberalists, nationalists too believe that supply of energy resources should be diversified; however, this does not undermine the importance of building strategic reserve piles to reduce imports as well as an assurance of energy efficiency. Though nationalists encourage fuel diversification they differ with liberalists on the account that security fears prevail over economic sense, i.e., coal would be used to substitute oil even though it is cheaper to import oil.

Again, though they encourage the gains of keeping energy prices "right" of lower energy imports and lower energy import bills, they prefer to keep the energy prices "wrong," i.e., price not reflecting the real cost of supply or externalities. They may manipulate price to encourage exploration or subsidisation.

One point where perhaps all theorists converge is the improvement of energy efficiency by effectively utilising energy intensity (i.e., amount of energy consumed per unit GDP). However this does not mean that they advocate reduced trade for energy transactions. Though no state adheres to only one spectrum of thought, China heavily borders on practising the nationalist perspective in their energy policies. The country's energy policy is determined by the Party State in consultation with its various agencies like National Development and Reform Commission, domestic energy companies, etc. The table below sums up the differences between economic liberalists and economic nationalists. (The above section is based on Downs, 2004)

Table 1.1: Economic Liberalists versus Economic Nationalists

Liberalism	Nationalism
States should not interfere in energy market	State intervention is absolutely necessary
Energy efficiency should be aimed at over self-sufficiency	Self-sufficiency is more important
Nationality of energy companies is of no relevance	State ownership of domestic energy companies is extremely important
Getting the prices "right"	Getting the prices "wrong"
Fuel diversification	Strategic pile reserves
Economic sense is supreme	Security fears prevail
Few takers of this theory among the Chinese but gaining ground like Song Guoqing, etc.	Vociferous Chinese supporters of this theory like Hu Angang, Yu Min, etc.

Source: Downs (2004).

Another understanding of energy issues is provided by the various energy economy policies which are basically derived from *energy economics theories*. These theories aim to solve the demand and supply gap in energy resources. In fact the first link between energy consumption and economic growth was studied by Kraft J and Kraft A in the 1970s. On similar lines a research was conducted in 2005 by Chinese scholars, Ma Hongwei and Zhang Tiaohui, who analysed the relationship between energy consumption and GDP in totality as well as of every industrial sector. In 2006 Zhao Yiping et. al realised that the characteristics of "decoupling theory" existed in its weak form in China. For a country in the midst of heavy industrialisation, urbanisation, globalisation and aiming to achieve well-off society, the pressure on energy consumption and environment were too much to avoid. Li Yongfeng (2004) believes that this link-up between energy consumption and economic growth is intricate and is not a mere exponent of cause and effect relationship. The energy efficiency of a product or a service on improvement will reduce the nominal energy consumption, but traditional view ignores declining energy prices and, alternatively, favours declining costs in energy usage causing a rebound effect in demand. This means that when efficiency of energy increases, it causes a relative fall in prices. Macroeconomists respond to this by increasing usage for better output and reduced costs of production for an overall economic increase (The above paragraph is taken from Zhao, 2008:6-15).

Wang et. al. (2012:70-72), Ji Jianjun (2011:26-27) and others have analysed the energy policies of China from a historical perspective where they have clubbed the policies based on the prevailing political ideologies of that time. The period between 1949 till the death of Mao which most people dub as the pre-reform era has been called as the era of self-reliance and self-sufficiency. It was a time when China had been stricken by scourges of external war and internal aggression and was practically isolated by almost all nations except some Soviet benevolence. Hence whether it was out of compulsion or out of ideology that China chose to be self-reliant is a matter of debate. The reform era has been called by them as multi-pluralistic energy development strategy which perhaps served the liberalists more than the nationalists though not *in toto*.

It oversaw a number of changes as ministries transformed into corporate, prices began to reflect the economic reality although regulation was still maintained and earning profits became a matter of glory rather than a political taboo. It was also a time which had witnessed the international oil crisis of 1973 and was feeling the heat even in domestic reserves. Thus, despite a liberalist approach, it maintained and in fact enhanced the levels of strategic petroleum reserves in China. However for Wang Qingyi (n.a:25) the cause for celebration is not the economy but the environment as he extols the highlighting of working with scientific concept and energy conservation. However, not all seem enamoured by the reform era as Ji Jianjun discusses the transportation costs which exacerbated after the government resorted to fully fledged economic development especially of the coastal areas. Tian and Wu (2005) are also not too happy with the era of the 1980s and 1990s which they believed continued the historical tradition of lacking in scientific temper and less investment which eventually led to China becoming an importer of energy.

It has been observed that literature on China's energy issues (both western and Chinese) widely believes that energy problem does not stand as a singular issue and cannot be analysed without encompassing the economic and environmental impact on its policy-making. This also means that energy analysts too have to widen their horizon in dealing with energy dynamics of the nation. Again it is imperative for other analysts too to understand the energy system before drawing conclusions and predictions over economy, policy or environment. APCO Worldwide (2011) talks about the current energy situation of China and future initiatives of China's energy policies. By taking the example of the Twelfth Five Year Plan it clearly outlines the government's focus on maintaining the environment quality and bringing in the industry and the market to assist in this direction rather than vice versa. However Wei Zhihong (2004) is not too upbeat about building renewable energy as a "one-stop" solution to the energy-environment dilemma. He cites environmental disasters and limitations to production as reasons for his non-appreciation of the renewable sector. Rosen and Houser (2007) have talked at great length about the trilogy of price, demand and market influencing the energy sector and in turn its policies.

Different Types of Energy Resources

Modern Chinese Dictionary (2009:990) defines energy resources as substances that can produce energy such as fuel, water, wind, etc. The destiny for China's energy is determined by its policy and for that it is imperative to understand what a policy is. *Oxford Dictionary (1992)* defines policy as "a course or principle of action adopted or proposed by an organisation or individual"; in short, policies guide our actions. They can be in the form of laws, rules, regulations, etc.

In the table below, energy is divided into two types: first level of energy resources (*yi ci nengyuan*一次能源) and second level of energy resources (*er ci nengyuan*二次能源). While the first level of energy resources are formed naturally, the second level of energy resources are formed after processing the first level of energy resources. The first level of energy resources are divided into conventional and non-conventional forms of energy. Conventional energy is divided into forms of commercial energy and non-commercial energy (traditional energy). Forms of commercial energy are large-scale water harnessing, nuclear and geothermal energy and crude oil. Non-commercial energy forms are primarily made by organic material. The non-conventional forms of energy are basically the new energy resources which have been released from processing renewable forms of energy and by processing of fossil fuels using advanced technology. The second level of energy resources are the coal and oil products derived from crude oil and coal (Cai, 2007).

Table 1.2: Different Types of Energy Resources

<table>
<tr><th>Type</th><th colspan="2"></th><th>Renewable energy</th><th>Non-renewable energy</th></tr>
<tr><td rowspan="2">First level of energy resources</td><td rowspan="2">Conventional energy</td><td>Commercial energy</td><td>Large-scale water harnessing, nuclear energy, geothermal energy</td><td>Burning of fossil fuels</td></tr>
<tr><td>Traditional energy</td><td>Organic material (firewood, straw, dung, etc.) Solar energy, water conservancy, wind power</td><td></td></tr>
<tr><td></td><td>Non-conventional energy</td><td>New energy resources</td><td>Methane released from burning organic material, ethyl alcohol, small-scale water harnessing, solar equipment, wind power, oceanic power and geothermal energy</td><td></td></tr>
<tr><td>Second level of energy resources</td><td colspan="4">Coal products—washed coal, gas, coking, oil products</td></tr>
</table>

Source: Cai, 2007: 5.

The above table shows that energy can be classified into various categories:

- Primary energy and secondary energy—primary energy is anything which exists in nature in its natural form and releases its energy capacity after being processed by humans. It involves fossil fuels like coal, crude, gas as well as natural ecological forms of energy like water, wind, solar energy, geothermal energy, oceanic energy, etc. Secondary form of energy resources are the products of original energy sources like coal and petroleum products, electricity, etc.
- Conventional and non-conventional forms of energy resources—energy gets classified here based on the historical time frame and technological expertise. Those forms of energy which have been used for a long period of time but with primitive technological expertise have been dubbed as conventional forms of energy and those energy resources which have begun to be employed only recently based on advanced technological resources are called non-conventional forms of energy. Conventional forms of energy are fossil fuels, hydropower, and new energy resources

are solar, wind, and geothermal, oceanic, etc. In the context of nuclear energy it is debatable whether to put it as conventional or non-conventional form of energy.

- Renewable and non-renewable forms of energy—those forms of energy which exist in a certain quantity and cannot be created are called non-renewable forms of energy and vice versa are the renewable forms. Renewable form of energy is like water resources, etc., and non-renewable forms of energy are fossil fuels, nuclear energy, etc. (Zhou Li, 2009:14).

Evolution of China's Energy Policies

Right from the period of liberation China has made energy development as one of its priority issues. Various tools like five year plans, long-term and short-term policies, laws and legislations, specific policy measures have maintained a continuous focus on development of energy resources. However the policies and the realities have always faced a tussle with each other, each trying to adjust and redefine the other to its own advantage.

- **Plan period:** This was a time when command economy was in vogue and both the supply and demand had a politically destined number. It was a time when the government played a key role in the planning of almost every aspect of China's present and future course which meant that the energy enterprises were completely centralised and had an assurance of survival regardless of production or business performance. It was the "pre-reform phase"—an era of closed development where self-sufficiency was the main motive (Wang et. al, 2012: 70), However the pace of development was slow. It was an exploratory phase where China coupled with Soviet technology was becoming aware of its own potential and "energy." Yet this period was also marked by lack of experience, political turmoil and high eulogising of "Mao thought," even in scientific and practical matters, that it led to large-scale inefficiency, wastage of resources and destruction of the environment (Ji, 2011: 26). In fact this period can be summed up in the following points: strive for self-sufficiency, single plan, simple policy, low energy efficiency, backward technology, and weak environmental awareness (Ibid).
- **Reform period:** "Reforms" of 1978 not only brought changes in the economy and politics of China but also in the thinking of the government and the people towards energy resources. Energy now became an important factor and commodity in the strategy of enhancing the socio-economic development of the nation (Ji, 2011:71). Energy industry now began to incorporate the adjustments of the market in determining

their production and consumption structure and major price reforms were introduced in coal, oil and electricity prices. Lessons were now learnt from foreign experiences and coal industry was released from tight central control, national oil companies were formed and state electricity grids were given more autonomy. (Dangdai Zhongguo de Shiye Gongye, 1988). Moreover it was also a period when investment became pluralistic, international cooperation in the energy fields was encouraged and energy conservation became an important part of the energy programme. The decade of the 1980s had begun with a slogan of "giving priority to energy conservation in the fight between energy conservation and development." (Zhao 2001:6). This period also saw the passage of many laws in favour of environment protection, laying the route for a policy for "sustainable development." (Wang et. al, 2012: 71)

- **The Tenth Five Year Plan onwards:** A period of maturity and holistic development. Energy policies since the Tenth Five Year Plan have become more streamlined in their aim of not only what they want to do but also what not to do in their drive for self-sufficiency. The policies of the recent times have focused on ensuring energy security, optimising energy structure, enhance energy efficiency, protecting ecological environment, continue to expand opening up and accelerate development of the western area. (*White Paper on Energy*, 2007) It was in 2005 that the Energy Leading Group and a Renewable Energy Law was passed charting the course of future energy policies of China. Yet years of experience and unrelenting reliance on high consumption of material resources has highlighted that China still follows the extensive mode of growth, which possesses the characteristics of high investment, high consumption, high emissions, and uncoordinated, non-recycled, low efficiency. (Wang et. al, 2012:71) By the Eleventh Five Year Plan the directions of action were "guided by the theory of Deng Xiaoping" and the "Three Represents," utilising the scientific development concept and harmonious society to oversee the work of energy, assiduously build up a clean, stable and economic energy structure and through the sustainable development of energy support the socio-economic sustainability of China (Ma Kai, 2006).The Twelfth Five Year Plan explicitly details its energy aims "To establish a secure, stable, economic and clean modern energy production structure." (*China's Energy Policy*, 2012)

The four words secure, stable, economic and clean are now considered the main support of China's energy structure which reveals to us the inherent interdependence of economy and environment ensconced in the policies made to preserve the stability and security of energy. The figure below sums up the trend analysis of energy policies of China highlighting the characteristics of various phases of energy policies while at the same time maintaining a relationship of cocooning and nurturing the previous as well as the future policies of China. This meant that no matter how diverse the opinion was during the changing phases of energy policies, the subtle thread of unity lay among them where the later policies drew inspiration from the energy policies of yesteryear.

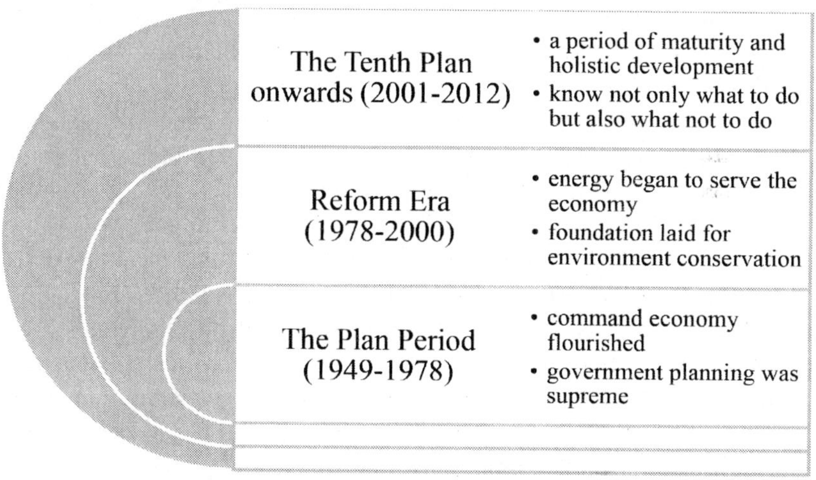

However policies are not formed in isolation of various pressure groups, and energy policies are no exception. Six major domestic determinants (actors and factors, three each) have been identified which have been instrumental in both giving directions to and getting directed by energy policies of China. They not only determine the domestic sphere of influence but also bear influence on the overseas activities of China in the energy sphere. However for the purpose of this study this aspect has not been discussed and neither has the role of extraneous factors like foreign governments, institutions or corporations been calculated. The identified determinants are:

- *Bureaucratic Control:* In China the party and the government are considered synonymous to each other yet hold difference of aspirations in their functioning. The CCP during the liberation period held a very strong influence on the government and political ideologies had strong bureaucratic bearings. Moreover at this time China itself was in a bewildered state and apart from its specified targets had no framework for any sort of government institutional functioning. China's energy production oscillated between the pinnacles of "learn from Daqing" to the nadirs of "Cultural Revolution" till the abolishment of energy ministry in 1993. Since then the energy sector operates under the NDRC. Issues related to why the energy ministry was abolished and never got reconstituted will be discussed here. Moreover the influence of changing political ideologies on the various ministries of China and vice versa shall also be pursued here. The nexus of Small Leading Group and Politburo control and the issues related to government diktat, the local governments, will be talked about. Also the institutionalisation of NDRC and the power struggle between NEA and NEC will also be highlighted.

- *Energy companies:* Most fossil fuel energy companies in China were formed out of conversion of ministries and hence their functioning still depends largely on government and its policies. This is not to say that they have no autonomy of their own or government's will is their command. In fact it is analysed that a mutual understanding exists between the government and these corporates which is reflected in the energy policies. While most equate national oil companies as the only worthwhile energy enterprises in China this work shall also delve into various coal and power companies who have a subtle but unique bearing on government psyche. A special mention has also been made of various renewable energy companies who mostly have been in the private sector but have created enough ripples in both domestic and international market to make the government rise from its "inactive state" and look up to it as a future potential.
- *Market mechanism:* Energy resources can be utilised in two forms either as an end product or as a raw material. The market of energy too maintains these two distinctions. While it is easy to administer production through bureaucratic control and association with energy companies it is tough to determine the vagaries of the market and demand of the consumers. Market for each energy resource shall be discussed separately in consonance with the income elasticity, price, GDP and other economic variables. China has ridden on its high energy consumption industries to become the "factory of the world." Issues of energy intensity in such industries along with the questions of "why China can produce" shall be addressed here. The impact of levels of investment, price reforms and international petrol price rise on the domestic energy market cannot go unnoticed here.

- *Environment:* Energy and environment have long been seen as potential enemies where the prosperity of one sounds the death knell for the other. Having said so, it is also true that both have a strong bearing on the economy and isolating one at the cost of the other is an impending disaster no matter from which side it happens. Recently various studies have been initiated to draw a solution of harmony between energy, economy and environment and lay a strong foundation for concrete progress in the theory of "sustainable development" and "well-off society." There has been a spate of laws related to environment protection and construction of renewable energy hinting on future endeavours of the government. This section shall cover the topic of energy efficiency and differences in regional intensity across provinces and across time. The correlation between energy companies and environment which is an annual feature of their sustainability report shall also be examined. The provisions of various environment laws which have stood both for and against the energy policies will also be categorised.
- *Advanced technology:* Technology can be a big factor in determining the direction of energy development. While Soviet technology had helped to explore fossil fuels and laid the foundations of a coal structure it could never pave the way for what China really wanted, i.e., technical prowess (*Dangdai Zhongguo de Shiyou Gongye*, 1988:631).When China now decides to shift to a structure of "low carbon economy," which it defines as a sustainable development mode of low energy consumption, low pollution, and low emission involving various industries on clean energy, industrial energy conservation, high efficient energy conversion, energy storage devices and carbon capture and storage, it needs to break its shackles of technical backwardness and adopt large-scale usage of advanced technology whether through foreign import or domestic innovation (Zhang, 2009:1). Various economic initiatives and political measures are discussed here which strive for optimisation of resources especially in the solar industry.
- *Consumers:* Having identified the different type of consumers, the rising living standards of China's consumers is the main theme here. Are they actual determinants of production and consumption of China or they are just at the receiving end. Can they make a contribution in alleviating energy scarcity scare or are they mere passive viewers, or rather victims as China gets embroiled in the typhoon of gluttonous demand and dwindling resources, are some of the questions which will be answered here.

Perceptions on Determinants

Yu and Houlden (2013) argued that bureaucracy as a determinant has stemmed from history. They have identified the trajectory of energy in political and government circles and the reason why energy was given so much of importance by the bureaucracy. However Zhao (2001) prefers to discuss the period after the reforms and the politics of the 1980s and the 1990s which was fluctuating in nature and witnessed a period of not only economic explosion but also energy scarcity. In this Downs (2008) makes an analysis of why the energy ministry was dissolved and especially at a juncture when it was needed the most. Lee (2012) on the other hand takes the route of the party analysis and its hierarchical set-up to draw a conclusion on the real decision-makers within the government. Martin (2010) (taken from Lee (2012)) also believes that the government and the party in China cannot be bonded into watertight compartments and analysing any one makes it imperative to understand the other.

However Burke et. al. (2009) have analysed NDRC under whose direct scrutiny is energy and analysing its inner politics is a faster and better approach than taking a bird's eye view of the party. Qiu and Li (2012) also second it giving in detail the institutional framework of NEA and NEC. Liberthal and Oksenberg (1998) too blame the internal power struggle causing discrepancies and weakness in energy policies. However Rosen and Houser (2007) feel that the tussle is not only political but also economic in nature causing intra-regional rivalry due to increasing economic gap. In another opinion Yu (2010) and Qiu and Li (2012) feel that the flaw lies at the legal level which causes overlapping of jurisdiction resulting in conflict. However, another kind of tussle has been analysed by Major Lee (2010) and Lewis (2007) which is more professional than political, i.e., the struggle for influence over the government between the national oil companies. CNPC, Sinopec and CNOOC have not only shaped the present of China but also possess the power to determine its future despite their dwindling resource. However Xu (2008) and Downs (2008) are quite sceptical of this professional relationship which they believe is sometimes detrimental to national interests. Wang (2012) also supports this scepticism as he feels that despite tall claims of production China's imports have been escalating unabated. Liu (2003) also feels that despite coal being in dominant position China's energy mix has shifted its base from coal to oil.

However Chen (2008) seeks interest in coal and power companies which till date form the bulwark of China's energy structure. Mathews and Tan (2012) believe that China has already reached its peak position in coal consumption and nothing new is left to explore. Austin (2005) discusses

China's energy issues from the investor point of view which she believes not only have the opportunity of profit but also the compulsion of maximum risks while investing. Song and Zheng (2012) also explore the various economic variables like capital, income, price in relation to energy. However Zhao (2001) makes a distinction between prices of the pre-reform era and that of reform era. Yi et. al. (2007) too draws a periodic analysis of the relation between energy consumption, investment and economic growth. They focus less on foreign investment but on various domestic sources of investment which are mostly also the consumers of energy. Yan et. al. (2009) too reiterates the findings of Yi. In fact rising energy prices at an international level have brought out a lot of response from energy analysts. Yang (2005) dubs it as a starting point of future instability, uncertainty and threat.

On a similar spectrum have been the researches on environment conditions of China in relation to energy. Zhou (2009) believes that after the economic growth it is time that environment is also developed, based on Chinese characteristics rather than blindly aping the West. Wu (2011) compares China's environment conditions not only related to other nations but also amongst its own undeveloped and developed provinces. Hyung and Seong (2006) think that in analysing the relationship of energy and environment all other determinants like state, market and companies should also be kept into the focal point. Song and Zheng (2012) find the difference in regional efficiency by introducing an energy gap variable. In an interview to Xia Lihong (2012) Ceng Xinqiu reiterates that actual energy development can be achieved only by bridging the energy availability gap between the rich and poor, urban and rural, etc. Ling et. al. (2010) too believes that the wave of urbanisation and rising living standards have sparked a lifestyle which is strewn with high energy consumption expanding the energy consumer base in China. This is seconded by Churchill (1993) who also feels that resorting to energy efficiency is the actual cause for increase in energy consumption. Tao and Xue (2008) on the other hand feel that it is the tax factor which is responsible for changes in energy consumption by the consumers. Cui and Wang (2010) says that it is not one factor but a plethora of factors ranging from production to consumption, prices to income and politics to business which determines the energy structure of China.

Having identified various domestic determinants we shall attempt to draw an analysis of the complex relationship between them through various prevalent models like the CGE model (Wei, 2009), PREEST model (Cai, 2007), etc. Domestic determinants not only carry an impact on the provisions of various energy policies but also other policies which in turn have a bearing on the energy policies. Lester and Steinfeld (2007) are not too happy with the ground realities in China and highlight the hold of the local governments and the bureaucracy as the major determinant overriding all other determinants in China. Xiao Guoxing (2010) too highlights the discrepancies and the status of energy in China's legislation both in itself and in comparison with other policies which are formulated by the governments at all levels.

There has been a debate among many energy economists regarding how far China has been able to decouple itself, i.e., ability to sustain economic growth without being affected by negative impact of environmental conditions. Thus the ratio of "economic gains" to "environmental losses" in the energy market has now begun to gain ground beyond intellectual debates and boardroom conferences. The Greenpeace Report by Fang Lifeng (2013) analyses the decoupling effect of economic growth on energy industry and specially that of coal which is the base of China's energy basket. Lee (2012) on the other hand believes that China's energy strategy is less based on decoupling and more on hedging strategy where supply is the main focus. Also the environmental costs in achieving economic profits are also identified of each industry by Zhao (2008). In all this the role of renewable energy is discussed in detail identifying the pros and cons of developing each renewable resource. He is also a bit sceptical of considering renewable sector as a foolproof method for conserving the environment and highlights the negative impact of renewable sector if the production techniques are not used carefully. Xina Xie (2010) on the other hand has taken interest in exploring the complex relationship between China's domestic energy companies and rising prices which she believes are not just an outcome of market vagaries but a connivance between corporate and government officials to gain more export at the international front and more profit at the domestic front. Leung (2011) on the other hand believes that energy security issue has attained a larger than life image and has deviated from the government from focusing on the real issue of achieving self-sufficiency. At this juncture it is also imperative to read the regional capacities of China and analyse their losses and gains, not just based on their own economic and ecological activity but also of their neighbouring provinces, done by Wu and Li (1995). Chen et. al. (2011) has also attempted to draw an analysis of intra-regional energy production and consumption based on regional capacities.

The nexus between market, investment and technology is also considered especially when the latest policies have begun to harp about "green GDP" and "green trade," in this case the direction of energy investments both domestic and foreign have been analysed by Pang et. al. (2011). They have also highlighted the risks of Chinese domestic market which are often on the "leeward side" due to the glitter of the economic growth. Wang and He (2009) transfer their focus on technology affecting energy intensity, efficiency, industry and eventually the market. Sinton et. al. (1998) and Chen and Lin (2008) talk about optimum utilisation whether in fossil or non-fossil fuels as an answer to reduce energy intensity and eventually consumption. Andrews (2013) considers economic motives to spear application on this direction by both residential and commercial users of energy. Gangadar (2012) has laid her focus on nuclear energy which they believe is lying dormant only because of environmental apprehensions, and the right kind of technology can mitigate the panic. While rising living standards have often been blamed for creating the scarcity scare, Swartz and Oster (2010) have believed that this is a natural phenomenon and like all other developed nations, China's voracious demands shall also peak and then begun to decline.

Lastly the provisions of the latest White Paper on energy security, how much China pollutes for production for other countries and what it can learn from other countries, is also discussed here. Li (2003) in an interview cites Chen Xinhua as a vociferous supporter of domestic determinants in being the major stakeholders of China's energy policies. He believes that although China's energy policies are getting increasingly affected by international aspects of China's energy policies, yet it cannot be denied that the actual impact is that of the domestic determinants. However Fan (2006) thinks that China has still a long way to go in solving its energy dilemma and should in the meantime learn from the experiences of other developed nations.

The Beginning

The book was written as an attempt in understanding the different kinds of energy, different schools of thought for energy policies and different energy policies of China. Analysing the literature regarding the energy policies of China led to examining the theories of economic nationalism and economic liberalism in the context of energy policies. Any theory needs to stand the test of practical reality and China's energy policies have gone through myriad changes to provide a dais for testing of international energy theories. Hence, the trajectory of China's energy policies and its changing priorities during various circumstances and change in leadership has been constituted as the very first chapter of this book. It shall also analyse the focus of various five year plans in the context of energy and China's transformation from being an exporter to becoming a net importer of energy. It shall also analyse the shift of energy policies from targeting energy production, to targeting energy efficiency, while maintaining their aim of self-sufficiency in the energy market. The changing priorities from conservation of energy resources to reduction in energy intensity and then to innovation in production and utilisation of energy resources to achieve the aim of self-sufficiency will be discussed in this chapter.

It is evidently clear that China's energy policies have abided by the maxim of "change is the only constant." However a larger issue (which incidentally is also the main theme of the book) is that *who or what can make those changes?* It would be too simplistic to believe that only people or, on the other hand, only circumstances can determine or alter the prevailing ordain. No country can function by clinging on only part of the spectrum and China is no exception. The book has outlined six determinants which can guide or influence the direction of energy policies. However a distinction between energy actors and factors has been taken to evaluate the scope of influence and limitations of each determinant. The determinants identified are bureaucratic control, energy companies, and consumers as the actors which can be influential over China's energy policies. However this is not to say that China can evade its domestic compulsions or be wary of its interactions with the globalised world while formulating its energy policies. Hence another set of determinants has been listed which have been constituted as the factors which play a decisive role in shaping the energy structure and henceforth the policy of China. They are the market mechanism, environment and advanced technology. A relation between the changing domestic situation of China and the position of speakers in influencing the energy policies of China has been drawn constituting the last but the most important chapter of this book.

It shall talk about the way the domestic determinants impact and influence the energy policies of China as well as in turn get affected by them. It shall discuss about the various models which analyse the connection between the determinants. A separate analysis of each major energy resource in context of the identified determinants shall also be done. Moreover the issue of energy laws and various other laws which though unrelated to energy but can affect its policies are also taken up. Lastly the discrepancies between various regions in the context of energy intensity and other issues of China learning from other countries instead of just competing are also raked up.

The concluding section outlines the main conclusions on China's energy policies and various decision-makers.

2. Historical Vicissitudes of China's Energy Policy

This chapter delves into the history of energy (since 1949) in China, history of not energy as a resource but history of when and how energy became a resourceful factor in China's growth trajectory. When and why did energy become an issue of discussion? How did it become an issue requiring specialised experts and department for formulation of its policy? Was it only the scarcity scare? But China exported energy till the early 1990's, then why did the leaders think of conservation as early as 1978? Did the base laid by Mao Zedong in China's energy structure hold worth or was he short-sighted? Did Deng Xiaoping exchange economic growth for energy starvation? Was Mao a better visionary in championing the environmental cause? Answers to all these questions are weighed down by opinions, by different conclusions due to different methods used for assessment and also, perhaps subtly, by the experts' own predilection for a certain time frame.

A policy of a country especially its basic policies are guidelines to a country's direction, speed and success of the development of that nation (Ji, 2011:1). Energy policy of any country is an important aspect of its decision making and China is no exception. It is a mirror to the emphasis, research and development of the energy resources of that country.

Throughout history China's energy policies have been instrumental in determining the speed and capacity of energy cultivation, the basic changes in the energy structure, the pattern of energy development, the R&D of energy technology and other important aspects related to the energy field. Liu Zhiyan and others have defined energy security as "a nation or a region enjoying an adequate supply of energy in order to ensure sustainable economic and social development" (Liu et. al., 2008:3). Another paper highlights the complexities associated with formulation of energy policies: "the formulation of energy policies is an extremely complicated process, especially because energy policies have a widespread impact on society. It involves the difficulties of coordination between different departments, the different appeals of collective interests as well as the varied market information which are often misleading" (CASS, 2006:36 cited in Wang et. al., 2012). It is also true that energy policies can also not be oblivious to prevailing domestic conditions and the changing international environment around.

China's energy policies have gone through the rigmarole of constant adjustment and restructuring subjected and changed according to changing requirements and conditions of China's energy demands. Hence it can be divided into three phases:

The First Period (1949-1978)

Self-sufficiency and Energy Policies of China

The first period belonged to the command economy and believed in the spirit of self-reliance, planned structure, simple policy, low consumption, backward technology and low awareness about the environment (Ji, 2011: 26). It was an environment when industrialisation developed at a slow pace within a closed and confined space. It was a phase of exploration where the industries produced only to survive and there was little incentive to optimise quality more than quantity. On September 25, 1949 Yumen oilfields were liberated *(Dangdai Zhongguo De Shiyou Gongye,* 1988:629) and on the historic day of October 1, 1949 both the People's Republic of China and Ministry of Petroleum Industry were created together (Ibid). Foundations were laid in the ensuing period as by March 20-27, 1950 the basic principles of exploration of oilfields were discussed, also planning was made for exploration between the period 1950 to 1952 (Ibid). Many dignitaries from Beijing and Russian experts visited the conference. It led to the establishment of Sino-Russian Petroleum Share Company (Ibid). On April 13, 1950 the first Industrial Petroleum Conference was promulgated issuing guidelines and tasks for China's Petroleum Industry (Ibid: 630). Petroleum Administrative Bureau was set up in the North West where quality scientists dealing in petroleum exploitation were to be nurtured and by 1951 exploration in Shanxi had begun (Ibid). In the trial period of the First Five Year Plan, i.e., during 1952 to late 1953, Soviet help was greatly encouraged and appreciated as Mao Zedong authorised the ninetenth battalion of the People's Liberation Army to undertake exploratory engineering of the petroleum industry (Ibid: 630). A Summit meeting regarding specifications for oil products was held in Beijing where two drafts were issued, namely, "all China temporary standards for petroleum products specifications" and "all China temporary standards for trial methods of petroleum products." (Ibid: 631) By November 1953 Russian experts at the invitation of China investigated Gansu petroleum resources to assess its utility for Lanzhou electrical factory (Ibid). By now the targets had been set and from March 1954 the First Five Year Plan set down its exploration tasks: intensify exploration at Sichuan basin and to continue in other places in order to pave the way for the Second Five Year Plan (Ibid: 632). The date of July 30, 1955 dismissed the Industrial Fuel Department and in its place established the Industrial Petroleum Department, Crude Coal Department and Electricity Department (Ibid: 633). In February 1956 Ministry of Petroleum Industry at the summit meeting in Beijing proclaimed its aim to "concentrated efforts to be made to explore large basins both on surface and underground" and on March 6, 1956 Chen Yun announced the target for the search of two large basins within a span of two to three years (Ibid). The Eighth National Congress spoke about the contradiction not between the proletariat and bourgeoisie but the contradiction between need and the requirement for economic and cultural development. "The chief task confronting the entire nation was to concentrate all efforts on developing the productive forces, industrialising the country and gradually meeting the people's growing economic and cultural needs" (Report of Eighth National Congress, 1956).

The newly liberated China in 1949 was confronted with two major arduous tasks: restoration of production and re-establishment of society. The role of energy in this mission was to build up the economy and ensure a guaranteed supply of energy to maintain the country's security. The period from liberation to reformation (1949-1978) worked under the dictum of self-reliance and self-sufficiency (*zi li geng sheng zi ji zi zu*) (Wang et. al., 2012:70). This policy of China led it into making great strides in the energy sector as it opened up new vistas of energy resources in its domestic domain. At a time when oil had begun to dictate its terms over other energy resources Xinhua reports of the establishment of Yumen oil deposits as China's first natural oil base in October 1957 (Dangdai Zhongguo *De Shiyou Gongye*, 1988: 634) and the Daqing discovery of 1959 (Wang et. al, 2012:70) were obviously considered as the biggest accolades and celebrated victory across China, as it marked the end of impoverishment of China in the oil domain and laid the foundations of its petroleum department. During the end of February 1958, Deng Xiaoping gave the basic thought and principles behind exploration and industrial production of energy resources *(Dangdai Zhongguo De Shiyou Gongye*, 1988: 635) which he believed should be like a good assault relying on the combination of strategy, campaign and tactic and the ensuing visit of Zhu De to various oilfields began to give momentum to the exploration phase of China, especially for oil (*Dangdai Zhongguo De Shiyou Gongye*, 1988: 635). Although the policy of reliance on iron and steel (*yi gang wei gang*) (Wang et. al, 2012:70) in the Great Leap Forward of 1958 and the Cultural Revolution of 1966 did wreak havoc on China's economic structure, yet the principle of self-reliance and self-sufficiency of the energy policy never changed and domestic production was more or less able to satisfy the domestic requirements of society, sometimes even generating a recurrent surplus. Perhaps that is why the international oil crisis of 1973 could not collapse the rudimentary energy structure which China had begun to build just a few years earlier (Ibid). With the rock solid production of its various oilfields China was cushioned from the volatilities of oil prices in the international market. The "learn from Daqing" model now engulfed the government as many important dignitaries made frequent visits to it. Deng Xiaoping's visit of Daqing as the party secretary in 1961, and then that of Premier Zhou Enlai on June 21, 1962 (*Dangdai Zhongguo De Shiyou Gongye*, 1988:638), was encouragement for local officials to replicate the Daqing example in other parts of China. In fact on December 3, 1963, Zhou Enlai even promulgated the principle of self-reliance and announced the period as an era of kerosene (*yang you*) (Ibid: 639). Subsequently, on January 3, 1965 saw the promulgation of a certain number of measures in order to solve the "petrol problem." (*Dangdai Zhongguo De Shiyou Gongye*, 1988: 640) They were: exploitation of oilfields, maintenance of stable production and profound development of oil refining technology (Ibid). In June 1965 at Sichuan a strategy was decided: "to exploit gas and search for oil (*kai qi zhao you*)" (*Dangdai Zhongguo De Shiyou Gongye*, 1988: 640) However this strategy was abandoned in 1967 in the wake of the Cultural Revolution. In December 1966 Liao He basin began to be exploited on the lines of Daqing and consecutively in April 1969, Wang Jinxi (the mastermind of Daqing, also called "the iron man") attended the meeting of the Ninth Party Congress only to be felicitated by both Chairman Mao and Premier Zhou Enlai (Dangdai Zhongguo *De Shiyou Gongye*, 1988: 641-642). Although on June 26, 1969 the State Council endorsed the work of Ministry of Petroleum Industry but Daqing production had begun to dwindle, hence on March 10, 1970 Zhou Enlai asked for the restoration of Daqing production which would not only integrate the worker and the farmer but also the city and the country (*Dangdai Zhongguo De Shiyou Gongye*, 1988: 642). To do so the Central Party Secretariat decided to amalgamate Industrial Coal Department, Industrial Petroleum Department and Industrial Chemical Department and formed a whole new department, the Industrial Chemical Fuel Department in June 1970 (*Dangdai Zhongguo De Shiyou Gongye*, 1988: 643), and on May 13, 1974 Daqing Chemical Fertiliser Factory started operation (*Dangdai Zhongguo, De Shiyou Gongye* 1988: 645). In subsequent years of 1975 and 1976 the Party Congress decided to revoke

Ministry of Chemical Fuel Industry and to establish (in its place) Ministry of Coal Industry and Ministry of Petrochemical Industry (*Dangdai Zhongguo De Shiyou Gongye*, 1988: 645-646). These efforts began to bear fruit as the first wave of modernisation led to the establishment of 100,000 tonnes of deep water oil port at Dalian (*Dangdai Zhongguo De Shiyou Gongye*, 1988: 646). In fact by 1978 China's oil production had reached a hundred million tonnes and it began to be considered as one of the major oil exporting nations of the world (Wang et. al., 2012:71). Perhaps that is why despite the experts continuous positioning and the government's measures the common citizen of China did not acknowledge energy scarcity as an issue and failed to use it judiciously (Wang et. al., 2012:71).

It is universally agreed that China had undergone a rapid exploration phase during the thirty years before the reform era. The reasons for doing so perhaps lies deeply embedded in its history. Historically, China always believed itself as being the centre of the universe (the Middle Kingdom theory), and this theory has a psychological imprint in the Chinese mind which has focused excessively on the contribution of the "individual" to the development of society (Wang et. al., 2012:71). This was expected at a time when the average Chinese individual was oblivious to the objective laws of society and also did not fully understand the scarcity and strategy issues associated with energy (Ibid). In fact the 1958 "Great Leap Forward" movement was the culmination of this people-centric mindset in its extreme forms bordering on delusional decision (Wang et. al., 2012:70). It was the extensive promotion of iron and steel production which was done to satisfy the industrial demand during the "Great Leap Forward" that the major energy resources like coal and electricity got a major boost of government investment, Soviet innovation and the media attention at that time (Wang et. al., 2012:70). Another major aspect was that because of the tremendous alienation and economic embargoes faced by China at the initiation of its development, it was left with no other option but to explore its own resources to fend for its development needs (Wang et. al., 2012:70). In fact in comparison to the first thirty years of China's development it seems to have done exceptionally well at the energy front, as the following table indicates.

Table 2.1: Comparative Data of Energy Production in the Pre-reform Period

Year	1950	1980
Total energy production (hundred million tonnes)	0.3	6.4
Coal (per cent)	96.7	69.4
Oil (per cent)	0.9	23.8

Source: Wang Yanxing et. al. (2012:71-72).

From the above table it can be seen that the total energy production, in a very short span from 1950 to 1980 had almost increased by twenty times. War ravaged China—which had just been out of the clutches of Japanese invasion and centuries of feudal mindset—was now eager to assiduously lay the foundations of heavy industry. Under this policy the main focus of energy policy was in and around the areas of Northeast China and the industrial bases of eastern coastal China as well as the original mines which needed to be restored for production (Ji, 2011:26). By 1952, China had more or less completed the task of restoration of its industrial bases and production mines and then initiated its First Five Year plan from 1953 to 1957 (Ji, 2011:26). The First Five Year Plan was instrumental in laying the foundation of energy bases at Huabei, Northeast China, etc., as energy industry alone received 156 projects under Soviet assistance (Ji, 2011:26). Hence began the chapter of modern industry in China in the energy sector in its truest form. However all the good work laid in the First Five Year Plan got undone as un-mindful energy bases were established in various parts of the country leading to excessive resource wastage and environmental destruction (Ji Jianjun, 2011:26-27). Actually before 1978 China did not have a problem of researching on strategy of energy development. At that time, the principle was "economic development requires lots of energy resources, hence no amount of production could be considered as excessive or even sufficient production" (Xu Shoubo, 2008:8). Thus the Chinese economy, for the first thirty years of its liberation since 1949, was relying almost completely on its energy supply. It adopted a policy of an "intensive resource exploration strategy" (Ibid). However this energy policy of China at that time was not the anomaly but the norm of that time followed even by most of the developed states. Demand was met readily and easily with free and available supply and the price was nominal too (2-3 dollars per barrel) (Ibid). It was this skewed ratio of demand supply praxis which culminated in what we know as the "Oil Shock" of 1973. To understand the impact of this energy crisis on a closed economy like China which, at that time, was still quite under-developed one should keep in mind the backdrop of domestic energy situation.

Domestically in China, wastage of resources was the norm (China was still recovering from Mao's "backyard furnaces strategy" during the Great Leap Forward), energy intensive transport was in vogue (although on a personal consumption level China was still the bicycle country), ecologically not just pollution but indiscriminate cutting down of forests (the Great Proletarian Cultural Revolution had built excessive population pressure in the rural areas) and growing burden of energy investment all existed (Xu, 2008:9). As a consequence, energy consumption in China's GDP kept on increasing while energy efficiency kept on decreasing. The "exploration phase" in the history of China's energy policy wasted to the amount of 35.5 hundred million tonnes standard coal of energy accruing 5.85 billion Yuan (1980 price) loss of GDP (Ibid). No wonder one of the first steps of reform was to embark on energy efficiency strategy. Actually the period from 1963 to 1979 underwent a series of adjustments and rearrangements of the energy policies to make up for the massive loss undertaken during the previous years (Ji, 2011:26). The energy policy now centred around the "three line approach," the discovery of Daqing and various other oilfields had already brought a massive change in the energy consumption basket of China as it now began to think more about oil than coal despite retaining its coal-based structure (Ji, 2011:27). The policies now also intended to turn around the transfer of coal from the north to the developed south which involved a heavy wastage of resources and an aggrandisement of costs (Ji, 2011:26).

However this is not to say the energy policies from the period of 1949 till before the reforms relied only on fossil fuels. In fact the pressure of burgeoning demand had been felt as early as the establishment of heavy industry in China and renewable energy resources like small-scale water electricity, methane pools, solar cooking stoves, small wind operated machines, etc., had begun to appear in rudimentary forms (Ji, 2011:26). Basically the low temperature geothermal energy resources and solar operated products were consumed by residents and spaceflight operators were given lot of impetus by the government for development (Ji, 2011:26). However, because of the limitations of low technology, poor investment and strained relations with the Soviets, which led to withdrawal of technical and intellectual support, China was unable to formulate a comprehensive energy policy related to the renewable energy structure and nor was it able to build a sound and competitive base for the development of the renewable energy industry (Ji, 2011:26). Also because the energy policies of that time were unable to foresee the future, the development of the energy industry was in a pathetic condition and in the dogged pursuit of raising the GDP levels it was forgotten that steady and speedy environment deterioration had in fact been escalating the costs of production, on the other hand (Ibid).

The Second Phase (1980s Onward till the Tenth Five Year Plan)

Multi-pluralistic Energy Development Strategy

The Third Plenum of the Eleventh Party Congress marked a major shift and adjustment in the energy policy. Energy had now come to serve the economy rather than society. Major reforms came in the industrial management of the energy, energy price structure, the energy market structure, etc (Wang et. al, 2012:71). Also the coal-based structure of the Chinese economy demanded not only oil but also became electricity-centric (*yi dianli wei zhongxin*). (Ji, 2011:26) The energy production now was a transition from a "balanced approach" (*jun heng*) to an "inclined approach" (*qing xie*) as newer energy production bases were established in Shaanxi, Inner Mongolia and Xinjiang (Wang et. al., 2012: 71). The period from 1986 to 2005 has been dubbed by the petroleum industry as the period of "stabilising the east and developing the west," *wending dongbu fazhan xibu*'. (Dangdai Zhongguo *De Shiyou Gongye*, 2008: 392). In fact since 1985 Xinjiang oilfields have been particularly instrumental in maintaining the rhythm of "keeping reform at the centre of all undertakings and achieving harmonious development." (Ibid: 108) By the Seventh Five Year Plan the oil production from Xinjiang oil fields reached 292 million tones (Ibid: 109). The Eight and the Ninth plan revised their strategy for "western development" by bringing in the focus on investment and scientific development (Ibid).

Figure 2.1: Gas and Oil Reserves in Various Parts of China

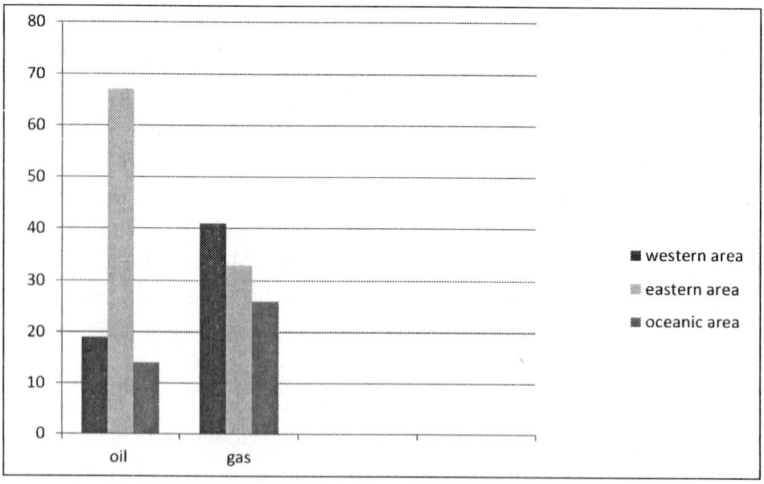

Unit Per cent

Source: *Dangdai Zhongguo De Shiyou Gongye* (2008: 10).

The above table gives a glimpse of oil and gas reserves found in various parts of China during the period 1986 to 1991. It has been found that while oil reserves were dominant in the eastern part of China (67 percent as opposed to 19 percent and 14 percent in western and oceanic areas respectively), gas reserves were almost evenly spread throughout China, being a little more in the western areas (41 percent as opposed to 26 percent and 33 percent in oceanic and eastern areas respectively).

The energy development strategy was now a rearrangement of exploration and conservation phase as China entered the Sixth Plan period (Ji, 2011:26-27). The Sixth Plan explicitly pointed out the need to continue with exploration and conservation where energy saving would now be the main priority (Ibid). This was perhaps the first time when the equation between energy exploration and energy conservation was highlighted by the government in one of its important documents (Wang et. al., 2012:71).

The second period was the period after the reforms where the industrialisation process was right out of the clutches of planned production and was expected to adjust to the production and consumption patterns of the market economy. The decade of the 1980s for the first time promulgated the concept of conservation along with development of natural energy resources (Wang et. al., 2012:71). It was now that conservation and efficient consumption became a part and parcel of social and economic plan. A number of laws and measures were passed, namely, China's Energy Conservation Law (*zhong hua renmin gong he guo jieyue nengyuan fa)*, number of stipulations related to development of thermoelectric output, administrative methods of legalising conservation products, plans for building standard residential houses with energy conservation, etc (Wang et. al, 2012:71). A number of measures which can be considered as rudimentary but pioneering steps were taken towards attaining sustainable development. On March 5, 1978 Petrochemical Industry Department was revoked to form Ministry of Petroleum Industry and Ministry of Chemical Industry and the dawn of December 12, 1978 saw the establishment of China's Petroleum Institute at Beijing (*Dangdai Zhongguo De Shiyou Gongye*, 1988:647-648). By May 1979 China began exploration in its eastern sector from the Shengli fields and by September 1979 China forged into international agreements and signed cooperation agreement with Vienna at an international meet in Romania (*Dangdai Zhongguo De Shiyou Gongye*, 1988:648). In 1979 China's Academy of Sciences (hereafter, CAS) started an organisation of experts who would conduct research on formulation of a structured energy policy (Wang Qingyi, n.a: 25-29). The backdrop of the "lost decade" had a subtle influence of redeeming the lost resources. The first summit meeting on energy, held in the same year, was met with great enthusiasm by experts who critically pointed out energy crisis as a product of failure of years of planned economy and the Cultural Revolution. The following conclusions were derived in the meeting (Ibid):

- The ratio of total population to total available energy resources was not good. Although the per capita consumption was less but supply was erratic and insufficient.
- Village resources were especially deficient in energy resources as excessive utilisation of twigs and fuel wood aggravated the ecological balance.

The motto of the meet proclaimed by Deng was *po you jian di* (being insightful) (Wang Qingyi, n.a: 25-29) as energy can determine the destiny of China's modernisation. In 1980, Deng declared that "energy is the biggest problem for economy" a wisdom achieved by loss of millions of economic worth of GDP and scientific persuasion. In China modernisation and energy share a cause and effect relationship (Ibid).

Mao's idea of "proletarianism" in the initial years of China was mostly fuelled by Soviet holdout of energy assisting China in widespread electrification. By May 1980 PetroChina began exploration in southern and western sea areas of Bohai and signed exploration agreement with French Oil Company for the central sea area of Bohai (*Dangdai Zhongguo de Shiyou Gongye*, 1988: 649). On the other hand China's first gas reserve began to function in Daqing (Ibid). This reserve was constructed in 1975 and was under experimentation since then (Ibid). This led to the announcement of formation of Ministry of Petroleum Industry for the Regulations of Petroleum Industry Department Work for Environment Protection at the Daqing meeting of 1981, where Ministry of Petroleum Industry discussed exploration directions, technical policies, tasks and measures for oilfields required in the wake of economic adjustment of the national economy (Ibid). National Energy Council too held a meeting in Beijing to discuss the question of petroleum exploration at Bohai (Ibid). The State Council decided that the Petroleum Department after producing a hundred million tonnes of oil for the state can use the conserved and the excess production for its own use thereby reducing the wastage of crude oil export making the difference between international domestic price as a fund to be utilised for exploration and exploitation of oilfields (Ibid: 650). In January 1982 State Council standing committee also passed the regulations for agreement with foreign countries for exploration of offshore petroleum resources and hence on February 25, 1982 the China National Offshore Oil Corporation

(CNOOC) was born in Beijing (Ibid). In 1982 the Twelfth Party Congress declared energy as the basis for socialist modern construction (Wang Qingyi, n.a: 25-29). This was the first step towards formulating a structured energy policy. The Energy Department of CAS in 1981 had organised a research on formulating a comprehensive structured economic policy involving five hundred experts of one hundred and seventy departments and organisations and gave a report titled *Zhongguo Nengyuan Zhengce Gangyao Jianyi Shu* (The Formulation of Guidelines for China's Energy Policy) highlighting the current situation and future tendencies, urgently asking for structuring for a policy (Ibid). This project was the beginning of the change in the Chinese perception as China began to graduate from concentrating on being politically systematic to also being scientifically comprehensive.

Later in January 1983 major discussion was undertaken by planning committee and economic committee over the policy on energy technology (Ibid). The result came out in August 1985 (Wang Qingyi, n.a: 25-29) as (*Nengyuan Jishu Zhengce Yaodian)* Main Points for Policy on Energy Technology. It focused on the following points:

- An overall healthy development of energy industry
- Those industries around Shaanxi should switch to being oil or gas based
- Developed areas which are energy deficient should focus on being nuclear based hubs
- China should focus on building village energy resources.

This whole period from 1981 to 1985 was fortunately not limited only to paperwork. The scientific implementation led to enhanced production, crude coal production jumped from 6,200 million tonnes of crude coal in 1980 to 8,500 million tonnes of crude coal, 1,250 million tonnes of crude oil and 4,060 billion kWh of power production (Ibid).

It also conserved energy the equivalent of 1,700 million tonnes of standard coal overtly exceeding the planned economy target of 70 to 90 million tonnes of standard coal (Ibid). In fact in 1982 the core of the Twelfth Party Congress adopted a series of political measures taking concrete steps for energy development (Xu, 2008： 8):

- Formulating law on the development of National Energy Science and Technology Development
- Establish National Energy Committee
- Building Shaanxi energy base
- Lay equal stress on both development and conservation of energy resources and to formulate conservation based policies (*yi jieneng wei zhu*) in the near future

- Every department of every industry and occupation should establish energy administration structure
- Conservation festivals should be actively organised and pursued all over the country
- Formulate energy conservation policies.

The period from 1981 to 1985 which was the Sixth plan period could be claimed as a golden period where there was coordinated development of economic growth and energy conservation (Ibid).

China's energy administration is divided into "three harnessed horse carriages" (Mo Bei):

- National Energy Committee
- National Reform Committee
- National Energy Bureau

They have broken traditional rigmarole administration processes and introduced innovative concepts like raising quality standards, illustrative expansion of number of employees, etc., attracting the attention of every other energy department in the world. The year 1983 witnessed various new events in the changing energy circuit of China. This was new as ice had begun to thaw in the Sino-American relations and 19 American geologists came to conduct research in Wennan area of oilfields of central China (Dangdai Zhongguo De Shiyou Gongye, 1988: 651). In June CNOOC announced the floating of new oil companies, namely, Bohai Oil Company, South Yellow Sea Petroleum Company, Nanhai (eastern part and western part) Petroleum Company (Ibid: 652). Sino-American joint exploration and production was conducted at Tarim basin and three units of geologists were sent in Takla Makan desert (Ibid). This led to the birth of another future stalwart of China on July 12, 1983 in the form of China Petrochemical Corporation in Beijing (Ibid). By April 8-13, 1984, Premier of State Council Zhao Ziyang had proclaimed that China's oil industry has entered a new phase of development and would contribute a lot more to the building up of the nation (Ibid). In July 1985 China imported technology from a Texas company to assist in oil exploration at Xi'an and within the next month China managed to produce 200,000 tonnes of oil for the first time, and on December 21, 1985 gas from Huabei oilfields began to be transported to Beijing (*Dangdai Zhongguo De Shiyou Gongye*, 1988: 653-654). CNPC was also established in the same year (Ibid). It was in the decade of the 1980s that problems of energy in rural areas were also given consideration. Economic incentives like subsidy allowances, tax revenues, assured prices, credit guarantees, leasing of land, etc., were done to promote the utilisation of renewable energy resources and a framework had begun to formulate the renewable energy policy (Ji, 2011: 27). By 1993 China had turned from an exporter to net importer of oil. Scholars believe that the coinciding of abolishment of energy ministry by Premier Zhu Rongji and the transformation of China turning into a net importer of oil (both in 1993) have been because the leadership very strongly believed that China's self-sufficiency issues could be managed better without the requirement of an administrative bureaucratic structure (Erica Downs, 2006:6). Obviously when, a decade later, in 2003, the country was reeling under the pressure of incessant power shortages and frequent "blackouts," the government was badly shaken from its state of inertia as it rushed to make amendments for its follies regarding the bureaucratic structure (Ibid). That the energy ministry has not been set up till date, despite continuous proposals, is another question. In fact since 1994 China's energy policies have begun to focus less on development (*fazhan*) 发展 and more on increase (*zengjia*)增加 (Wang et. al, 2012： 71). The question of energy was now an embodiment of an assured quantity and high quality and China, having turned a net importer of oil just the previous year, entered in to a large number of oil trades with various nations. By 1998, the focus of energy bases had shifted from the coal and oil rich eastern China to the western and central regions of the country. Energy policies now needed to be developed under the following guidelines "suit measures to local conditions, mutually reinforcing, comprehensive utilisation and being cost-effective (Ibid). It was also around this time that various laws related to the energy sector, like the Environment Protection Law 1989, Energy Conservation Law 1998, etc., were strengthened and work in the energy sector began to be more organised and legalised under the provision of various laws and promulgations (Wang et. al., 2012： 71). By the Ninth Five Year Plan China's energy policies had expanded its objectives not just serving the economic demands and the societal needs but also in considering the ethics of environment protection and maintenance of security of energy supply (Ji, 2011:27). The government functionaries had by now grown from the inception stage of exploration to establishing a framework for market supervision (Ibid). The decade of the 1990s was different for the energy sector of China in many ways. It had marked the transformation of energy policies from a planned economy to a market driven structure, encouraged investments in not just the fossil fuels but in the pluralisation of the energy structure and the theories of sustainable development, and development of renewable energy structure had now become such an important aspect of China's energy sector that all future energy policies from now on drew inspiration from them (Ibid). By 1996,

China's crude coal production was first in the world; power capacity was the third and oil industry was the fifth (Men Kepei, 1996:16) and by 2000 the total energy production released was 1,287 million tones of standard coal, and consumption was 1,482 million tonnes of standard coal (Ibid), a gap expanding from five million tonnes of standard coal to 200million tonnes of standard coal. However during the Ninth Plan (1996-2000) the energy structure of China was not a happy one. In order to solve the problem a comprehensive energy development policy was required, in which reserve strength of oil, coal and electricity industry was to be developed, which increased the intensity of construction of energy investment while at the same time went all out to excavate the latent capacity of conservation (Ibid). Since liberation, China's energy industry has had a lion's share in contributing to the development of its national economy (Ibid). But, since many years, rise in China's energy production is lagging behind rise in the economy. It is this mismatch of growth which has led to shortage of energy supply becoming the "bottleneck" of energy development arresting its growth. In fact growth rate of China's energy production has been constantly decelerating (Ibid). The production fell from 3.7 per cent to 1.9 per cent during the period from 1979 to 1996 (Men Kepei, 1996: 16-18). On the contrary demand has been rising much above production. Different indicators have time and again expressed the threat of energy scarcity. Scientists have suggested various measures of how energy industry should grasp the opportunity to intensify reforms and adjust with exceeding demands of economy to maintain its growth rate of industrialisation and modernisation.

Table 2.2: Distribution of Domestic Energy Consumption across the Two Decades

Item	1980	1990	2000
Total consumption	2,508	4,753	9,350
Household consumption	2,233	4,178	8,134
Consumption by society	275	575	1,216

(Unit: 100 million yuan)
Source: Lu Yinzhong (year unavailable:31).

The above table shows the consumption pattern of China's energy requirements spanning two decades. It can be seen that energy consumption has been increasing in tandem with rising living standards. Social consumption (row 3) is clearly on the rise while the bulk of energy is consumed by households (row 2).

However the realisation of the last few years of the twentieth century had dawned too late as by the turn of the century China was saddled with grave issues like erratic electricity supply, the exploration and utilisation of energy resources had led to grim problems of environmental pollution, the dependency rate on oil imports continued to escalate, strategic petroleum reserves were fast depleting, energy supply was unstable and unreliable (Ji, 2011:27). Energy was now again the biggest bottleneck in the development of the economy. China was already riding on the accelerator of twenty years of growth and its rising living standards meant that energy consumption had risen to unprecedented levels. Moreover, voices for environment protection and reduction of carbon-emitting pollutants were gaining enough ground and China could not ignore them anymore. On the other hand, the issue of energy security was already gaining prominence especially when it had been a decade since China had turned into an importer of oil. The tussle between increased energy consumption and scarcity of energy resources was brewing and China's energy imports are not only unstable but are also located in the most politically volatile regions of the world. It was increasingly felt that now the time required a targeted social development and lifestyle without adverse effects on energy (Ibid).

The Third Stage (from the Tenth Five Year Plan onwards)

The third stage which roughly can be stated from the Tenth Five Year Plan saw China's energy policy achieving an experience of maturity and globalisation. The Tenth Five Year Plan explicitly reveals that China's energy policies have come of age. It unequivocally highlighted its agenda at its promulgation which was to "ensure energy security, optimise energy structure, enhance energy efficiency, protect ecological environment, continue with expansion of the exploration of energy resources and speedily develop the western areas" (Ji, 2011:27). The technology related to cleaning of coal before and after utilisation was gaining ground and the transportation of gas and electricity from the backward western areas to the industrially developed east were the two most important tasks undertaken during the Tenth Five Year Plan (Ibid).

Table 2.3: Analysis of Domestic Energy Consumption during the Various Plan Periods

Plan period	Year	Total Consumption (10,000 standard coal)	Yearly increase in consumption (10,000 standard coal)	Yearly increase in consumption (per cent)	Rise in GDP (per cent)	Consumption/GDP	Situation of restrictions due to energy	Energy and economy coordination
Fifth plan	1980	60,275						
Sixth plan	1981-85		3,281	4.93	10.7	0.46	Restriction not visible	Good A
	1985	76,682						
Seventh plan	1986-1990		4,404	5.18	7.87	0.66	Slight restrictions	Satisfactory C
	1990	98,703						
Eighth plan	1990-95		6,495	5.85	12.0	0.49	Slight restrictions	Good A
	1995	131,176						
Ninth plan	1996-2000		-176	-0.13	8.3	-0.02	Restriction clearly not felt	Very Good AA
	2000	130,297						
Tenth plan	2001-05		18,434	11.3	9.48	1.19	Restriction felt heavily	Satisfactory C
	2005	222,468						

Source: Xu, Shoubo (July 2008:10).

From the above table, it is visibly clear that energy consumption has increased continuously since 1980 which is also in tandem with rise in GDP, except the year 1996. It is strange enough to see that China never felt restricted by energy scarcity till 2001 despite turning net importer as early as 1993. However it had begun to encourage a coordinated development as early as 1981 perhaps for reasons beyond scarcity like pollution, etc. However this is not to say that the energy sector was in complete doldrums and had become completely dysfunctional. Its conservation efforts which had now continued for quite some time did lay fruit by expanding its domestic energy supply although not to that extent as would have been expected by the government. By 2005 China's energy productive capacity had expanded to 2,250 million tonnes of standard coal which had increased by 3.7 times since the reforms period (Wang et. al.., 2012:71). China's energy consumption basket now represented a coal-based structure where oil, gas, electricity and other new forms of energy resources replenished the energy supply and by the culmination of the Tenth Five Year Plan (Ibid), it was able to satisfy at least the basic domestic demands. In fact the consumption of oil and gas has been continuously rising making China one of the major energy importing and consuming nations of the world (Ibid).

In fact the core aim of the Tenth Five Year Plan was to establish a settlement between the energy consumption and energy supply structure of China (Ibid). It also aimed to establish an energy structure which supported rather than impeding the economic growth of the fastest growing nation of the world, as well as safeguarding the pluralistic energy supply system of the global energy security pattern. Many Chinese scholars state that after the year 2000 as China gained more experience in interacting with the rest of the world, it realised the natural value of energy resources; the trade and exchange of energy resources, commodities and technology made China aware of its own strength and failures in the energy sphere and prompted it towards a more sincere and sustained approach towards energy conservation and expansion of newer energy resources (Ibid). In 2005 an international conference on renewable energy resources convened in Beijing, in which the then president Hu Jintao noted down the responsibility, the desire as well as the prime responsibility of each and every nation of the world (be it big or small) to strengthen international cooperation, appropriately handle the challenges posed by economy and the environment and to realise sustainable development (Ibid). The culmination of this meeting led to the issuance of the Beijing protocol which redirected the Chinese policies from focusing on the pattern of economy rise to taking measures related to enhancement of energy efficiency (Ibid:71-72).

The Eleventh Five Year Plan had another bout of adjustments and changes for the energy structure. The highlighted aspects were: "priority to energy conservation (坚持节约优先 *jianchi jieyue youxian*), based on domestic conditions（立足国内 *li zu guo nei)*, pluralistic development（多元发展 *duo yuan fazhan),,* strengthen international mutual cooperation（加强国际互利合作 *jiaqiang guoji huli hezuo),* build up stability of economy（构建稳定经济 *goujian wending jingji)* and the clean energy structure（构建清洁能源体系 *goujian qingjie nengyuan tixi)* and to promote the sustainable development of energy resources in order to maintain the sustainable development of economy and society 以能源的可持续发展支持经济和社会的可持续发展 *yi nengyuan de kechixufazhan chixu jingji he shehui de kechixu fazhan)* (Ji, 2011:27-28). China had by now been considered as one of the major countries of the world and the policies of energy conservation and energy efficiency were promulgated not just to ward of the delusional fears of energy scarcity and ecological pollution but also to showcase to the world that China is capable of maintaining the responsibility of a "big nation." During the Eleventh Five Year Plan China issued a policy related to long-term scientific and technological development (*guojia zhongchang qi kexuehe jishu fazhan guihua gangyao*) which had a heavy emphasis on the energy sector and the promotion of pluralism of energy structure, enhance energy supply, simultaneously augment the technologies related to oil and gas exploration and the development of hydropower, strive to develop technology related to nuclear power, formulate a voluntary development capacity of nuclear power system technology, achieve breakthroughs in renewable energy technology like wind and solar energy and to realise the large-scale utilisation of these technologies (Ji, 2011:28).

The Changing Face of China's Energy Policies

The current scenario of China's energy policies has clearly reflected on the importance of technology in the renewable energy sector to capture the future global energy market. China's energy policies have also advanced with the passage of time in keeping in tandem with the changing requirements and priorities of the country's socio-economic needs. Perhaps the most visible change in the energy policies has been the shift in the basic attitude of the decision makers in establishing a "new, independent. self-made energy policy" (Wang et. al., 2012:73). China has always linked its energy security with the economic security and sometimes even border security in case of war. Its Soviet experience had given it enough lessons to not rely on foreign resources for its basic needs and China began its first and perhaps the most important mission of achieving self-sufficiency. Another major change which occurred in the policy structure was the introduction of various legal clauses and protocols which not only enhanced its authenticity but also justified its scientific importance (Ibid). This was an important change as energy policies were now formulated not just by the whim of the top brass but through debate and discussions between various administrative departments, energy companies and intellectuals from various science and social science institutes dealing with issues of energy security (Wang et. al.., 2012:73). This now not only gave a better approach to comprehensive planning for long-term exploration of energy resources but also helped to draw on the experiences of various developed and developing nations of the world, initiate the establishment of strategic energy reserves and set up mechanisms for price regulation of the energy market. (The above section is based on Wang et. al.., 2012)

The issue of energy security and the ensuing formulations of energy policies to mitigate its effect have had an indirect impact in bolstering up the economic structure of China as well as give a subtle boost to the issues of global warming and environmental deterioration. Energy policies have been instrumental in taming down the "wild growth" of China's economy by adopting restrictions on companies and their commodities which are highly polluting in nature (Ibid). This has not only helped China to assuage some of its fears of "overheating economy" but has also been instrumental in striving for a "healthy" economic structure which is more conscious of its environmental conditions. Moreover this has also been a political trump card for China by showing its contribution in the abatement of conflicts which have arisen out of exploration and exploitation of global energy resources. Energy policies have been instrumental in inspiring innovation and research in energy saving technologies and lately have even aroused the government to snatch the position of domination by foreign countries over such technologies (Ibid). The government has been extremely active in promoting energy saving products and has even given large-scale investment to establishing R&D institutes meant exclusively for innovation in energy saving technologies (Ibid). It has also tried to balance between the costs and the prices of energy saving products and to products of those companies who are strictly adhering to energy saving norms. The target of "green development" which was especially highlighted in the Twelfth Plan has also encouraged the participation and supervision activity of various conscious citizens of Chinese society (Ibid). (The above section is based on Wang et. al.. 2012)

The most important aspect for the viability of any policy is the comprehensiveness of its provisions which can prove effective in their practical application. The trajectory of China's energy policies have revealed that despite aiming for grandiose objectives, it never lost its touch with the actual conditions and requirements of that particular period of time. However, whether it managed to achieve or even touch its targeted aims is another question altogether.

The period in and around liberation was a tumultuous phase and it demanded development right from scratch and the energy policies of that time focused on concrete restoration of energy production in China which had been devastated during the civil war and other domestic and international political turmoil faced by China. The "dragon" at that time was the "sick man of Asia" and focused only on what was available in abundance within its territorial boundaries and hence the energy policies then were heavily fossil fuel-centric concentrating almost wholly on coal, oil and electricity (Ji, 2011:28). The basic aim at that time was to cater to the basic energy needs of the people and to guarantee the initiation of at least a minimum level of socio-economic development (Ibid). However problems arose when the energy policies focused only on the supply issues without taking care of the costs associated with the "self-reliant and self-sufficient" supply. This led to tremendous economic losses, ecological losses and more importantly the loss of opportunity for developing indigenous technological innovation and promoting large-scale investment in technical breakthroughs (Ibid). Apart from technological dilemmas, China was also saddled with problems of innovation as there was no marriage of convenience between its supply areas and major consumption areas, and China spent most of its investment in not just exploring but also transporting the energy resources from the explored areas to the industrial consumption bases (Ibid). Also the continuously fluctuating economic policies constantly disturbed the industrial layout of the energy sector and added an unnecessary burden on the exchequer funds allocated for the exploration of energy resources. The influence of an organised system was extremely influential on the decision-making ability of China's energy policy (Ji, 2011:28). However although China was operating under a planned economic system the energy sector never had an integrated administrative office due to which its initial policies were never in accordance with the vision of long-term benefits in the process of complete development for China (Ibid). On the other hand during the transformation from planned economy to the market economy the energy sphere was saddled with two major problems of a weakening macroeconomic regulation capacity from the government and of a novice market whose adjustment role was not being unleashed up to its full potential due to lack of experience and the necessary groundwork in the domestic sphere (Ibid). Hence it would not be an exaggeration if it is said that too many and too soon reforms in the administrative structure of the energy policy had heavily compromised on guaranteeing the domestic energy security as well as the competitiveness of the production capacity of the energy industry (Ibid). In the sixty odd years of China's liberation and formulation of policies it can easily be distinguished that they have been heavily influenced by the aspiration of maintaining energy security, the many other related and unrelated strategies regarding China's development issues, the level of economic development, energy production technology which most acquired through import or grant (in the Soviet case) and the living standards of the general population (Ibid). However which factor or actor had more influence than the other differed with different levels of economic development at different time frames. Yet it is also true that China while pursuing any form of economic model had to heavily rely on its energy policy in order to maintain a balance between its economic developments or in meeting the rising demands of the residential population (The above section is based on Ji, 2011).

The example of power is taken to illustrate the requirement of "responsible social development" and not just "rising living standards" as the policies have propagated time and again.

Table 2.4: Electricity as an Example to Study the Changing Nature of Energy Structure of China Especially after the Reforms

Item	1980	1990	2000	2010
Total energy production (billion Kwh)	3,006	6,000	12,000	21,500
Coal electricity (per cent)	62.9	76.8	73.4	60.5
Hydro-electricity (per cent)	19.4	21	20.8	20.9
Petrol electricity (per cent)	17.7	2.2	1.6	0
Nuclear electricity (per cent)	0	0	4.2	18.6
Electricity consumed in total energy consumption (per cent)	20.46	26	26.3	28.6

Source: Lu Yinzhong (year unavailable: 33).

From the above table it can be seen that China's energy structure is still largely coal based. China's largest consumers of energy are its heavy manufacturing units, yet, despite this, it has not been able to achieve complete industrialisation due to various reasons. One of the main reasons is that generally when a country enters into manufacturing phase it automatically shifts from coal-based energy structure to cleaner sources like oil, gas and even renewable energy sources. However this is not true for China; easy accessibility and copious availability of coal has made it fall back on its traditional consumption pattern whenever it feels a paucity of material or scarcity of time (Lu Yinzhong, n.a： 33). Yet it is also true that no country can or would be able to achieve industrialisation relying solely on coal and hence China is forced to look for better and cleaner options onshore and offshore.

Hydro-electricity on the other hand has maintained a modest growth rate despite China has built large-scale dam building projects (Ibid). Petrol, once used to produce electricity, showed a sharp decline within a decade to almost nil by the turn of the twentieth century (Ibid). Nuclear electricity is increasingly gaining ground though it is still modest in growth compared to other sources of energy. Electricity consumption increased by six points within a decade and stabilised after that with modest increases (Ibid). This reveals that bulk of changes happened in China in the decade of the 1980s when reforms were most enthusiastically sought after (Ibid). It has lately been increasingly advocated that development of renewable energy resources is not just an option to be used as a complementary resource but an essentiality as a replaceable resource. At the same time a socio-economic structure and a lifestyle need to be created that is based on less energy consumption, which suitably consumes and protects energy resources and reforms the degraded environment. (The above section is based on Lu Yinzhong, n.a:33-34)

China has a variety of energy resources, however per capita availability is low exploration capacity is low and distribution uneven. Moreover increasing energy consumption is invariably linked with rising living standards (a base from which China's leadership draws authenticity to authority). As it is the Great Leap Forward had brought a shift in industrial base to iron and steel, disturbing the balance between energy and economic development. It is an irony that China despite being rich in the material base for economic and social development (read energy) is starved of its own resources due to economic growth and energy development mismatch as well as burgeoning population leading to decreasing per capita availability of resources. In fact energy supply was a question of constant worry though China turned net importer only in 1993. The reason was the emergence of the basic problems which surfaced together, vacillation between intensive exploration and extensive conservation. These shifting policies without some concrete research and assessment wreaked havoc on the minds of the people who did not know what to do or what not to do. Many of the major consumer cities of China (e.g., Beijing) depend upon supply from outside its geo-boundary adding to the cost of transportation. For example in the 1990 figure Beijing used 26.48 million tonnes of standard coal which was second largest in the whole of China and 89 per cent of supply came from outside the boundaries (Li Rugan, n.a:11). In the 1990s and before that China had to conserve not because of scarcity of resources but because of pollution wreaked by its coal-based structure (Ibid). By 1996, China's crude coal production was first in the world; power capacity was the third and oil industry was the fifth (Men Kepei, 1996: 16-18). Hence, it was projected that till 2000 total energy production released would be 1,287.1 million tonnes standard coal and consumption was 1,482 million tonnes of standard coal (Men Kepei, 1996: 16-18), a gap expanding from 5 million tonnes of standard coal to 200 million tonnes of standard coal.

China's Energy Footprint on the World Map

Energy demands are rising in huge proportions. However while every year the world energy demand rises by 2.5 per cent China's goes up by 8.8 per cent (Wang Jian, 2012). Naturally, for a country with ravenous consumption it is imperative for it to build up an energy efficient society. Wang Jian (2012) in his article explained that China's energy consumption elasticity in the 1990s is 0.4, i.e., for every 1 per cent of GDP increase, China's energy consumption increased by 0.4 per cent. By this estimate it was predicted that China's energy consumption elasticity by 2020 would be 0.5. However, by 2004 China's energy consumption elasticity was 1.6. This should have been no surprise as "the factory of the world" had long before entered the heavy manufacturing phase before it was actually ready for it (Wang Jian, 2012).

Until now what we discussed was the changes that energy policy went through in the fifty odd years. However policies are difficult to implement. Why? Most people sign it off as a case of government procrastination and bureaucratic impediments. But execution conditions do not just work on will. Most policies in actuality are too good to be true. Apart from that the government targets focusing on economy expansion are to be met by hook or by crook. Also policies usually carry a "should" burden on them without giving concrete directions of what to do and not to do. All the above factors, lead to making crass decisions, focusing only on short-term gains while consequences of such decisions are borne by the people. Hence it would do well for the top brass to deviate from "to do so" orders into "do like this" directions. Certain measures need to be adapted to and before that certain psyche has to be changed. Below we shall discuss both concrete measures and psychological dispositions which will also help in breaking widely accepted rationale. According to Li Rugan (n.a:11-12):

- It is always believed that decline in agriculture and rise of secondary and tertiary sectors in GDP share is the step towards well-off society. Usage of bio-fuels and renewable forms of energy not only cleans the environment but also gives a fillip to the agricultural base by creating a market for it while at the same time expanding the tertiary sector.
- It is easy to say that investment should be increased in conservation of energy. However what is not clearly defined is what investment is required in what aspect of conservation. One way could be conservation technologies which are usually imported. However developing countries should focus more on innovative indigenous products than costly technologies from outside. What could be made perfunctory is deposition of a certain amount of capital for the purpose of conservation from the profits reaped after utilisation of energy.
- Developing central heating system reducing pollution and conserving energy by reducing the cost and consumption of heaters.
- People using coal for cooking purposes/heating purposes to be encouraged to use coal briquettes instead of coal balls. They have evenly spaced balls mixed with lime and coal and allow fire to go upward in straight formation saving energy by 10 per cent. During the Seventh Plan period 198 briquettes were produced saving thirty thousand tonnes of coal.
- The Sixth Plan period had constructed 2,683 chain boilers enhancing their heating capacity by 10 per cent and saving 320,000 tonnes standard coal.
- Revamping the technologies of high consumption appliances like air-conditioners and generators could save 145 million watts of electricity.
- Industries should be encouraged to adopt "targeted responsibility systems approach towards energy conservation. In the seventh plan forty-nine high consumption products were especially identified and targeted bringing down consumption by 66.6 percentage points (Li Rugan: 11-12).

The most important task for any energy policy is to maintain a balance between the sustainability of the economy while at the same time transforming its energy consumption habits to an inexpensive and more ecologically friendly one. China's energy resource base on the global front is not a very happy one and it is counted as one of the least resource possessing country. The main reasons have visibly been the extensive economic growth and excessive reliance on high consuming industries. Despite having a copious availability of coal and relying on a coal-based structure, the position of oil and gas in the domestic energy configuration is far from satisfactory. Due to this the energy consumption basket of China is highly skewed towards coal which it consumes 41.5 per cent more than the world average, while oil and gas is consumed 16 per cent and 20.5 per cent less than the world average respectively (Ji, 2011:24). Geographically, China's oil and gas reserves are located in eastern, central and western parts as well as the coastal areas. Hydropower projects though quite developed in the south lie primarily in western and central parts of China while its coal reserves are located in northern China and northwest and the southeastern coastal areas which are economically developed. Due to this China's transportation routes follow the route of transportation of coal from north to south, gas from west to east, electricity transmission also from west to east and oil again from north to south, which is extremely strenuous on the total cost of production (Ji, 2011). Liu Zhiyan and others (2008) in their work are extremely vociferous about this dichotomy of large distance between supply and production of resource areas throughout the paper:

> "Ninety per cent of coal reserves lie north of Dabei, Qinling and Kunlun mountain ranges, 70 per cent of hydroelectric sources are in the southwest and 80 per cent of natural gas reserves are located in the central and western regions, as is the majority of wind and solar resources. Key issues for energy security are how to exploit these resources, control disorderly exploitation by business, increase production efficiency and make effective use of rich renewable sources of energy" (Liu et. al., 2008:7-8).

The Eleventh Five Year Plan even suggested laying down of intra-country power pipelines from west to east to avoid transport bottlenecks (Ibid, 2008:8). It has also asked the affluent rich to contribute to the development of the west which is adept in the renewable energy sector (Ibid, 2008:9).

Leaders had realised by now that parroting of China as a resource abundant country when there is actual deficiency could not solve the problem until and unless long-term and continued efforts were made to maintain it. China's Energy Law explicitly speaks of "Energy is the most important commodity for sustaining economic and social development. Because the existence of a pluralistic international society, the energy strategy reserves has become an important component not only for realization of well-off society but also for revival of China"

(Tong Yuanchun, 2008:100). The Energy Conservation Law of China which became effective from April 1, 2008 explicitly pointed out the economic dimensions of energy conservation (Ibid). It held various provisions for energy conservation in industrial production, construction, transportation, public institutions and various energy intensive units. It also included incentive measures for energy conservation as well as legal liabilities for non compliance (Ibid).

Given below are the aims and measures adopted in the three successive plans from Tenth and Eleventh Five Year Plans. The aims of Tenth Five Year Plan (2001-2005) (Shi Dinghuan:n.a) :

- Raising funds to support the development of renewable energy
- Supporting works on localization of manufacturing equipment and speeding up the industrialization process.
- Establishing scientific research and translation from scientific results to standardized production of renewable energy
- Enhancing international cooperation in promoting advanced technology and financial aid

It was evident that the Tenth Five Year Plan focused on development of renewable energy. However rising and unavoidable energy consumption led to shift in the focus from conservation to reducing the amount of energy intensity (i.e., energy consumed per unit of GDP). Hence the following measures were initiated in the Eleventh Five Year Plan (China FAQs World Resources Institute, 2011).

- The Ten Key Projects programme, which focused on using economic incentives and technical strategies to improve the efficiency of everything from coal-fired industrial boilers and motors, to promoting "green" lighting and alternatives to oil-based fuels
- The Top 1000 Energy-Consuming Enterprises Programme, which mandated a suite of energy-saving steps for the biggest firms in nine industrial sectors
- Building energy efficiency programmes, which aimed to make newly-constructed buildings more efficient and to retrofit older structures
- Small plant closures, which targeted the most polluting and least energy-efficient facilities for closure
- Appliance standards and energy-efficiency labels, which aimed to curb energy use by new appliances and provide consumers with more information
- Expand the enforcement of building energy standards that have been effective in large urban areas to the rest of the nation, and continue to

emphasise energy management of large-scale public and governmental buildings

- Combine explicit market mechanisms, such as energy pricing reform and tax incentives, with administrative measures, such as binding targets and controlling market access through permits, to encourage a structural shift away from energy-intensive, low value-added production.

Given below is the data of China's energy production and consumption during the period of its "China rise" dictum.

Table 2.5: The Structure of China's Energy Production

Year	Total energy production (10,000 tonnes standard coal)	Coal produced (per cent)	Oil produced (per cent)	Gas produced (per cent)	Renewable sources (hydro, nuclear, wind in per cent)
1991	104,844	74.10	19.20	2.00	4.70
1992	107,256	74.30	18.90	2.00	4.80
1993	111,059	74.00	18.70	2.00	5.30
1994	118,729	74.60	17.60	1.90	5.90
1995	129,034	75.30	16.60	1.90	6.20
1996	132,616	75.20	17.00	2.00	5.80
1997	132,410	74.10	17.30	2.10	6.50
1998	124,250	71.90	18.50	2.50	7.10
1999	125,935	72.60	18.15	2.66	6.59
2000	128,978	71.95	18.05	2.80	7.19
2001	137,445	71.80	17.04	2.93	8.23
2002	143,810	72.25	16.59	3.02	8.14
2003	163,842	75.07	14.79	2. 84	7.30
2004	187,341	75.96	13.41	2.94	7.68
2005	205,876	76.50	12.62	3.20	7.70
2006	221,056	76.68	11.94	3.52	7.86
2007	235,415	76.60	11.30	3.90	8.20
2008	260,000	76.70	10.44	3.89	8.98
2009	280,000	77.50	9.40	3.84	9.26

Source Ji Jianjun (2011:24)

Table 2.6: China's Energy Consumption Composition

Year	Total energy consumption (10,000 tonnes standard coal)	Coal consumed (per cent)	Oil consumed (per cent)	Gas consumed (per cent)	Renewable sources (hydro, nuclear, wind in per cent)
1991	103,783	76.10	17.10	2.00	4.80
1992	109,170	75.70	17.50	1.90	4.90
1993	115,993	74.70	18.20	1.90	5.20
1994	122,737	75.00	17.40	1.90	5.70
1995	131,176	74.60	17.50	1.80	6.10
1996	138,948	74.70	18.00	1.80	5.50
1997	137,798	71.70	20.40	1.70	6.20
1998	132,214	69.60	21.50	2.20	6.70
1999	133,831	69.09	22.57	2.14	6.20
2000	138,553	67.75	23.21	2.35	6.69
2001	143,199	66.68	22.87	2.55	7.90
2002	151,797	66.32	23.41	2.56	7.71
2003	174,990	68.38	22.21	2.58	6.83
2004	203,227	67.99	22.33	2.60	7.08
2005	224,682	69.10	21.00	2.80	7.10
2006	246,270	69.40	20.40	3.03	7.20
2007	265,583	69.50	19.70	3.50	7.30
2008	285,000	68.67	18.68	3.77	8.89
2009	305,000	70.10	18.70	3.85	7.35

Source: Ji Jianjun (2011:25).

The year 2009 witnessed a new phenomenon as China not only imported oil but also more than a hundred million tonnes of coal, becoming the second largest country in the world to do so (Ji, 2011: 29). The above tables have clearly indicated that the conventional energy sources like coal, oil and hydropower have structural problems in China. While the petroleum reserves have been continuously depleting, the demand for oil reserves has been rising exponentially. The hydropower capacity of China has already reached its limits and the government has come under serious criticism for compromising on the local ecological habitat and the residents concern and consent while investing in construction of colossal dam projects (Ibid). Moreover, the transportation problem also remains unresolved as China's supply areas are far away from its beneficiaries. The declining quality of China's tradable coal reserves has also weeded out the "advantage of plenty" despite being the holder of the third largest coal reserves of the world (Ibid). Also the overall strategic reserves of China are not enough to sustain its speedy economic growth at the same pace as before. The data of 2006 has revealed that while American energy reserves can withstand for 150 days and the Japanese for 160 days, the Chinese situation is abysmal, lasting only for 7 days (The above section is based on Ji Jianjun, 2011:29-30).

It was only later that it was realised that conservation or reduction of consumption of energy would not be enough and it has to be combined with innovation to achieve the desired efficiency. The Twelfth Five Year Plan explicitly details its energy aims "to establish a secure, stable, economic and clean modern energy production structure" (China Energy Policy, 2012). The four words secure, stable, economic and clean are now considered the pillars of China's energy structure (*si wei yi ti*) which reveal to us the inherent interdependence of economy and environment ensconced in the policies made to preserve the stability and security of energy (Ibid). Another suggestion which has been implemented by National Development and Reform Commission in collaboration with General Administration of Quality, Supervision, Inspection and Quarantine of China (since August 13, 2004) has been the formal foundation of energy efficiency labels in energy consuming products as a performance index for energy efficiency (IHSEIA Track Environmental Intelligence Analysis, 2004).

In this context it would be apt to mention certain points made by *Nengyuan Jishu Zhengce Yaodian* (Guidelines for Energy Technology Policies) promulgated by State Council (Wang Qingyi, n.a:25-29):

- Reformation of energy structure by removing dependence on coal, firewood, etc. This has to be shifted to utilisation of gas, hydropower, etc., and expansion of exploration capacity. In 1984 the ratio of gas to petrol production worldwide was 1:1.17. Soviet and American ratios were 1:1 and China was 1:10. This discrepancy revealed that China in the 1980s considered gas as a low-cost subsidiary product and hence attached less or almost no value to it.
- Better electricity management and price reform should be given special impetus and focus should be laid on more and more electricity creation.
- Energy Economic Zones should be established based on each district's resources and markets.
- Reformation in the usage of oil and coal and expansion of its quality
- Increase in quality of energy technology imported and constructed indigenously. This requires revamping of administration structure, opening up of technology market, invitation of tenders for the best technology to be opened, development of quality protection standards and technology assistance system. This way environmental damage and wasteful consumption both would be stopped.

The policy believed that the thinking of "first produce then live" should be stopped and a balanced approach should be adopted. Energy is not a commodity but a process which starts from resource exploration, development, production, conversion, transportation, distribution to utilization (Ibid). In the 1980s and before that apart from imposition of leftist ideology, scientific temper was lacking too. It has been evident enough that China became an importer less for reasons of scarcity (as it is a coal-based structure) and more for the causes of less exploration and low investment (Tian and Wu, 2005:59). China has come a long way and its fast changing scenario needs speedier reforms not just in economy but also in energy. The government planning committee in 1994 gave the guiding principle to "capture opportunity, intensify reforms, expansion of opening up, promotion of development and maintenance of stability" (1995 White Paper:3-4). The White Paper also indentified four major high consumption industries (power, metallurgy, the chemical industry and building materials) and asked for a targeted programme to enhance their saving capacity. The following were the most illustrative points mentioned in the White Paper:

- Strengthening of legal system for energy conservation which should involve active support and involvement of Standing Committee of National People's Congress and help in early passage of "conservation laws of energy." However for this to materialise proper groundwork needs to be done encompassing both scientific knowledge and technical know-how. Also a permanent investment fund for energy should be initiated (1995 White Paper).
- A portion of energy policy should be devoted to drafting of conservation of resources. This requires not only scientific expertise but also a political and economic analysis of conservation technology. Preferential tax system and a viable financial policy could accelerate the utilisation of conservation technologies.
- Rising living standards implies changes in lifestyle, however this should not necessarily mean rise in consumption patterns of exhaustible energy resources. The passive approach to conservation should be diluted.
- Indulge in computerisation of energy management. This will enhance quality and quantity of energy management making it easier to gather information on trends and analysis of energy consumption.
- Encourage the market of clean energy and usage of products marked with energy efficiency labels

The table below compares the energy efficiency rates of India, US and China since the reform period of China.

Table 2.7: Comparative Analysis of Energy Efficiency Rates of China, India and the USA

Year	China	India	USA
1978	386	1,062	905
1979	441	1,139	983
1980	470	1,282	1,132
1981	445	1,260	1,302
1982	423	1,109	1,418
1983	430	1,127	1,541
1984	341	1,068	1,646
1985	339	1,026	1,739
1986	314	1,105	1,841
1987	343	-	1,724
1988	396	-	1,781
1989	-	-	-
1990	394	1,140	2,104
1991	358	805	2,025
1992	388	753	2,120
1993	-	-	-
1994	441	745	2,270
1995	534	866	2,396
1996	-	-	-
1997	652	1,015	2,619
1998	716	998	2,748
1999	762	1,046	2,853
2000	829	1,025	2,967

Unit: dollar/tonnes of standard coal.
Source: Xu, 2008:13-14

The table above shows the effective rate of China's energy efficiency strategy in comparison with another rising power (India) and an established superpower (read, the United States). In fact it can be seen that despite tremendous rise in China's EE (energy efficiency) rates, it still lags behind and is one of the worst conservers of energy. On the contrary America, although it is the biggest polluter of the world, has been able to conserve its own domestic resources. However this does not reduce its own obligation of turning the rest of the Third World, and especially least developed countries, into the dumping yard and resource material for its requirements. India thanks to its poverty ratios can still come under the category of satisfactory energy conservation as the bulk of its population either consumes less or relies on small-scale method of energy consumption preventing large-scale pollution. Similarly in the China case, while the demand for renewable energy sources is rising for all ethical and practical reasons, the lack of indigenous technology and experience is a big bottleneck in its smooth development. For example in the case of wind, the wind policy of China has targeted to build wind power bases in seven areas of China namely, Hami, Jiuquan, Hebei, Jilin, coastal areas of Jiangsu and eastern and western parts of Inner Mongolia by 2020 (Ji, 2011:30). These areas are expected to hold 78 per cent of China's total wind power capacity (Ji, 2011:30). However because the installation capacity and the costs involved for loading are extremely huge, these wind power bases have earned the sobriquet of being "the three gorges dam on land 陆上三峡" (Ji, 2011:30). Moreover the cost factor has also delayed the construction of these wind power bases and hence China's wind energy is still concentrated in pockets of northwest China. While the wind industry is developing rapidly, the low plant load factor of its supply areas has not only stifled its growth but has also caused the problem of "overheating" of economic trade in the industry (Ji, 2011: 30).

The Sixteenth Party Congress in 2002 declared the aim of well-off society which in principle was doubling the 2000 GDP by 2020 (Xu, 2008:9). This meant that Chinese GDP was targeted to rise every year by 7.18 per cent but it grew by 9.15 per cent (2001-5)(Ibid). At this rate it was estimated that the target of well-off society could be achieved by 2015(Ibid). However in this period energy consumption also grew at a very fast rate. In the Tenth Plan period energy consumption was 11.3 per cent, the fastest since the Fifth Five Year plan. (Ibid). Also apart from the First and Second plans, it was the highest ever in the period of the ten Five Year Plans, especially in 2003 and 2004 the consumption was highest ever since reforms—15.3 per cent and 16.1 per cent respectively(Ibid). This high rate of consumption led to high supply scarcities, massive import surges, environment deformities, etc (Ibid). In such a situation not only will GDP not increase at the targeted point but the current GDP rate will also slide down (Ibid). However it has been observed that high consumption rates in a particular time frame (especially the Tenth Five Year Plan) is a cumulative burden of the previous five year plans (Ibid). A vicious cycle then begins to move. This has been historically proven when high consumption rates in the Second Plan were also reflected in the "three year period of adjustment" (1995 White Paper： 3-4).

The 2008 financial crisis had a subtle affect on the psyche of the government of various nations as the oil prices slid and there was a rush to fill in the depleting reserves of the fossil fuels till the market was bullish (Ji, 2011:29-

30). While the financial reserves forced the developed countries to cut back on their demands and requirements, the prices of crude oil began to dwindle and countries whose economies were still tough and strong (like China) used much of their foreign exchange reserves to expand their energy security and especially the oil security base (Ji, 2011:29-30). Another development in the aftermath of the 2008 financial crisis was the technological boost to the renewable energy sector (Ji, 2011:29-30). It also brought the two biggest nations of the world China and the US closer into signing an energy cooperation agreement between them (Ji, 2011:32). This was imperative especially when not only the economies but the panics of energy scarcities also share the same resonance (Ji, 2011:29-30). Sceptics believe that China should follow the West (after the 2008 financial crisis) in pursuing a low economic growth strategy as it could not maintain the balance between high growth and energy conservation. (Xu, 2008:10) However it is an indisputable fact that China is still a developing country and pockets of it are extremely backward (especially western China) (Ibid). A low economic growth policy means pushing these areas towards greater impoverishment. In fact moderate or suitable economic growth with "high energy efficiency" is the only option for China. China has been vacillating between exploitation and conservation since the liberation. The only difference was that before 1978 it preferred exploration to conservation and after 1978 it was the reverse (Ibid, 11). However the conservation was done in a narrow sense. Narrow sense of conservation implies conserving coal, oil, gas, power and such exhaustible forms of energy in their natural state (Ibid). This restricts the scope of energy efficiency. The energy policies face the wrath of not just conflicting policies but also discomforting export-import policies where China has not only not been able to seal on its rising imports but has also not been able to control the escalating prices both inside and outside China (Ibid). By 2010, China's gross national product was four per cent to that of the total world GNP but consumption was 31 per cent of coal, 8 per cent of oil and 10 per cent of total electricity output of the world's reserves. China's restoration rate to the energy reserves is merely 30 per cent which is 20 per cent compared to other advanced nations (Ji, 2011:31). In 1974 China's energy efficiency was 28 per cent (Xu, 2008:11). The rest of the 72 per cent of surplus energy was wasted, while developed countries using the same measures were able to conserve 40-50 per cent of energy (Xu, 2008:11). Hence at that time the planning commission decided to transform boilers (used to start steam turbines), furnaces (used for processing bricks) and household kitchen ranges to enhance energy efficiency (Ibid). Another way was to retrieve the effective utilisation of energy efficiency. Such extensive measures incorporated both direct and indirect methods of technical know-how and economic conservation (Ibid). Apart from conserving energy in its natural forms (material resources) it also focuses on carriers like funds and capital (financial resources), transport capacity, human capacity and natural capacity brought by costs incurred on spent resources. Had such methods been practised it is estimated that China would have been able to increase its energy efficiency by 31 per cent (Xu, 2008:11).

One of the highest GDP grossers, China currently is one of the worst energy efficient states in the world. Adopting a broader sense of conservation would mean following a "comprehensive energy efficiency" package which would yield the following advantages (1995 White Paper):

- It encompasses conservation of human, natural, financial, material and natural resources expanding its benefits to the economy because all have come from change of energy.
- It involves mobilisation of each and every aspect of all professions and trade while exploration strategy focuses only on expansion of productive capacity.
- This method does not go for processing of resources and hence does not require large-scale investment of boilers, factories or fields.
- It focuses on acquiring energy (renewable or non-renewable) from the place where required and avoids transportation costs.
- It ensures effective utilisation of energy, is economically beneficial, pollution free, promotes investment on technology and focuses on expansion of administrative capacity.

Administrative capacity in the energy context is essentially the economic administration which in principle aims to seek less consumption, production according to market needs, reduced costs of energy production, enhancement of economic efficiency and competitiveness of factories, etc. This involves two or three concrete aspects of energy—one of them is price. When prices of energy were controlled producers had no incentive to produce and neither the consumers to conserve (Xu, 2008: 12). It was in fact the market forces of demand and supply which gave the concept of suitable price and optimised energy structure focusing on rise of nuclear and other renewable resources (Ibid).

The Seventeenth Party Congress had given a new expansion to China's growth and development strategy which was tabbed as "the scientific outlook of development" (*kexue fazhan guan*)—an anagram for balanced, energy efficient, technology intensive and eco-friendly mode of growth harping not just on fast escalating GDP growth rates but also slowing down for its after-effects (Wang and Zheng, 2007:3). However the objective seems to have few takers as China still focuses on GDP rate in evaluation of its success parameter. No wonder after aiming to quadruple GDP from 2000 to 2020 in the Sixteenth Party Congress, Hu Jintao vowed for quadrupling per capita income from 2000 to 2020 in his next term (Wang and Zheng, 2007:1). "Scientific development" has been referred to as the brainchild of Hu (Wang and Zheng, 2007:3)—it could be considered a confession of the previous decades of an exotic but extremely wasteful growth. "Scientific outlook" has been incorporated into the revised party charter on October 21, 2007—a well accomplished feat believed by Wang and Zheng as Jiang Zemin had to spend an excruciating thirteen-year wait for his "Three Represents" to be incorporated in it. Even in the illustrative "sound and rapid economic development" China seems to have shifted its priority from quantity (read: at any cost) growth to quality (read: innovative and efficient) growth (Ibid:5). It is clear that Hu's usage of "development" at places of "growth" in his speech reflects the jeopardy of China's GDP-ism a clear demarcation at least on paper from "it is glorious to be rich" (*xiang qian kan*). On October 24, 2012 China had issued a White Paper titled *China's Energy Policy 2012.* The paper outlined that China's energy consumption increased by 5.82 per cent from 1981 to 2011 in the background of China's annual growth rate of 10 per cent. It also boasts of China having built a comprehensive supply system of energy with better utility and service conditions since the reform period.

Table 2.8: Statistic for Total Energy Production in 2011

Raw coal	3.52 billion tones
Crude oil	200 million tones
Refined oil products	270 million tones
Natural gas	103.1 billion cubic metres
Installed electricity generating capacity	1.06 billion kilowatts
Annual output of electricity	4.7 trillion kilowatt hour
Total primary energy output	3.18 billion tonnes of standard coal

Source: Government White Paper titled China's Energy Policy 2012.

The Twelfth Five Year Plan (2011-15) too reiterates the White Paper estimates that by 2015 China shall lower its energy consumption per unit GDP by 16 per cent of 2010 and carbon dioxide emission per unit of GDP by 17 per cent. Also the non-fossil fuel installed generation capacity to be increased from 11.4 per cent to 30 per cent by 2015 (Government Work Report, 2011).

> China will push forward its agenda of clean development of fossil energy in an effort to protect the environment and attain its goal of energy conservation and emissions reduction. It will make unswerving efforts to develop new and renewable energy to protect ecological environment and achieve sustainable development. (White Paper on Energy Policy, 2012)

In an entry posted in Green Energy and Clean Technology Intel, Shen Hongpo believes that the basic problem with China is its energy mix which constitutes the domination of coal. The only correction to that problem is investment in clean technology which can be achieved by appropriate market competition between state owned enterprises (SOE) and private enterprises in this field (Hongpo, 2012). It was also notified that China is going in a big way in building nuclear reserves and aims to enhance its nuclear power capacity by 2015 (White Paper on China's Energy Policy 2012). Another White Paper on energy conservation released outlines China's commitment towards developing an energy saving society focusing on the Twelfth Five Year Plan target of achieving 16 per cent reduction in energy consumption (Mao Yaqing, 2012). It is also hailed as the greenest five year plan so far with binding targets aiming towards a direction of concrete implementation than lofty paeans being sung about. China's emphasis on low carbon economy seems to be surpassing the USA especially in industries like electric vehicles, wind turbines and solar panels (APCO Worldwide, 2011).

Table 2.9: China's Estimated Energy Consumption in Comparison from 2010 to 2015

Energy	2010 (per cent)	2015 (per cent)
Coal	70	63
Oil	20	18
Hydro	7	9
Natural gas	4	8
Nuclear	1	2
Wind/solar	0.8	2

Source: APCO Worldwide (2011:5).

The above data clearly defines the government's strengthening resolve to improve the energy security. It has even announced a cap on usage of coal to 4 billion tonnes by 2015 (APCO Worldwide, 2011:5), something it did even in the previous five year plan but failed to achieve. While the previous leaders of China had focused on building their nation into a "world factory" with emphatic focus on state owned enterprises (SOEs) the current plan wants to shift from "made in China" to "designed in China" (APCO Worldwide, 2011:5) and is therefore relying on building strategic emerging industries (SEI) which incorporate the "clean energy syndrome" against the state owned enterprises which are considered as the old pillar industries of China's industry.

Table 2.10: China's Old and New Industries

The old pillar industries	Strategic and emerging industries
National defence	Energy saving and environmental protection
Telecom	Next generation information technology
Electricity	Biotechnology
Oil	High end manufacturing (e.g., aeronautics, high-speed rail)
Coal	New energy (nuclear, solar, wind, biomass)
Airlines	New materials (special and high performance composites)
Marine shipping	Clean energy vehicles (electric cars)

Source: Lewis (2011).

These sectors are expected to become the foundation of China's future economy and help expand on a global scale. The government aims to increase its contribution into GDP from the present 5 per cent to 8 per cent by 2015 and 15 per cent by 2020 (APCO Worldwide, 2011:5). The Strategic and Emerging Industries would help in reducing energy intensity targets which have been pegged at 16 per cent for the Twelfth Five Year Plan (Wee Kean Fong, 2012). This was 19.06 per cent for the period of 2006-2010 (Eleventh Five Year Plan) (Wee Kean Fong, 2012). Measuring energy intensity implies energy consumption per unit GDP which is measured in tonnes of coal used to produce 10,000 Yuan of GDP (usually referred to as standard coal) (Ibid). This involved many efforts with explicit orders from the Centre like closing down of inefficient industries, retrofitting of existing industries, etc (Ibid). It has also been observed that general global meltdown has led to slowing down of the Chinese economy which has reduced production from high energy intensity industries and has also closed down sick, loss making industries which were engaging in wasteful consumption of energy (Ibid). This is also accompanied by shift of energy intensity industries into central and western regions which are rapidly developing as the more developed areas of China are now increasingly foraying into the service sector (Ibid). This provides both an opportunity and challenge for China to enhance its overall low carbon economy (Wee Kean Fong, 2012). An opportunity of engaging in Clean Development Mechanism (CDM) projects in relocation and building up of industrial base of backward areas of China and a greater challenge of energy conservation if this opportunity is not taken properly (Ibid).

Table 2.11: China's Energy Consumption Province-wise

Provinces	Energy consumption per 10,000 Yuan GDP tce/10,000 Yuan GDP	Energy consumption per 10,000 Yuan GDP Increase or decrease from 2010 (+-per cent)	Energy consumption per 10,000 Yuan industrial added value (Increase or decrease from 2010 +-per cent)
Beijing	0.459	-6.94	-18.50
Tianjin	0.708	-4.28	-7.48
Hebei	1.300	-3.69	-6.68
Shanghai	0.618	-5.32	-7.33
Jiangsu	0.600	-3.52	-5.41
Zhejiang	0.590	-3.07	-2.40
Fujian	0.644	-3.29	-1.16
Shandong	0.855	-3.77	-7.67
Guangdong	0.563	-3.78	-5.13
Hainan	0.692	5.23	12.53
Shanxi	1.762	-3.55	-5.82
Anhui	0.754	-4.06	-9.54
Jiangxi	0.651	-3.08	-6.87
Henan	0.895	-3.57	-8.60
Hubei	0.912	-3.79	-6.88
Hunan	0.894	-3.68	-8.61
Inner Mongolia	1.405	-2.51	-4.39
Guangxi	0.800	-3.36	-6.13
Chongqing	0.953	-3.81	-5.31
Sichuan	0.997	-4.23	-7.78
Guizhou	1.714	-3.51	-8.02
Yunan	1.162	-3.22	-9.92
Tibet	n.a	n.a	n.a
Shaanxi	0.846	-3.56	-5.60
Gansu	1.402	-2.51	-1.96

Qinghai	2.081	9.44	9.62
Ningxia	2.279	4.60	14.72
Xinjiang	1.631	6.96	9.28
Liaoning	1.096	-3.40	-5.02
Jilin	0.923	3.59	-4.19
Heilongjiang	1.042	-3.50	-5.17
China	0.793	-2.01	n.a

Source: Wee 2012

The above table gives details about the energy consumption of different provinces in China in terms of its economic costs and total carbon emissions. The table also highlights the changes in energy consumption within a span of two years from 2010 to 2012 and also gives data about industrial added value. It has been seen that relatively undeveloped areas like Qinghai, Gansu, Ningxia, Heilongjiang, Inner Mongolia are consuming more energy than Beijing, Shanghai and other developed places. Moreover these areas have also had the maximum increase in industrial added value like Ningxia (14.72 per cent), etc., while developed areas have had a reduction in industrial added value, with Beijing being the maximum at 18.5 per cent.

China's energy policy 2012 White Paper sums up China's present energy position and future goals to achieve energy efficiency.

> As a country with a large population but relatively insufficient resources China must take the path of energy conservation. China will make unswerving efforts to develop new and renewable energy to protect ecological environment and achieve sustainable development. The reform is expected to give full play to the fundamental role of the market in allocating resources. The nation will develop the coal industry in a safe and highly efficient way to spur the development of thermal power in a clean and highly efficient manner (White Paper on Energy Policy, 2012).

At the World Energy Forum 2012 in Dubai, Jin Xiaoming Director General of the Department of International Cooperation of China's Science and Technology Ministry said "there is still a considerable gap between China and developed countries in energy efficiency and capabilities. We have launched a host of energy efficiency furnaces, electric mechanical equipment, buildings and lighting" (*China Daily*, 2012). Reform in the energy sector implies reforms from within the energy system which China's White Paper claims to be "a requirement for perfecting the socialist market economy." Statistics have shown that 25 per cent of the rise in oil demand during the last decade of the twentieth century has occurred because of rise of only one nation—China (Sascha Muller-Kraenner, 2008:3-5). China's own domestic sources (in this case oil) like Tibet and Xinjiang have contributed little to its growing appetite which is more industrially "producer" based unlike the USA where consumers are the main energy guzzlers (Ibid).

In an analysis done keeping the year 1978 as the break-even point, a survey was done of the period between 1953 to 2006 and it was discovered that before the reform era energy consumption and pollution emissions reflected a phenomenon of fluctuating rise while after the reforms both consumption and emissions revealed a rising trend while the intensity was on decline.

Figure 2.2: Pollution and Energy Consumption from 1953 to 2006

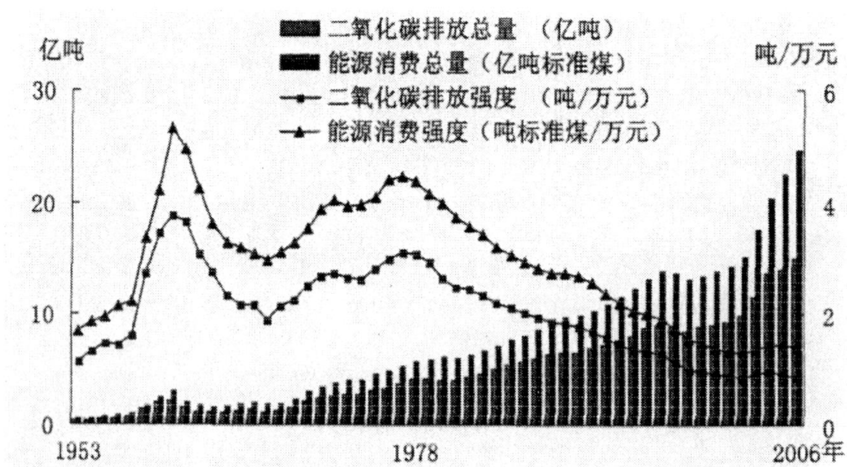

Source: Zhou Li (June 2009:2).

LINE 1: total carbon dioxide emissions (hundred million tonnes)
LINE 2: total energy consumption (hundred million tonnes standard coal)
LINE 3: intensity of total emissions (tonnes/10,000 yuan)
LINE 4: intensity of energy consumption (tonnes/10,000 yuan)

The table is a juxtaposition of energy consumption and carbon emissions intensity and the total amount from the period of 1953-2008. The table shows that the pre-reform era was in sharp contrast to the reform and post-reform period showing high and fluctuating tendency of energy consumption and emissions which have had a steady decline since 1978.

In a preliminary analysis it has been revealed that the reformed economy focused more on reduction of intensity of emissions and energy consumption than the complete reduction of actual figures. However it has been evident that energy, environment and economy have always been intricately linked together. It has been increasingly felt that mindless FDI is not the only solution to better economic growth (whose fruits are now being wearied down by environmental costs) what is required is proper rationalisation of import and export of products which cater towards energy saving. It has been increasingly seen that China's energy policies are usually in conflict with each other. If we analyse the Chinese economy between the period of 1980-2000 we can see that China's GDP has expanded 6.3 times in the two decades (Wei, 2004:1). It is no secret that China's industry has been the main contributor towards its "rise" especially the growth in manufacture, metallurgy, chemicals making China enter into a heavy and chemical industry stage (Wei, 2004:5). China's energy consumption increased up to 1996 and then supply began to exceed demand especially for coal and electricity (Ibid:6). However by the turn of the century the consumption rebounded and supply shortages shot up. This led to different implications on different resources especially their prices. While coal price was subjected to market forces from 2002 since the state gave up its rights to monitor the price (Ibid:7). However the state has retained its control over prices of thermal power (Ibid).

This led to a situation of double whammy for the coal-based power generators to the extent that provinces like Shaanxi which were one of the biggest coal producers also began to face power shortages (Wei, 2004:7). This had repercussions over oil and diesel supply which was now stored by many enterprises for self-generation of power to continue with normal production. China's demand and supply pattern reveal some special characteristics (Wei, 2004). Primary among them (apart from others) is lower per capita availability of energy reserves due to being *numero uno* in population. China has suffered from overall lower per capita availability of reserves despite being one of the main producers of major energy resources. While China was the third largest producer of coal averaging around 200 billion tonnes (1996 data), its per capita availability even by 2000 was merely 90 tonnes (Wei, 2004:7-8). Similarly in 1994 China's oil production was 93 billion tonnes and gas reserves were 38 trillion cubic metres yet the per capita availability was merely 11.1 per cent and 4.3 per cent of the world average respectively (Wei, 2004:8). With the turn of the century one can analyse the trends of the first ten years of energy demand and draw inferences at least for its next ten years.

Table 2.12: Energy Demand in the Last Ten Years

Item	2000 (per cent)	2010 (per cent)
Coal	65.9	59.6
Oil	24.5	22.2
Natural gas	2.4	8.7
Hydropower	6.7	6.6
Nuclear power	0.4	1.8
Renewables	0.1	1.1
Total	100	100

Source: Wei Zhihong (2004:6-7).

From the above table one can observe that despite declining demand, coal still dominates China's consumption structure. Other fossil fuels like oil and natural gas are pulled back by international supply patterns and China's own exploration adventure. As far non-fossil fuels like hydro and nuclear power are concerned, they are usually limited by their capacity to produce and accompanying large-scale impending environmental disasters encouraged by their over-exploitation or unattended distribution. The rise in consumption of renewable sources shows the government's commitment towards energy conservation which it started as early as 1981 (Wei, 2004:11). The energy development strategy of 1981 aimed "to produce and save energy simultaneously with priority on energy saving" (Ibid). The proposal of Ninth Five Year Plan in 1995 also adhered to the reiteration of the same strategy of 1981 (Ibid:11). Energy conservation goes beyond the purview of energy efficiency or non-utilisation of fossil fuels as it also encompasses labour force and funds, control of population expansion, increasing productivity and benefits of industrial enterprises, optimisation of industrial product mix, etc., the government has even institutionalised its conservation commitment by establishing China Energy Conservation Investment Corporation (CECIC) and State Energy Conservation Information Dissemination Centre (SECIDC) for leasing of conservation equipment. Energy Saving Corporation (ESCO) gave advisory services to users of Integrated Resource Programme (IRP), Demand Side Management (DSM) (Wei, 2004:12-13), etc. However China's energy conservation programme is not all a dreamy silhouette but is gutted with problems larger than the system itself. China's transition towards market economy has many a time hindered more than facilitated the energy conservation mission. Grant of autonomy and simultaneous loss of authority of the central management system has meant weakening of the macro control and consequent lack of stringency in implementation of government measures. Again the restructuring of ministries sometimes meant axing down of relevant departments and organisations which performed the mundane but extremely viable task of collection of data for future policies. Also policies granting incentives for energy saving like tax subsidy, low interest loan, etc., were little, if existing. Aggravating the situation were the loopholes in "energy conservation law" providing ambiguous statements retarding its effective implementation. ESCO too failed to fulfil its desired aim due to market inaccessibility, lack of funds, lacuna of integration of information regarding various projects and existence of inexperienced and insufficient managers, etc. (Wei, 2004:13).

The development of renewable sources was another major issue troubling the policymakers of the energy department. Hence three commissions: State Development Planning Commission (SDPC), State Science and Technology Commission (SSTC) and Ministry of Science and Technology (MOST) collaborated to formulate "guidelines on renewable energy development programme (1996-2010)" in 1995 (Wei, 2004:20). Following the guidelines China had established thirty wind farms by the year 2002 in Xinjiang, Guangdong and Inner Mongolia. This was also inspired by the 1999 strategy of "development of the west" which seeks to eschew the principle of "production first and environmental protection to be followed" (Ibid). It is common knowledge that the issue of energy intensity reduction is not a mere post-reform enlightenment but also an absolute necessity provoked by Soviet-style industrialisation which China was dragged into, "kicking, screaming and sometimes starving" (Rosen and Houser, 2007a:6).

Figure 2.3: Energy Consumption from 1952 to 2009

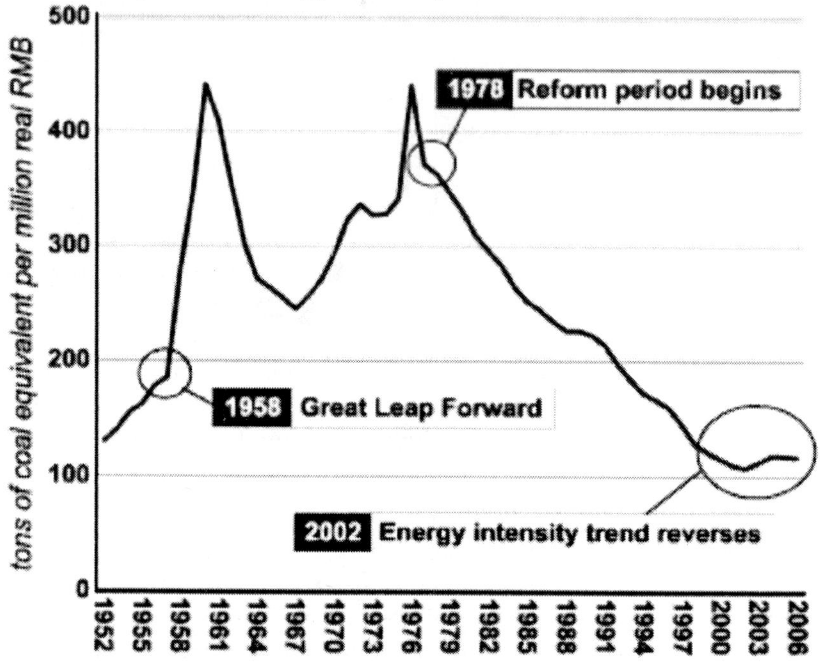

Source: Rosen Daniel and Trevor Houser (2007a:6).

The above graph shows that Chinese economy's energy intensity accelerated since 1958, the Great Leap Forward and peaked till the early 1960s after which it declined as the Soviet assistance began to decline and China embroiled itself in multiple wars. This again gained momentum in the 1970s until the reforms of 1978 and a series of conservation laws which steadily brought down the energy intensity figures. However the advent of "China rise" reversed the trend and all the good work was left undone as China again reverted its focus on economy only (Rosen and Houser, 2007a:6-8). Despite the post-reform period witnessing a meteoric rise which has been widely publicised, it was actually the pre-reform period from 1949 to 1978 that raised the industrial output in a streak of blitzkrieg often at the cost of energy which kept on escalating (and even tripled) to produce each unit of economic output (Rosen and Houser, 2007a:6-8). The reform period which was an economic incentive in spirit not only allowed people to retain profits but also made them aware and bear the costs incurred, including energy. The introduction of free-market forces to prices of fossil fuels left the companies (state owned enterprises) with no choice but to learn, and to learn fast the management of their growing energy bills. The mood was set by competing domestic private sector and energy efficient foreign firms. However, this is not to say that Chinese firms bear full brunt of the cost but National Development and Reform Commission (NDRC) fixes the prices, varying according to provinces in consultation with local officials and local pricing bureaus (Rosen and Houser, 2007a:11). This implies that all industries of a particular region or area pay the same price despite large differences in the quantity of their consumption. NDRC, although wanting to increase prices for most of the energy consuming industries, has failed to do so because of local resistance and non-payment issues (Rosen and Houser, 2007a:11).

The institutionalisation and price liberalisation of the reform period did contribute to reduction in energy consumption and enhancement of energy efficiency. With the result that China in the early 1990s maintained its exporter status (Rosen and Houser, 2007a:6). The 2002 reversal of investment into economy-led growth without adequate or even considerable investment in efficient technologies or conservation measures and nascent rise in consumption-led energy demand has been instrumental in putting the energy supply into reverse gear (Rosen and Houser, 2007a:6).

Figure 2.4: Energy Demand Growth Period-wise

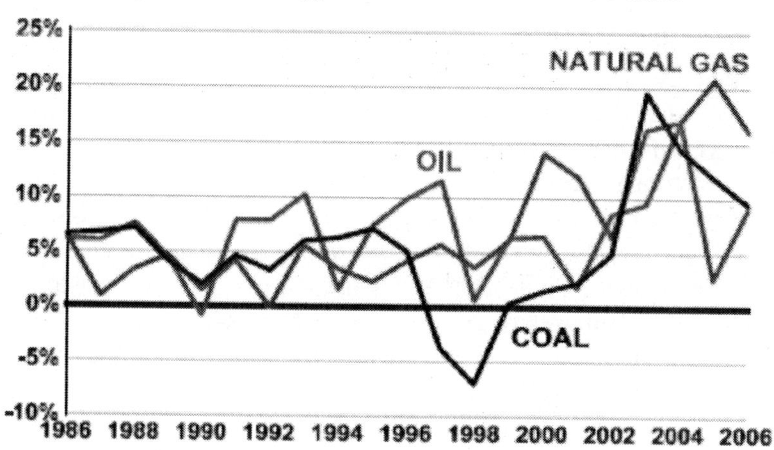

Source: Daniel Rosen and Trevor Houser (May 2007a:17).

The above graph detailing the fluctuating demand structure of fossil fuels (coal, oil and gas) more than anything else has confirmed the accelerating rise in fossil fuel consumption since the turn of the century. Juxtaposed between the plan and the market, fossil fuels of China (needless to say, which have not been able to be displaced by renewable sources/non-fossilised fuels as the base of China's energy structure) are more focused on supply expansion than demand management (Rosen and Houser, 2007a: 16-17).

Conclusion

From the burning of wood by primitive society to the burning of coal and now of oil, energy consumption by society has continued unabated and the energy structure has never remained unchanged for a long time. Changing living standards, changing economic symbols and changing political concepts have all been contributing to the construction, expansion, destruction and restoration of the energy structure from time immemorial. This continuous revamping perhaps metaphorically links energy resources to the phoenix which has been rising from its own ashes. The industrialisation of the economy, urbanisation of the society and dawn of the information age has all been detrimental in deciding the development pattern of energy resources of not only China but also of the world.

The main objectives of China's energy security have been to ensure price stability, supply stability, energy efficiency, energy self-sufficiency and to diversify its supply sources. The issue of price stability was given special impetus in the Eleventh Five Year Plan which demanded less interference in the prices of oil and gas so that the actual gap between the demand and supply of fossil fuels could be assessed (Liu et. al., 2008:3). Also since China possessed only 7.7 per cent and 7.1 per cent of the world's total oil and gas reserves, it would be feasible for China to invest in the supply infrastructure and delivery mechanism to reduce the costs of production (Ibid). This plan was also instrumental in making the local governments more accountable for the wastage of scarce energy resources within their jurisdiction and the deteriorating environment conditions due to the production or consumption of fossil fuel sources. China's energy industry is caught between conflicting positions of different interest groups, especially the tussle between coal and oil (Ibid: 6-7). The abundance of coal within the domestic confines has made it lose its lustre in the government eyes as the policymakers spend all their attention on the investment in the oil industry. Naturally, private players are kept away from the "black gold" and state owned oil companies enjoy windfall profits which are mostly left with them for further investment in the maintenance of oil security (Ibid). Coal industry not only gets a step motherly treatment from the government because of the oil factor but also faces harassment because of the constant bickering between its mining industry and the electricity generation industry (Ibid). Continuous shift in price structures are of no help as the mining industry is unable to pick up despite increased payment from the electricity generation companies. The electricity generators too are caught in their own embroil with the distributors as heavy competition has forced them to drastically reduce the price while selling to the state grid (Ibid). China also faces day to day brawls between the local private producer and the state owned company, local resources and far established industries, consumers and distributors which can perhaps never be solved by any energy policy dealing only with macro perspectives (Liu et. al., 2008: 6-7). China's energy policies have a unique characteristic of giving its industries a superior position than its supply areas which is incomparable to the policy of any other country in the world. One of the foremost reasons for this policy is the "demand surge" of energy resources during the "double digit" growth of China's economy. This meant that China's energy producing industries were given generous investments by the government to maintain the stability of supply for all other energy consuming industries (Ibid). However, what these investments missed out was focusing on the research and development of these areas to achieve "technical breakthroughs" (Ibid, 7-8). It cannot be discounted that with the advantage of inexpensive labour and an excellent industrial base China should begin to concentrate not just on production but efficient and effective production.

The above discussion can help us build a trajectory of the analysis of China's energy structure from the period of 1949 till present date. China has constantly been oscillating between industrial demands and conservation policies never being able to bring the two together in consonance rather than divergence with each other. Though the China rise can be blamed for rising demand yet it is clearly evident that it is not the rising living standards but the demand to maintain double-digit growth rates which bears an impact on its policies. Hence, while the spirit of self-sufficiency has percolated through all the energy policies, the ways and means to achieve it have been inconsistent, vacillating between extreme priorities of allowance of unproductive consumption for the sake of economic growth to stringency on optimum utilisation even at the cost of stifling production. Note that in its vision a "modern energy system," China is still carrying the historical mindset of self-reliance and self-sufficiency as it chooses to "rely mainly on domestic supplies" despite "increasing international cooperation." This chapter gave a discussion about the energy policies which are affected by changes in energy sector through the efforts of the domestic determinants. It has been shown that government policies were always in tandem with the growth and prospects of the energy sector whether during the self-reliance phase or the current "green GDP" phase. Also many domestic determinants like the intelligentsia, industry, etc., could create enough pressure on the government to redirect the provisions and targets of the energy policies. How they did so shall be discussed in the ensuing chapters.

The government is also cautious about not committing the old mistakes of its liberation period as well as of the developed countries in their road to industrialisation and hence time and again harps on the underlying issue of "strengthening energy conservation," the national action plan of 2007 on climate change, the ex-president Hu Jintao's speech during the 17th National Congress of "improving China's capacity for independent innovation as well as energy and environmental conservation" and the extra emphasis of the White Paper on development of science and technology speak about China's commitment to "protect the environment" (*Beijing Review*, 2008). However Erica Downs believes that this "Chinese rhetoric" not only needs serious commitment but also abolition of historical obstacles like a strong bureaucratic department so that it can withstand the heavy pressure of the state owned energy companies and yet champion the environment cause (Erica Downs, 2006:16). The years before 1978 focused only on establishing the investment structure for energy so that it is able to cater to the demands of the emerging heavy industry as well as maintain its stability through the continuous supply of energy. Energy hence was given a supplementary role and was still not considered one of the basic fundamental policies of China. It was for the first time in 1978 that the industrial development policy separately dealt with issues of the status of development of fuel industry, power industry and industries of raw energy resources (Shi Dan, 2000:20-26). The issue of transportation bottlenecks was also discussed for the first time (Ibid). The 1982 report on economic and social development and the report on the Sixth Five Year Plan also focused on policies regarding the construction of infrastructure and removal of transport problems (Ibid). By 1988, in the annual policy report the emphasis had shifted to investment in the power industry which was fast becoming a reality (Ibid). In 1989 the State Council took a major decision regarding the prevailing production policy (ibid). The decision was to use collective capacity in developing the basic production units for developing agriculture, energy, transport and the raw material industry (Ibid). By 1992 when China was on the verge of becoming the net importer of oil, it issued the policy of "stabilising the east and developing the west" (*wenzhu dongbu, fazhan xibu*) (Shi Dan, 2000: 20-26). The Tenth Plan was the manifestation of the conflict of development between resources, environment and economy. It has been regularly felt that in order to give space to new and developing enterprises it is imperative to reduce the pressure on energy and environment. The year 2004 witnessed a new promulgation by the State Council called guidelines and laws for medium and long-term development of energy (*nengyuan zhongchangqi fazhan guihua gangyao, 2004-2020*). It is a known fact that China's extensive economic growth patterns have been spearheaded by foreign direct investment and international trade. Grossman and Krueger (1993) (cited from Zhou, 2009:1) have always believed that decline in air quality of China is precisely because of this investment which usually happens in the dominant production sector which, in China's case, was the industry. This led to a frenzy of competitive market encouraging low-cost production at the cost of environment quality. The White Paper titled "China's energy conditions and policies" issued on December 26, 2007 had come out after almost a decade of highlighting the direction of the government's future plans. This paper was the combined work of Energy Bureau and Institute of Macro-Economics (both of which are under the supervision of NDRC) and their officials have been in media limelight since then, especially when the public and the whole world in general wants to know what China would do next to save itself from the scarcity scare. Xinhua News Agency in an interview quoted the officials of NDRC, considering the previous White Papers issued in 1995 and 1997, as mere "annual reports of industrial sector in the government department" (*Beijing Review*, 2008). They believed that a comprehensive analysis and ensuing publication was long overdue and coinciding with the theme of the Twelfth Five Year Plan, this was the best time to publish it. Also a country which is time and again hackneyed for non-transparency in government dealings would also allow the international community to learn the Chinese understanding (*zhongguo tese*) of energy security. Moreover the NDRC is also publishing reports on individual energy resources (report on coal industry was published in November 2007), as additional supplements to its White Paper to grant more transparency to its energy policies (Ibid).

China's future energy strategy consists of the goals of "strengthening energy conservation, relying mainly on domestic supplies, exploring new energy resources, giving a bigger role to high technology, protecting the environment, increasing international cooperation and building a stable, economic, clean and safe energy network" (*Beijing Review*, 2008). The January 28, 2010 Xinhua report of the decision taken by State Council to set up National Energy Commission with Premier Wen Jiabao as its head and Li Keqiang as its deputy head (Yu and Houlden, 2013:10) and the October 24, 2012 releases of the White Paper on energy policy marking a sharp difference from state owned enterprises to strategic emerging industries have shown that perhaps it would be in the best of China's energy interests if it adopted extensive measures to curb industrial energy consumption which has been its biggest consumer throughout history. It can do so either by pushing for stringent administrative controls, especially over factories which are using obsolete techniques for exploiting or producing coal, chemicals, electricity, petrol, gold or other construction materials. These industries can also be the biggest pollution makers if they do not adhere to environmental regulations. Another measure could be to introduce major reforms in the supply and price pattern of the industrial consumption structure. However in doing so energy policies should not forget to ensure the competitive edge of these industries, as well as the Chinese economy. The government has been trying to bank upon the fluctuating price mechanism of the energy resources to raise the awareness and conscious level of citizens in general and companies in particular about the misery of the energy resources and the urgent collective will required for conserving them. Various blogs and media discussions are publicised highlighting the gap between the taxes paid by the citizens and the consumption pattern. The internet is also becoming a medium for transmission of information between the central and the local governments, the energy suppliers and the distributors as well as the think tank and the government departments reducing the costs to some extent. In the case of China it has been evident enough that the present has come out of the past and history shall repeat itself in future, yet to what ferocity is only in the store of time's belly.

3. The Domestic Determinants of Energy Policies: The Actors Involved

Self-sufficiency of energy resources has always been the basic aim of China's energy policies. The base of economic security and perhaps a country's security is embedded in energy security. Energy has descended really fast from being a luxury to a necessity and has permeated all spheres of human activity. Energy industry is a special industry in the sense that in providing public goods and services it has attained monopolisation over all other industries. An enterprise now requires energy equipment at all levels of production. No industry can be built without energy. China's energy production and consumption has increased six times since 1978 which was 600 million tce (total carbon emission) in 1978 and became 3,500 million tce by 2011 (Zhou Hongchun, 2012: 5-12). The first and foremost step is to formulate an energy policy based on advantages possessed by China, a policy which is not fathomed from the fear of market or short-sightedness but a policy which believes in China's strengths as steps to achieving energy sufficiency. Recently China has transformed its policy of "wealth for country first" (*guo fu youxian*) to "wealth for people first" (*min fu youxian*) (Lin Jenny, 2012: 1).

China is avidly promoting "inclusive growth" (ibid.). This automatically brings us to the question of the determinants of China's energy policies. A determinant is a thing that decides whether or how something will happen (*Oxford Dictionary, 1992*), a domestic determinant is obviously one that happens inside a particular country or holds influence within the territorial confines of a country. In the case of China, the latter does not hold so much true as the former explanation. *Modern Chinese Dictionary* (2009: 1620) defines a determinant as a component of a product or the cause or condition which decides the failure or success of a product or phenomena. Anthony Wanjohi (2011) claims that domestic determinants of policies are those internal factors which focus attention on "variations in states' attributes." Note that while Western dictionaries do not define the outcome of a process which is based on a determinant, the Chinese definition considers the "determinant" as instrumental in deciding the outcome of a process. This chapter shall identify the various domestic determinants of China which are influential in determining the contents of energy policies and direct the development of the energy sector.

The determinants here constitute the actors instrumental in formulation of policies, the economic factors which invariably lead to the cause of the problem and environmental repercussions of energy management. For the purpose of this study we shall not discuss the issues of geopolitics and other extraneous factors which can indirectly influence the domestic policy structure.

The actors in the energy context are what make the bulk of the Chinese population. It is entrenched amongst all strata of society ranging from government which also involves the bureaucracy, the employees of the energy companies as well as the actors at the receiving end, i.e., the consumers.

Bureaucratic Control: Bureaucracy (*guanliao zhuyi*) is a term which evokes more emotions than reason in the Chinese psyche. While Oxford puts it as "a system in which most of the important decisions are taken by state officials rather than elected representatives" *Modern Chinese Dictionary* defines it as a system divorced from reality and the masses, does not bother about mass benefit and only knows how to give orders without undergoing research or leadership styles (*Modern Chinese Dictionary, Xiandai Hanyu Cidian*, 2009: 503). Perhaps the corrupt officials of the Qing dynasty and afterwards had a deep-rooted impact on the Chinese. When the Communist Party took over China it had a nation to build from scratch whose "energy levels were low" literally. It evolved various ministries creating, destroying and re-creating to boost up its energy production. The transformation of energy policies have been reflected in its ensuing plans. Coincidentally the changing plans were also earmarked by changing leadership which saw a shift not only in the policies but also the methods and mechanisms adopted to pursue it. For this purpose it is imperative to understand the shift in the institutional framework of China's decision makers. An obvious transformation in this bureaucratic structure has been rise and fall in the number of ministries since the Mao and Deng era. There has been a gradual shift from the "individual leadership charisma" to "informed study group." Moreover changing ideologies in the political front meant that the energy sector too developed in the similar pattern ranging from centralisation to marketisation of resources. Between 1993 and 2003 the decisions of the top brass were fragmented and piecemeal in nature owing to duplication of authority and contradiction of control (Yu and Houlden, 2013:7-8). It was not only the influence of the echelons of the party like the members of the Leading Small Group or the NDRC who were instrumental in manoeuvring the provisions of energy policies but even the local governments who were left with the main task of implementation (Ibid). In June 2005 Leading Group was established to submit its recommendations to the State Council (Burke et. al., 2009:3). Meanwhile China's strengthened policies and regulations have seen a radical shift from 'resource exploitation strategy' to 'synthetic enegy efficiency strategy'(Xu, 2008:8).

Energy Companies: It is a known fact that China's energy companies are no routine state enterprises but a conglomeration of government interest and experts acumen into generating energy resources for the nation. While universally the government is one of the shareholders in a public owned corporation, in the Chinese case the Government is not only the shareholder but also retains full ownership of the company (*Modern Chinese Dictionary, Xiandai Hanyu Cidian*, 2009). As the main producers of the nation, China's energy companies specialise in different sources of energy to earmark their scope of expansion and harnessing of energy resources. The research institutes of companies like China National Petroleum Corporation (CNPC), China National Offshore Oil Corporation (CNOOC), China Petroleum and Chemical Corporation (Sinopec), etc., coupled with State owned energy companies and State Power Economic Research Centre not only have the voice of expertise but also strong powerful influence. Another important energy company group is the coal and power companies like ChinaCoal, Shenhua Group, etc., which have been catering to a large section of domestic needs since their inception and form the bulk of China's energy consumption. When the whole world is clamouring for China to take a deeper dig in its environment contribution, the influence and control of these fossil fuel companies should not be doubted as they have been the backbone of China's energy structure withstanding the changing political stands, changing hands only at the administration front.

Consumers: The consumers are not just the common man but also various interest groups and social communities. The state owned enterprises, the industrial stakeholders the non-governmental organisations and the media reflect the voice of the people who directly bear the brunt of energy scarcity and its issue. China's consumers of the pre-reform era were the poor of the country who consumed to satisfy their needs. In the coal dominated consumption structure and political dogmas of self-sufficiency it was widely believed that coal would last enough for all and forever. However as China became more integrated into the world economy the demand structure of its citizens expanded and rising living standards descended many luxuries into necessities demanding more fossil fuel consumption. How much a consumer contributes to energy scarcity and how much it can do to promote energy conservation is primarily discussed here.

The Bureaucratic Control with Embedded Aspirations of CCP

The policymakers of any country occupy a pivotal position. Being at the helm of affairs they get to decide who gets what and by how much. China is dominated by one party, the Communist Party, and so naturally gets to be its decision-makers in all aspects, with particular scrutiny, of issues dealing with security, like energy. At a time when China had just emerged from the ravages of civil war and its energy sector was in the nascent stage of development, China was heavily focused on satisfying its immediate needs rather than adopting a long-term strategy for the growth of its energy sector. Moreover the influence of the Soviet Union was not just limited to political ideologies but also to import of technology and machinery as well as the administrative structure of a centralised planning approach. Due to this factor the institutional structure of the pre-reform era was a rather confusing one as ministries constantly evolved and dissolved and power kept on oscillating from the central to the local and the provincial governments. The ministries at that time were (Yu and Houlden, 2013: 5-6):

- Ministry of Fuel Industry—this Ministry had seen the dawn of the day with paeans of liberation sung in the air in 1949. It was instrumental in channelising and allocating the production and distribution of various fossil fuels like oil, gas and power till 1954.
- State Planning Commission—while this institution established in 1952 was mainly responsible for economic supervision, it also played a major role in supervision of matters related to energy.
- The four ministries—the Korean war in 1955 led to the end of the Ministry of Fuel Industry in China as it got divided into separate ministries related to each energy resource, namely, Ministry of Petroleum Industry, Ministry of Coal Industry, Ministry of Chemical Industry and Ministry of Electric Power Industry. However these ministries were again merged during the Cultural Revolution.
- Another bifurcation—although the Ministry of Fuel Industry had been reinstated it was left devoid of any powers as the Cultural Revolution had shifted the political mileage to the rural areas as well as power to the local governments. No wonder it faced another bifurcation in the form of Ministry of Coal Industry and Ministry of Petroleum and Chemical

industry in 1975. The latter mentioned ministry again got sub-divided into Ministry of Petroleum Industry and Ministry of Chemical Industry in 1978.

Jimin Zhao (2001: 5) observes that during the period of Cultural Revolution not only political turmoil, but decentralisation also was the cause of reduced production of energy resources. Moreover the planned period, despite adopting a centralised planning approach, had no long-term vision for development of its energy resources. Zhao cites that the fifteen-year electrification programme of the 1950s was the only exception to this approach. However this mentality had a change with government restructuring in the periods of 1981 to 1983 and 1985 to 1989. This governmental reorganisation which had led to pulverisation of various energy ministries into energy corporations and companies were funded by a special fund called the coal for oil substitution fund (*mei dai you*) (Zhao Jimin, 2001: 5-6). This fund was financed by the profit earned from the high price charged on the export of oil and low price paid to domestic sources of production (Ibid). The China Energy Investment Corporation formed in the year 1988 deserves a special mention as by the virtue of its responsibility, it had access to all domestic and foreign capital and could command banks to issue bonds both at the home turf and abroad (Ibid). This was unique to a corporation as the Ministry of Energy which, although superseded it on power, had no such effective powers and was limited to building energy strategies and policies (Ibid). Even in this aspect says Zhao (2001), electricity was the only scope of action as the rest all operated under their own corporations and institutions concerned only about their sector's interests. This lack of unification delayed China in achieving its lofty goal of reducing wasteful consumption.

While the reforms gave a greater autonomy and in hand revenue to the local governments over their supervised energy projects, it did little to alleviate the sagging regional energy industry from cash crunch situations or technological imbalances (Ibid). This was because the revenue was redirected by the local governments into investing in industries which brought windfall profits in the short term like the light industry, real estate, etc., hence the proceeds from the energy industry were utilised less in energy production industry and more in energy consumption industries aggravating the situation even further (Ibid). Thus, despite massive political and economic reforms the "donor and beggar" relationship of the central and the local governments remained in the energy domain (Ibid). Moreover the self-sufficiency policies of the Mao era had taught the local governments to view other regions with a spirit of rivalry and competition rather than coordination and cooperation (Ibid). This hindered the intra-economic trade and led to duplication of resources resulting in cases of "too much" or "too little" production across China.

All these inherent weaknesses of the 1980s led the central government of the 1990s to adopt the "control and release" approach (*shou and fang*) regionally rather than holistically (Ibid, 7). This meant that not all local governments were given freedom but only those who deserved it and could handle it "with responsibility." The institutional settings of China's energy sector have undergone a number of reforms and adjustments which are generally consistent with China's broader administration reforms (Yu and Houlden, 2013:6-8).

The reform era meant the rule of the market and no sector was left untouched of this ideology including the very important sectors like energy. With the market came the corporate, and a string of national oil companies were established in the pursuit. The havoc of the Cultural Revolution had burnt the institutional structure of China and National Energy Commission was established to hide the scars in 1980 (Ibid). Nothing worked leading to dissolving of this ministry in 1982 and "ruling the future" was considered a more viable option than "restoring the past" (Ibid). On the other hand the Ministry of Petroleum Industry had begun to gain unforeseen impetus due to international tumult and soaring appetite in the domestic sphere. The SOEs dealing in oil which were still affiliated to the Ministry of Petroleum Industry were granted autonomy as never before and became pioneers in engaging in overseas activities as part of the overall "opening up" (*kaifang*) strategy (Yu and Houlden, 2013: 7-11). In fact Sinopec is a protégé of the merging of various enterprises which were under various ministries and had clubbed to form the China Petrochemical Corporation in the year 1983 (Ibid). On similar lines CNPC was established through the abolishment of Ministry of Petroleum Industry in 1988 (Ibid). This SOE especially dealing with the onshore drilling activities like its predecessor was reporting directly to the State Council. However oil was not the only sector where the experiment of turning ministries into SOEs was undertaken (Yu and Houlden, 2013: 7-11). National Coal Corporation and National Nuclear Corporation also emerged from the demise of Ministry of Coal Industry, Ministry of Water Resources and Electric Power and the Ministry of Nuclear Industry (Ibid: 7). As the "coordinating body" of all state owned energy enterprises, the Ministry of Energy was established in 1988 to look after the entire energy sector. However, the decision was revoked by Premier Zhu Rongji in 1993 as the creation of this ministry had led to political tussles as well as "duplication of authority with NDRC" as was officially cited (Yu and Houlden, 2013: 7-8). Erica Downs (2008:42) has stated that energy, despite being a major issue, has not able to achieve its own separate ministry because of opposition by NDRC who would not only lose its sphere of influence but also its direct relation with the party leadership. Now, China operated under the National Development and Reform Commission which operates by the directions of State Council (the highest executive organ of China) which in turn is a firm believer of CPC's guidance and policies. By 1998 the influence of market in establishing the Chinese economy in its pristine position had begun to be endorsed even in government circles and any administrative structure which hindered or neutralised the effect of the growth in the economy, such as any redundant government official, ministry, or institution, were completely scrapped. The year 1998 was a landmark year as it saw the dissolution of about fifteen ministries which were related to the separate energy resources (Yu and Houlden, 2013:8). The State Planning Commission by now had become the State Planning Development Commission (SDPC) and Oil and Chemical Industry were given a specialised industry under the name of National Bureau of Petroleum and Chemical Industry in 1998 (Ibid). This Bureau had usurped the government powers of CNPC, Sinopec and Ministry of Chemical Industry leading to political bickering, and hence faced an early demise in 2001 (Ibid). The fag end of the twentieth century gave the oil and gas industry a big boost as the National Oil Corporations (NOCs) were upgraded from being mere enterprises to listed companies and were granted more autonomy and power through "central administrative assets allocation" (Ibid). Yu and Houlden (2013) believe that this move was taken under the policy principle of "separating primary industries from secondary industries, separating superior assets from non-performing assets and separating corporate functions from social functions" (Yu and Houlden, 2013: 9).

After the major restructuring in the year 1998, the current government departments dealing with energy have reduced from 40 to 29 (Zhao, 2001: 9). Jimin Zhao (2001) lists the major ministries, the departments under them and their scope of work.

Table 3.1: The Functions of Various Ministries Dealing With Energy

Ministry	Department	Function
SDPC	1. Department of Basic Industry involving • Division of Transportation • Division of Coal Industry • Division of Electricity • Division of Energy Conservation and Renewable Energy 2. Department of Investment 3. Department of Foreign Financing Utilisation 4. Department of Regional Economic Development also involving the • Office of the National Coordination Group for combating climate change	1. It formulates strategies, policies and plans for energy and transportation development and energy efficiency. 2. It also supervises the national energy investment projects and policies for foreign investment. 3. It not only coordinates the domestic efforts related to climate change but also signs treaties with other foreign partners.
SETC	1. Department of Electric Power 2. Department of Resource Conservation and Comprehensive Utilisation involve • Division of Energy Conservation and New Energy 3. Department of Industrial Policy 4. Department of Sector Planning and Sector Associations	1. It engages in formulation of policies, planning and regulation related to electricity and electricity saving and renewable energy. 2. It promotes technology innovation for energy saving and formulates policies for management related to sectors like oil, gas, petrochemicals and coal.
MOST	1. Department of New Technology and Industrialisation involving 2. Division of Energy and Transportation 3. Department of Rural and Social Development	It formulates policies and plans and manages R&D programmes related to energy. It also deals with research, deployment, development and demonstration of renewable energy.
MLR	Department of Mineral Resources Department of Mining Management Department of Geological Exploration	It engages in planning, management, protection and sustainable use of all natural resources.
SQBTS	Department of Standardisation	It establishes energy efficiency parameters for all commercial and non-commercial products and processes.

SEPA	1. Department of Pollution Control 2. Department of Nuclear Safety and Radiation Management	It formulates policies for pollution control in the energy sector and nuclear control management.
MOA		Biomass, wind and solar
MWR		Hydropower
COSTIND		Nuclear power

Source: Zhao Jimin (November 2001:10).

A few others are:

State Energy Investment Corporation

One of the main government lending channels, this corporation lends after assessing the financial viability of a project. This assessment is done in collaboration with China International Engineering Consulting Corporation (Zhao, 2001: 13).

China National Nuclear Corporation

The nuclear head of China's government was split into two companies in 1999. While one was tasked out for establishment of domestic nuclear power plants the other had the responsibility of uranium extraction, nuclear processing for civil and military use, waste treatment and safety (Zhao, 2001: 15).

Chinese Renewable Energy Industries Association

A joint effort of UNDP and Global Environment Facility (GEF) project, this self-financed association plays an advisory role to the government in dealing with both national and international projects related to renewable energy. It has developed an online facility of "investment opportunity" through which it helps in technology transfer through its networking channels (ibid, 13-15).

CCP and the Government

China's policies are dissected into three major tiers. The first tier is decided by the central government, the second by the State Council and the third by the commissions, bureaus, provincial and local governments (Lee, 2012: 14). The policies made by the central government involve basic laws and five year plans. While most consider these policies as mere reiteration of party ideologies and manifestoes, there are other scholars who take them as "key indicators of the directions and changes in the development philosophy" (Lee, 2012: 16). The next in line are the laws issued by the highest executive organ of the country, the State Council. Hence they are called the administrative laws (*xing zheng fa gui*) (Ibid). They also involve the white papers and the national laws which are issued by specific ministries of the central government. Apart from this there are departmental and local regulations (*bu men he difang guizheng*) of the local and the provincial governments (Ibid). These policies are area specific and also have the maximum efficiency as they cater to local requirements and resources. Moreover they are also the most clear in their target and area of application and hence are implemented to the maximum (Ibid: 17).

Figure 3.1: The Hierarchy of Decision Makers of China

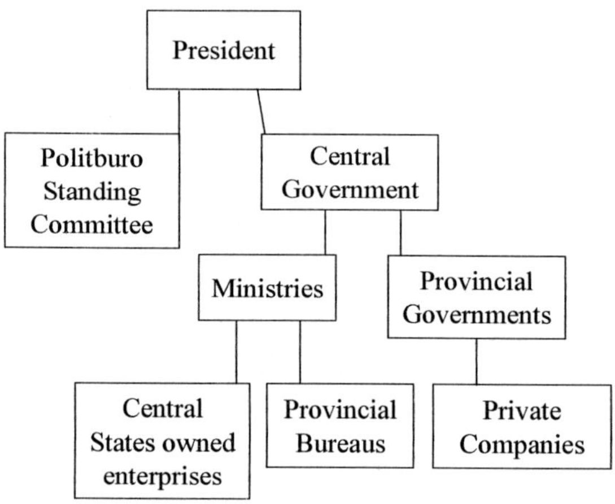

Source: Lee (April, 2012:23).

The above table is in the descending order from the most influential decision maker to the least influential decision maker. In the above flowchart it has been seen that even the most influential leader, is answerable both to the central government and the Politburo members.

> Bargaining and negotiations are important elements in the Chinese policy process. Consensus building has become the order of the day, such that even after a policy is adopted, negotiations do not cease, leading to possible changes made to the original policy (Lee, 2012:2).

From the figure it can be seen that despite being an influential group the Politburo members are also responsible to the central government as well as the Leading Group (*xiaozu*) of the party. The central government is responsible to incorporate the demands and the requirements for both the ministries and provincial governments. The central SOE does also hold the central government responsible for its needs. The private companies can at best only approach the provincial governments as their scope of business expansion is limited (Lee, 2012:23). Lee (2012:24) in her dissertation describes the description of Martin (2010) in the communist party and the government as two "vertically integrated, but interlocking institutions." In fact it is difficult to make a difference between the working and functions of the government and the party. There are many scholars both inside and outside China who believe that it is the party which is the "real" decision maker (Ibid). The party wields power not just through its leading group but also through its appointments both within the party and the central government (Ibid). In fact all government employees are party members and hence the will of the party is largely the agenda of the government (Ibid).

> Novice observers of Chinese politics are often confused by the notions of "theoretical" and "real" holders of power in the Chinese system of government. The main thrust between the real and the theoretical bureaucratic hierarchy is the level of influence the different institutions wield on one another and their ability to make significant decisions that affect policy (Lee, 2012: 25).

Michelle Lee (2012:25-30) has also identified the actual distinction between the party functioning as projected to the world and the party which functions in practice. Through graphical presentation she has represented the pretentious position of the Politburo Standing Committee. While theoretically the Politburo is subservient to the National Party Congress, in reality it is the one which wields the actual power directly within the party and obliquely within the central government (Ibid). When power lies in the hands of the Politburo Committee, it means that the decision makers in the central government and in the party are the top echelons of the communist party (Ibid). This means that despite all grandiose speeches of devolution of authority, power is still centralised and concentrated both within the party and the government. However, constant bickering and factionalism within the party has forced the expansion of politburo seats to accommodate the newer top brass and the changing times and stature of China (Ibid). Expansion of the seat base also means that the Politburo still has the whole and sole control and has not diffused it among different sections of the government. Despite all secrecy about the real position of power of the Politburo and the decisions undertaken in the meeting, speculators have time and again drawn analysis from the background of the who's who of the Politburo Committee (Ibid). The work profile and the background of the members can reveal in which direction the future of China's major decisions shall go. This becomes more explicit when the Politburo members are also the top brass of the government ranging from positions of current President and Premier to future President and Premier (Ibid). Lee (2012) has revealed that with changing times the Politburo is now divided between members of two backgrounds: those who rose from within the party and those whose paths were paved naturally because of their "princeling" statuses. Lee (2012:30-32) divides them into the "populist group" (*tuanpai*) and the "elitist coalition." In the energy purview while the "populist group (advocators of Hu-Wen brigade) are in favour of scoring energy over economy, especially the renewable sector, the "elitist coalition" (those of the Shanghai Gang) are the mentors of "coastal economy" who still believe that any change in the energy structure should be through the economy and especially through the industrialised east (Ibid). This faction within the politburo members has been very emphatically described by Lee who calls it as a system of "one party, two coalitions."

> PBSC will result in more balanced policies that aim to achieve both economic efficiency and social justice; the negotiations that go on behind the scenes will surely depend on the relative balance of power of PBSC members (Ibid., 31).

No matter who rules it is definitely clear that political experience and economic will are the two stalwarts who may chose to ally with or deny each other's presence. The 18th Party Congress is now under the tutelage of Xi Jinping and Li Keqiang. It would be interesting to see the evolution of the current leadership in the next ten years since the two leaders belong to two different factions where the former is the "princeling" and the latter belongs to the *tuanpai* (Ibid, 32). However it is also true that China is always cautious about its public image and its political leaders never wash their "dirty linen in public." Hence a situation of public spat is ruled out and despite ideological differences we can expect natural bonhomie to prevail.

Leading Small Group

Michelle Lee (2012: 36) defines it as "informal bodies of members in the State Council that generate information to advise the State Council on policy, and later aid in coordinating the implementation of policy decisions made by the top leaders with the relevant bureaucracies." The National Energy Leading Group was formed in 2005 and some of the top-ranking party officials were members of this group (Lee, 2012:37). Lee (2012:37) considers it as a window to the importance of energy sector which was gaining ground in political circles. It was the NELG which was instrumental in advocating the renewable energy resources which culminated in the formation of Medium to Long-term Development Plans for renewable energy in 2007 (Ibid:37). Yet not all agree about the invincibility of the LSGs. Lee cites Downs, who believes that it is short-sightedness to believe that LSGs are a solution for the energy woes of China.

Ministry and Bureaucracy

The NDRC has 26 departments under it dealing in diverse fields like industry, transportation, energy, environmental protection, social development, foreign enterprises, trade and employment (Burke et. al., 2009:8). NDRC not only makes energy policies but also deals with fiscal policies, price policies, investment policies, etc. (Ibid). An interesting angle in NDRC is the rise of NEA from the ashes of the Energy Bureau of NDRC (Downs, 2008). NEA operates as a vice ministry yet gets an official of ministerial rank to preside over it (previously the appointment of Zhang Guobao) (Ibid). It is a move which has never happened, for any other ministry, even in the history of China's bureaucracy (Burke et. al., 2009:9). Former director of NDRC Energy Research Institute Zhou Dadi believes that the formation of NEA is a rudimentary step towards formulation of an independent energy ministry and many second his opinion (Ibid). However whether NEA could gain precedence over NDRC is difficult to tell as despite possessing an independent office with its own foreign affairs department it still shares its personnel with NDRC(Ibid) and does not possess the requisite power (like setting up of energy price) to deal with the rancour of energy companies and overlapping bureaucracies (Downs, 2008).

National Energy Commission (the brainchild of National Energy Leading Group) is a supervisory body with some interactions with NEA (Burke et. al., 2009:10). SASAC, the technical owner of all the SOEs in China (including stalwarts like CNOOC, Sinopec and CNPC) and the major shareholder of all the enterprises is in reality like a titular king whose real power lies in the hands of its ministers (Burke et. al.., 2009). A commission responsible for the reform of SOEs has no control over the budget, no share of the earnings (the proceeds of which go to the Ministry of Finance) (Ibid) and no say in the offshore operations of the very same enterprises it stands as the proud owner of. However SASAC deserves accolades for introducing the concept of Corporate Social Responsibility (CSR) to its enterprises (January 2008) and not allowing them to fall for "crony capitalism" to achieve the profit motive and economic growth (Ibid). Annual release of sustainability reports along with their annual reports have become a norm for SOE executives.

However it is unfortunate that an extremely important industry of an extremely important country is devoid of any unified ministry but is looked after by a random assortment of ministries, commissions and companies who converge with their own individual interests and aspirations. The establishment of the "National Energy Leading Group" in 2005 and the subsequent establishment of National Energy Administration in 2008 can be considered as an initiative towards the establishment of a unified structure for the administration of the energy sphere (Burke et. al., 2009: 8-10). Two institutions emerged out of NDRC in 2008: National Energy Administration (NEA) and National Energy Commission (NEC), both strategic bodies which do not work on a day-to-day basis but are a conjunction between diversified energy authority and a coordinated energy ministry-cum-bureaucracy (a consolation for the Draft Energy Law which was proposed in 2007 but never surfaced) (Ibid). NEA though administratively devoid of a ministerial status is still operating under a ministerial head (Burke et. al., 2009: 8-10). The National Energy Commission (NEC) was established in 2010 as one of the first institutes which focused on "energy efficiency rather than energy production" (Yu and Houlden, 2013: 10). On paper the National Energy Agency is subservient to National Energy Commission, yet it wields significant administrative powers over its contemporary ministries and superiors (Lee, 2012:44). It is also the ministry which is renowned for taming the otherwise "wild SOEs," who thrive on profits and connections (*guanxi*) (Ibid). Its control over China's scarce Strategic Petroleum Reserves (SPR) and energy price fixations and adjustments are powerful tools to render it an omnipotent presence (Lee, 2012:44). Yet NEA is subservient to NDRC and the State Council and no matter what it is not allowed to override their powers (Downs, 2008). The current leadership has had a firsthand experience in dealing with energy provisions and institutions as Premier Li Keqiang was the deputy director of NEC before his takeover and some interesting decisions might come forth as his progeny (Lee, 2012: 40-44). (See Annexure 1)

While the NDRC and the NEA directly report to the NEC, other state owned enterprises like CNPC and others report to the SASAC which is a part of the NEC (Yu and Houlden, 2013:11). SASAC's power can be analysed from the fact that it has the power to "appoint and remove the top executives of the supervised enterprises." (Website of SASAC, 2003) Other ministries which play a role in the bureaucratic control of the energy sphere are Ministry of Finance and Commerce (MofCom) and Ministry of Land and Resources (MLR), which deal with issues like mining rights and issuing of certificates for imports and quotas (Xin Qiu and Li, 2012:10681) . Chinese energy analysts say that China has subdivided its energy legislation into coal, oil and natural gas, electricity, nuclear power, energy conservation and renewable energy (Xin Qiu and Li, 2012:10681). The below table has summed up the departments and the functions of the National Energy Commission:

Table 3.2: The Departments and the Functions of the National Energy Commission

Department	Function
The Bureau of Energy	Formulates plans, policies and strategies related to energy situations of the present and the future.
The Ministry of Land and Resources	It deals with licences and technological requirements dealing with mining and also stores geological information.
The Ministry of Housing and Urban Rural Development	It deals with construction price of energy projects as well as price of energy consumption in commercial and residential projects.
The State Administration of Work Safety	Safe production during oil and gas riggings as well as safety of production equipment and facilities.
The Ministry of Commerce	Dealing with both the domestic and the international market of the energy sphere.
The Ministry of Environmental Protection	Environmental issues in energy concerns dealing with exploration, production and distribution.
The State Bureau of Tax	Collection of taxes related to energy consumption and other taxes.

Source: Xin Qiu and Honglin Li (July 2012:10681).

In China, policymakers are heavily dependent on information holders especially in the energy sector and government statistical departments and public think thanks, especially government sponsored information holders which play a vital though oblique role in the decision-making process (Lee, 2012:45). China National Renewable Energy Commission established by the joint collaborative effort of NEA and NDRC is viewed as one think tank who could take a position of eminence in the future (Ibid., 46-47).

However it is tough to draw a consensus when ministries, companies, commissions and SOEs all pull strings in different directions and engage in diversified interests and NEA seems to lack the requisite capacity to do it (Burke et. al., 2009). CCP is aware that energy dynamics works through unitary work in conjunction with the economic motive of its suppliers and hence established State Assets Supervision and Administration Commission

(SASAC) dealing exclusively with investor relations of the 150 energy related state owned enterprises (SOEs) (Ibid). Another major player or rather aspirants of influence in CCP's energy policies are its energy companies (discussed in a separate section) which can indirectly dictate and sometimes even get dictated to about certain nuances of energy policies. In fact these energy honchos were former energy ministries themselves and their leaders were once top echelons within the CPC (Ibid, 15). Other major actors are the government research institutions especially those within the NDRC whose updated knowledge and innovation breakthroughs can cumulatively usher in a landslide shift in energy policies (evident in the Twelfth Five Year Plan with heavy focus on renewable resources) (Ibid, 15). Development Research Centre (under State Council) and Energy Research Institute (of NDRC) are some of the ones worth reckoning (Burke et. al., 2009: 13-14).

To a layman outside the CCP, formulation of energy policies seems to be mysterious and opaque. Enveloped layers of governance, hierarchy between ministries, complexities of interests, laxity in administration and sensitivity of security have exacerbated this non-transparency. However this is just one of the general perceptions. Another perception is that of the rationalist approach who believes that solidarity among the CCP is a force to reckon with (Ibid:4). A force which controls the nation, all its nuances, its past present and future, its politics, economics, internal and external security (Ibid:4). Complete control and complete knowledge is a policymaker's paradise in achieving simplistic solutions to the country's problems (Ibid). This rationalist approach is what the western media believes. It is a rationalist belief, which is instrumental in creating convulsions of paranoia and xenophobic tendencies amongst the developed and the emerging nations. China does not face power struggles (unlike democratic nations) and hence populist measures do not encrypt its long-term visions and policies. However, it is a plain truth with only in its half self being exposed to the world. In party fighting, bureaucratic politics are invisible to the heavily censored media. Lieberthal and Oksenberg (1998) under their model of "fragmented authoritarianism" believe that China's inherent weakness of energy policies is their bureaucratic power struggle (Ibid:4). However it has been seen that Deng's reforms and Jiang's "Three Represents" have contributed to a large extent in reducing factionalism within the party and reducing internal pluralism (Ibid).

When governance over energy sector is discussed, a few unrelated ministries also deserve a special mention due to their oblique influence over the energy policies (the below section is based on Burke et. al., 2009: 11-12). They are:

- Ministry of Finance—for a ministry responsible for the economy of the nation, it has an obvious concern for its star revenue generators, or its "three giants," CNPC, Sinopec and CNOOC, and hence an obvious control over a few of their economic policies. The Ministry of Finance functions in the following way in the budget of the three companies: determining the rate for windfall tax, rebate on vat imposed on crude imports to compensate for domestic refinery losses, setting up rates for various taxes like corporate income tax and resources tax, tax subsidy for equity shares sale and allocation of fund technical innovation. Apart from that various taxes on fuel consumption are also managed by it (Burke et. al., 2009: 11-14).
- Ministry of Commerce (MofCom)—the biggest utility of MofCom is its power over all offshore operations and all overseas employees (even those of Chinese private companies) and hence automatically gets a say in energy operations also (Ibid).
- Ministry of Land and Resources (MLNR)—for the possessor of land and its resources, MLNR acquires natural importance by virtue of its creation. Under the statuette of People's Republic of China MLNR can supervise the operations of energy companies but only within the confines of the domestic boundary. It issues permits for upstream activities in oil and gas areas and maintains the strategic centre of oil and gas resources (Ibid: 4).
- Ministry of Environmental Protection—with State Environment Protection Administration (SEPA) acquiring the ministerial status and with five year plans increasing focus on clean and green energies, China's energy sector is both a detrimental challenge and wonderful opportunity for the development of the environment sector and SEPA is there to administer just that (Ibid).
- Development Research Centre of State Council (DRC)—one of the primary research institutions of China working directly under the aegis of state council. The institute deals with all kinds of research regarding all sorts of policies related to macro, strategic and long-term research of the socio-economic policies of China. DRC's industry department works in areas of energy policies and its implications (Ibid).
- Energy Research Institute (ERI)—the benchwork of NDRC is done here and it would be no exaggeration to say that ERI is the right hand of NDRC. Research done here, input gathered here and data analysed here all serve as food for thought for the national energy policy shelved on the table by NDRC. As a researcher and advisor to energy policies formulated by NDRC it covers a wide range of issues (famous researches

being "China's Medium to Long Term Strategy" and "China's National Energy Law") (Ibid).

However, no research, exploration, production, marketing and collaboration activities of energy rely on allocation of finance and the financial institutions which disburse them, and hence comes the role of China's heavily regulated banking sector like China Development Bank (CDB) and China Export Import Bank (EXIM) as the main ones providing financial support under the name of "development assistance" (Burke et. al., 2009: 13-14, 17).

- China Development Bank (CDB)—this bank has been instrumental in funding China's activities in Africa and other places.
- China Exim Bank Energy Initiative (EXIM)—this bank has funded China's initiatives in Africa and other areas. It has even been lending to energy honchos like PetroChina for their projects outside China.

These banks, like the energy companies, are also increasingly complying with the rules of corporate social responsibility through various means by not financing energy intensive and highly polluting industries and abiding by "equator principles," i.e., identifying not just economic but also environmental and social risks associated with the projects financed by it (Burke et. al., 2009:18-20). It seems that as the maker of the energy policies China's government has adopted a macroeconomic approach as it seeks to craft an energy sector which has renewable playing a greater role in its structure, which relies less on imports and has clean technologies to fortify it. This upgradation of industrial structure would also mean a step towards the establishment of a "well-off society" by relying less on unmanaged growth and getting more people inclusive into the range of higher living standards. The NDRC already follows a bifurcation of department of Energy Bureau and Price Bureau where lawmakers do not preside over pricing decisions (Chen, 2008). It has been increasingly seen that more energy is lost in the bureaucratic fighting between NDRC and various ministries than in the consumption process (Ibid). An attempt was made by ex-president Hu Jintao to relegate some of the powers of NDRC to some new "super ministries"—a move heavily contested by NDRC members (Ibid). Hence the defeated proposal of establishing a new "energy ministry" is letting out its steam by establishing Ministry of Environment Protection (upgradation of SEPA) and Ministry of Industry to empower the industries in enforcement of industrial policies and regulation of power utilised in large industrial projects (Ibid). NDRC in theory has to abide by the guidelines laid down by government advisory bodies like State Energy Leading Group (headed by the Premier) and State Energy Leading Group Office (Ibid). However reality is far from it as NDRC possesses an unquestioned monopoly over energy policies (Ibid):

> In general the changing composition of China's industrial structure is less the result of concerted national aspirations (as it was under Mao Zedong) as competition among provinces, counties and cities to grow GDP, the capital stock, tax revenue and corporate profits (Rosen and Houser, 2007a:9).

Rosen and Houser make an emphatic statement drawing a deep analysis of the nature of political and economic functioning over the decades. To validate their point they have also been extensively quoting stalwart works like Barry Naughton's *The Chinese Economy,* Andy Wedeman's *From Mao to Market* and Scott Kennedy's *The Business of Lobbying in China.* All these works reflect a strong understanding of the western perspective who believe that China's policymaking and decision-taking process has reduced to a mere play of rabble-rousing and tug-of-war where the strongest and the loudest are also the most boisterous. It is not just in decision making but also in decision implementing that economic might clouts or, rather, thwarts the idealistic aspiration. Left on local officials and provincial governments, the state owned enterprises get a free ride in having their whim, especially so when the parameters of good governance are just accumulating numbers in the profit quotient. Most energy hungry industries fall under the domain of SOEs earning the advantages of being a public property while salvaging corporate interests. A few of the financial benefits they garner (as a commodity in public interest) are huge depreciation on Greenfield investments, absence of dividend payments to the government, transfer payments, etc.)(Ibid:10). Moreover, basic fixed costs are negligible with land being free, air and water quality measures not applied, an in-built plant set up with the gestation costs being borne by the government, subsidies and tax holidays, lower loan rates from the banks and the freedom from accountability of ill-invested projects (Ibid). To know more about the functioning of the various major energy SOEs it is imperative to discuss them in individual detail.

Local Governments

It is widely viewed that the local governments are mere followers of the high command orders having no say or role in their area of jurisdiction. This is a virtual reality which was an actual reality till leaders like Mao and Deng ruled and "cult worship" ruled. In the recent period it has been seen that despite a cadre system where local officials are judged by their superiors for their performance, the local bureaus still "lend more ears" to the provincial governments than central institutions and government's orders (Lee, 2012:52). The reasons lie in geographical proximity as well as the effect of a microscopic institution which is less verbose and more explicit in orders (Ibid). The hierarchy system sometimes delays the dissemination of information from the top to the bottom level. Many a time data gets outdated, orders get twisted and information gets complex due to which local officials are either confused or are unable to implement the order verbatim. This gives them enough space and time to leverage their own judgement and an implicit authority to impose their own will and decisions in actual implementation (Ibid). As it is targets in the national policies are often written in "grandiose and eloquent" speeches while less is highlighted about how to perform them. Such ambiguity is used in full advantage by the local officials.

Policy and Law

Yu Xiaojiang (2010) has divided China's energy law system into nine sub-parts namely, constitution, energy laws, legal administrative energy institutions, administrative energy regulations, local energy legal regulations and administrative regulations, energy-related provisions in other laws, energy standards, international energy treaties and other regulated documents. The office of the National Energy Leading Group had closed on February 2008 after formulating the draft provisions of the energy law (ibid).

> The purposes of the energy law are to standardise the development, use and administration of energy, create a stable, economic, clean and sustainable energy supply and service system, increase energy efficiency, ensure energy security, promote the development of a resource efficient and environmentally friendly society and promote the coordinated development of energy, economy and society (Yu Xiaojiang, 2010:2162).

However Xin Qiu and Li (2012) have identified four major areas where China's energy laws need to work to improve upon their viability and effective implementation factor.

Given the tradition of policy overriding legislation on energy regulation in the country, the emergence of energy laws is a big step forward. However compared to the more advanced energy laws and regulations in the developed countries, the country's system still has four areas that can be improved significantly Xin Qiu and Li (2012:10682).

- Heavy intermix of "political will" and government authority'—as a one-party rule China's energy interests have intrinsically been bounded by political ideologies and bureaucratic conflicts. Xin Qiu and Li (2012) have identified three basic responsibilities of administrative management in the energy sector. Firstly, energy management means management of the state property which thrives not on windfall profits but value addition. Secondly, since the government deals with establishing a long-term policy perspective for the whole country it deals with formation of a macroscopic energy policy. Nonetheless, political regulatory authority also deals with economic regulation and market control. In a study it was found that while both the American and the Chinese possess "regulatory bodies" the Chinese allow complete political interference in the regulatory bodies due to which it just becomes a puppet dancing to the tunes of popular political dictums. (Xin Qiu and Li, 2012:10682-10686).

- All captains, no crew—while China is already suffering from lack of distinction between politics and professionalism it is also facing the problem of overlapping regulatory authority due to which there is duplication of both tasks and decisions. The biggest example of sector suffering from this major problem is the electricity sector where SERC and NDRC are at constant loggerheads with each other. While NDRC looks over the macro policies it sometimes overlooks its micro responsibilities whose brunt is borne by the SERC. Moreover the appointment and dismissal of senior officials and personnel is in the hands of SASAC due to which SERC is unable to wield some real authority on its employees, price or market (Ibid).
- China's current separation of political authority and the regulatory authority is incomplete because many policymaking departments still enjoy the power to conduct several market regulatory practices which is nowhere close to independent regulation. Hence SERC is often seen as a judge who has no authority (Xin and Li 2012).
- Over-regulation somewhere, no regulation in others—despite an NDRC control it is widely viewed by Chinese scholars that China has left oil and gas and industries almost wholly on the listed companies (who report directly to the State Council). Also separate regulatory authorities for similar energy resources promote overlapping of jurisdiction as well as employment of redundant personnel and authorities (Ibid).
- "Regulated market" is an oxymoron—any enterprise entering the energy market of China requires a licence and has to pass through stringent qualifications and rigmarole process to start a business. China offers two types of licences, one which prevents risks, i.e., regular licensing and one which prevents price and quality control, i.e., special licensing.

Chinese practice is to grant regular licences to areas where there is no natural monopoly like electricity generation and special licences in areas where there is natural monopoly like oil and gas production, electricity transmission, etc. While in the former case licence issuing authorities are more bothered about economic worth rather than considering technology and environmental risks. In the latter case special licences means extra strictness of regulations due to which licences are often given or renewed only to existing players due to which monopolisation is encouraged which is exactly against the spirit of the special licences. Moreover the regular licences too are extremely stringent and interfere in matters which are not related to the public (like generation capacity, operating hours, etc.). This not only hinders the growth of private capital investment but also does not allow free and fair competition in the market (Ibid).

- Price and regulation—China follows the model of "capital cost repayment price" which is unique only to China's energy sector. In China energy price is calculated as the summation of "reasonable costs, reasonable profits and taxes." This is done so that electricity units have adequate revenue not only to cover up the costs but also to repay the government loans avoiding the long gestation period." The main disadvantage of this system is the ambiguity of the word "reasonable" as the prices are not reflective of the true cost and also come in direct control of the NDRC to be used as a tool which can manipulate prices of other goods, domestic markets and international competition (Xin Qiu and Li, 2012:10682-10686).

Energy Companies and Fossil Fuels: The "Black" Market

Energy companies are state owned enterprises where "all assets are owned by the state" says the Chinese government (Lee, 2012: 54-55). The Chinese distinguish SOEs based on ownership and control. Hence China has SOEs which are controlled by SASAC, controlled by its owners and those who are controlled by its own branches or subsidiaries. Lee (2012:55) identifies four main parts of an SOE (which is cited from Lin and Mihaupt, 2011):

> The core company serves as an intermediary between SASAC and the firm, the listed company acts as the external face whose shares are publicly traded on stock exchanges. The finance companies help the SOEs to be exempted from general prohibitions on inter-company lending. The research institute was created so that each SOE did not overlook the central government's desire for increased technological development and competitiveness Lee (2012:55).

The national oil companies of China are "vertically integrated oil companies" (Lewis, 2007). Hence these companies compete not only with other international oil companies but also with each other to win the favour, capital and investment of the Chinese government.

> Their current competition over supplies is largely hidden from public view, but as they develop downstream and retail markets across China and in foreign markets, the needs of marketing and branding will push them to distinguish themselves among their peers in the eyes of the consumers (Lewis, 2007:3).

At a time when the country was fresh from liberation and was nursing its raw wounds after years of external aggression and internal disturbances, nobody but the government could make some semblance of development through its various ministries who directed the energy battle line in chaos. These ministries were institutions of enormous potential and worked in close proximity with the central authority. However the wave of reforms did not spare them and these government ministries were soon disbanded (read, privatised) to establish themselves as professional corporates of the energy sector. In 1988 Ministry of Petroleum metamorphosed into CNPC (dealing with upstream activities) and Sinopec Group (dealing with downstream activities) (Burke et. al., 2009: 18-20). Many experts believe that the rapport of these tycoons with the government has helped them to promote their interests even at the cost of national interests. Strangely the disorganisation of energy bureaucracy is in complete contrast to state activism in state owned enterprises (Burke et. al., 2009: 15-18). These companies regularly compete and contrast with each other but in a completely professional manner.

Oil and Gas Companies

A major crude oil and natural gas company engages in all activities related to exploration, development, production, refining, transportation, storage, sales and marketing of oil, petroleum, gas and their related products. Some of the major oil and gas companies in China are CNOOC, PetroChina and Sinopec.

PetroChina: PetroChina Company Limited was established in 1995 after the restructuring of China National Petroleum Corporation (CNPC), as the subsidiary looking into the domestic operations of CNPC and got listed in New York and Hong Kong stock exchanges (stock code 00857) after five years followed by Shanghai stock exchange (stock code: 601857) in 2007. One of the A share Market Company with CNPC as its major shareholder (holding 86.507 per cent of shares), PetroChina titles its corporate policy as "Caring for Energy, Caring for You." In order to create a "harmonious enterprise" the company claims to follow three ethics: long-term mechanism for work safety, environmental protection and energy conservation. Ranked sixth amongst the world's 2,000 largest public companies by Forbes 2011, and second in Fortune 500 China, PetroChina is a regular and important invitee to government discussions on formulation of energy policies, climate change, energy emission targets, determination of regulations and standards, attendance to public concerns, signing of cooperation agreements overseas and with domestic private enterprises. It also offers expert advice on professional issues and corporate responsibilities. The company has two level administrative systems, one stemming from headquarters to regional companies and another from headquarters to professional companies to regional companies. A unique feature of PetroChina is its annual general meeting where CNPC despite being the major shareholder is not allowed to vote to ensure equality amongst its other shareholders. The orange and red flower shaped logo of PetroChina is an amalgamation of the rising sun (the brilliant future) juxtaposed on the red base (strength and cohesion) (The above section is based on Annual Report of PetroChina 2011).

CNOOC: China National Offshore Oil Corporation was established on February 15, 1982 under the protégé of State Owned Assets Supervision and Administration Commission (SASAC) of State Council. Its logo consists of its initials with blue seawater ripples representing China Seas and the red capital letters represent an oil rig with the backdrop of a rising sun representing China's rising prowess in offshore oil industry. Another participant in government's national policies and updating of information, CNOOC has been ranked 32nd in one of the top 50 global oil companies and 162nd in global Fortune 500 rankings. The company operates under the company law of People's Republic of China and does not hold any investor assembly as all its investor obligations are completed by SASAC. It was only recently in 2011 that under the orders of central government, the company established the board of directors and separated the jurisdiction of chairman and the president. In fact it is not just the company but the government also who plays a major role in decision making in the company. For this the representative agency of the CPC Central Committee, the party committee participates in all the meetings about the company's internal affairs. Under the "regulations of People's Republic of China concerning the exploitation of the offshore petroleum resources in cooperation with foreign enterprises" CNOOC has been given special authorisation by the State Council to work in tandem with offshore partners for effective exploitation of oil and gas resources (The above section is based on Annual Report of CNOOC 2009-

11). It also has the status of being an investment organisation within the state. CNOOC and its subsidiary companies, despite being registered abroad like the Chinese Ocean Offshore Oilfields Service, CNOOC Insurance Limited, etc., prepare their consolidated financial statements in compliance with basic and specific standards prepared by Ministry of Finance (MoF) (Ibid).

Sinopec: It was established in 1998 and its structure was based on the former China Petroleum Corporation. Sinopec Corporation was incorporated by the Sinopec group in February 2000 and had issued a successful initial public offering at Hong Kong, New York and London by October of the same year. It issued shares in the ensuing year and also got listed on the Shanghai stock exchange. Since then it has acquired a number of companies like the China New Star Petroleum Company (August 2001), Hainan Petrochemicals Ltd. (October 2006). Headquartered in Beijing this state owned company has the state as the main shareholder. China Petroleum and Chemical Company (Sinopec Corp.) has been controlled by the Sinopec Group and has been listed on various major foreign exchanges in Shanghai, Hong Kong, New York, and London, etc. The total number of shares of Sinopec Corp. was 86.7 billion, in which Sinopec Group owns 75.84 percent; international investors own 19.35 per cent and domestic investors own 4.81 per cent. With the logo of the rising sun, Sinopec (*zhongguo shi hua*) defines itself as the company dedicated to S- Sustainability, I-international, N-national, O-oil, P-people, E-environment, C-cooperation. Ranked as one of the most admired and trusted brands by various prestigious magazines, Sinopec has the unique privilege of being a member of the United Nations Global Compact Organisation since 2004 due to its image of abiding by the principle of corporate social responsibility (The above section is based on Annual Report of Sinopec 2011).

Production Areas and Business Expansion of the 'Three Big'

PetroChina- PetroChina has been maintaining "oilfield development year" campaign since 2009 and has had major exploration feats in Tarim basin, Ordos, Sichuan and Bohai. Since these areas have mature oilfields, their permeability levels have been extremely low. As a consequence water flood technique was adopted where multi-stage horizontal wells and multilayered vertical wells were improved to stabilise production. With the result that Daqing has been producing on an average 50 million tonnes of oil even after twenty-seven years and Changqing has enhanced its production to 40 million tonnes of oil and gas. Sophisticated technology applied for recovery of reserves deserves all credit. The below map gives the details of the second west-east gas pipeline under the aegis of

PetroChina. An 8,704 kilometre-long pipeline it shall traverse from the areas of Huoerguosi, Lunnan, Shanshan to Shanghai, Zaoyang, Xiangtan till Hongkong, Guangzhou and Nanning (The above section is based on Sustainability Report of PetroChina, 2011:20).

Figure 3.2: Production and Business Areas of PetroChina in China

Note: The route includes the following places: Huoerguosi, Lunan, Shanshan, Zhongwei, Jingbian, Pingdingshan, Shiyan, Zaoyang, Shanghai, Nanchang, Xiangtan, Zhangshu, Guaangzhou, Shenzhen, Nanning and Hongkong.
Source: Sustainability Report of PetroChina (2011: 20).

Domestically, China's energy dilemma exists in transportation costs and inferior quality oil which is highly sulphur ridden (Ibid). The only way to solve this is to strategise refining markets and optimise resource allocation. Hence, PetroChina has engaged in a number of refining projects like Liaoyang Petrochemical refining project, Karamay Petrochemicals and Jinzhou Petrochemicals each with a refining capacity of 10 Mt/a. Sichuan Petrochemicals, Hohot Petrochemicals (each with refining capacity of 5 mt/a), Urumuqi Petrochemicals, Fushun Petrochemicals, etc (Ibid).

China's "western development strategy" has also been instrumental in manoeuvring the moves of energy companies in developing the energy reservoirs of Southwest China. Guangxi Petrochemical Company has been the first major refining project in southwest China since 2010 and has yielded 12 million tonnes of crude, 11 million tonnes of refined products and has paid 10.2 billion Yuan as taxes. This has not only worked out the problem of regional demand and supply but has also strengthened the economy of Beibu Gulf. PetroChina has been one of the pioneer companies not only in maintaining cross-border networks but also in improving the domestic pipelines: Zhangshu-Xiangtan branch line, gas pipelines in Shandong and Liaoning, Shaanxi-Beijing gas pipeline, Lanzhou-Chengdu crude pipeline, Naming-Liuzhou oil products pipeline, etc. The West-East gas pipeline has terminals in Jiangsu and Dalian supplying northeast and north China (The above section is based on Ibid) .

CNOOC: This thirty-year-old national oil company has made great strides in production and expansion of its petroleum resources which it generally refers to as the "First Leap Programme." Relying on the successful build of an "Offshore Daqing Field," the company aims to be "effective, dedicated and innovative." It now has launched its "Second Leap Development Programme," beginning from 2012, to promote stability with growth. Its major areas of operation are Penglai 19-3 oilfield, Bohai Sea and regions of western areas of South China Sea, Jizhou 25-1 and Lufeng 13-2, development projects in Qinshui (Shanxi province) and eastern areas of Ordos basin which led to a big boost in development of coal bed methane. The company has had a first on land gas exploration experience in Xiyangzi district of Anhui province. Turnkey projects like deep water risers (part of the highly sophisticated R&D Programme of China 863), project involving drilling rig "*Haiyang Shi You* 923/924," etc. CNOOC has not limited itself only to oil and gas production but also expanded its production into fertilisers and asphalts through its subsidiary company of CNOOC Chemicals Ltd. It owns three major brands "Fudao," "Tianye" and "Sakefu," which are one of the most trusted in the agricultural market and "CNOOC 36-1" as the leading asphalt producer. The two main networks for marketing of its refinery products are "two deltas and one bay" and "one river and two railway lines." China obtained a major feat in innovation through the deep sea indigenous technology of "*Hai Yang Shi You* 981"—a sixth generation 3,000 metres deep waters semi-submersible drilling platform, a design specially suited for unpredictable oceanic activity in the South China Sea (The above section is based on Annual and Sustainability Report 2011). The below figure, gives details about the business expansion of CNOOC showing the position of its various gas stations (Guangdong,Fujian,Zhejiang,Jiangsu, Shandong etc.) and its refinery factories. Since CNOOC concentrates on the offshore regions it has a lower domestic presence than the other oil companies. Nevertheless it still has a strong foothold in the entire eastern sector of China.

Figure 3.3: Business Expansion of CNOOC

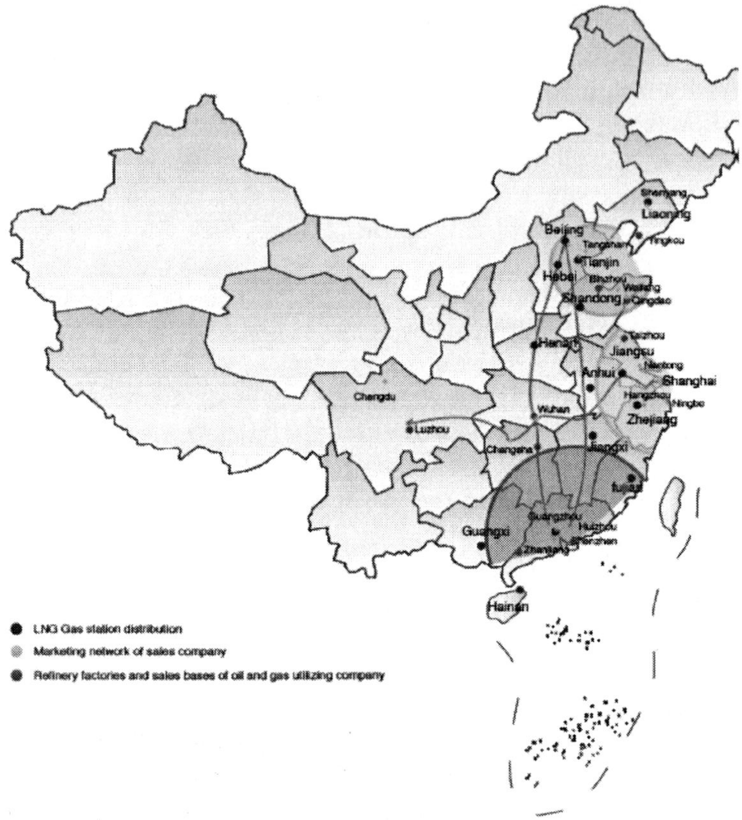

Source: Annual and Sustainability Report of CNOOC 2011:85.

Sinopec: As the second largest producer and the largest refiner of China, exploration breakthroughs in newer areas and enhanced intensity in mature areas, i.e., "stabilising production in eastern areas, expanding production in western areas, accelerating development in southern blocks, pushing forward offshore exploration and development, making breakthrough in unconventional resource development, depending on technologies and building up upstream strength," has been the bulwark of Sinopec Corporation production strategy. Northern rim of Jungar, western Sichuan depression, northern slope of Tazhong, newer areas of Songnan and offshore Hainan are its main areas of operation. Today is the demand for not just oil and gas resources but also the establishment of hydrocarbon reservoirs for establishment of production capacity of coal bed methane. With fluctuating international oil prices, Sinopec has adopted a two-way process of reducing crude procurement cost and increase crude receiving thereby reducd transport costs and hence the price. The "I safe" programme speaks of its commitment to "maintain safe production under complex operating conditions." The trump card of Sinopec has been the Shengli oilfields. Under operation for the last 50 years, it has spewed more than 100 million tonnes for the last 28 consecutive years, and an average aggregate of 5 billion tonnes, accounting for 20 per cent of the total domestic crude reserve of China since 1961. Optimisation of product mix demands diversification of energy mix especially in unconventional forms (CBM, shale gas and shale oil), and biomass energy (bio- diesel and bio-jet fuel, etc.). Latest reserves of shale gas have been found in Jianan (west Hubei and east Chongqing) and CBM in Yanchuan, Zhijin and Heshun blocks. It also recently discovered the Yuanba gas fields as the deepest marine gas reserves of China in northeast Sichuan with an average 100 billion cubic metres of gas. In a coal abundant and oil starving nation, the major task of energy companies is not just to explore and exploit what little is left, but also to indulge in refining of olefins which are the basic chemical feed-stocks and reap rich dividends through innovative refining technologies. Sinopec Zhonggyuan Petrochemical Limited has been successful in utilising the indigenously built S-MTO technology for 100 per cent conversion of methanol and 80 per cent of ethylene and propylene. This methanol to olefin technology has been a major contributor in fuelling China's economic growth. No wonder Sinopec's great wall lubricant was used to dock Shenzhou-8 with Tiangong-1. Besides exploration, marketing of crude and its binary products, maintenance of environment upgradation and concern for its employees, all corporate social responsibilities, also incorporate aiding backward regions like Tibet, Qinghai in establishing infrastructure and public development services regarding health and education apart from aiding disaster areas (The above section is based on Sinopec Sustainability Report, 2011).

In order to understand a company's expansion of operations and its stature, two basic dimensions of operations are studied: economic strength and ecological tenacity. An economic strength of a company (large or small) is its ability to withstand the vagaries of the market and yet earn profits for the company and economic growth for the country. The following tables explore the potential of Chinese energy companies through their economic performances under various parameters, in the recent years.

Table 3.3 Economic Parameters of China's Oil Companies (updated till 31 December 2013)

Item (yuan)	PetroChina	CNOOC	Sinopec
Overall Expenses	2,069,482	498,247	2,783,526
Overall Revenue	2,258,124	590,073	2,880,311
Net profit	116,653	71,982	70,289
Total Assets	2,342,110	1,041,650	1,382 916

Unit million yuan
Source: Annual Reports of PetroChina, CNOOC and Sinopec 2013

The below mentioned chart is for the year 2012

Table 3.4: Economic Parameters of China's Oil Companies, 2012

Item (yuan)	PetroChina	CNOOC	Sinopec
Overall Expenses	2,020,770	430,990	2,687,383
Overall Revenue	2,195,296	526,566	2,786,045
Net profit	130,620	74,787	66,796
Total Assets	2,168,896	818,097	1,257,944

Source: Annual Reports for PetroChina, Sinopec and CNOOC 2012.

Given below are the sources of crude oil processed from 2009-11 in million tonnes.

Table 3.5: Sources of Crude Oil Processed by Chinese Oil Companies from 2009-11 (million tonnes)

Year	Sinopec	CNOOC	PetroChina
2009	35.22	7.05	6.49
2010	35.13	5.10	6.91
2011	34.84	5.72	6.73

Source: Annual Reports for PetroChina, Sinopec and CNOOC 2009, 2010, 2011.

In comparison we can see that PetroChina seems to beat its counterparts in terms of total assets and net profit consecutively since the last recent years.. Sinopec despite a large (in fact, the largest) turnover has not been able to garner enough profits to acquire net gain and more assets. However this is not to undermine the fact that Sinopec has acquired the largest number of reserves for processing of crude oil (See Table 3.5).

PetroChina claims to facilitate socio economic development by providing basic energy demands and fuelling economic growth. The "Twelfth Five Year Plan" has earmarked the goal of setting up of a scientific and technological innovation system. It is a need imperative not just for economic benefits but also because the remaining resources do not possess the natural quality and need to be treated to be made market applicable. The energy companies and especially PetroChina have been instrumental in following this process diligently.

Given below is the list of proven and produced oil and gas reserves of PetroChina since 2007.

Table 3.6: Proven and Produced Oil and Gas Reserves of PetroChina

Year	Proven crude reserves (10^6 barrels)	Proven gas reserves ($10^8 ft^3$)	Crudeoil production (10^6barrels)	Marketable natural gas output ($10^8 ft^3$)
2007	11,706	571,110	846	16,277
2008	11,221	611,890	871	18,642
2009	11,263	632,440	844	21,122
2010	11,278	655,030	858	22,212
2011	11,128	666,530	886	23,964
2012	11,018	675,810	916.5	25,588
2013	10,820	693,230	932.9	28,019

Source: Various Annual Reports of PetroChina.

PetroChina claims that its total crude output represented an increase of 1.8 percent and total gas output to an increase of 9.5 percent for the year 2013 (Annual Report, PetroChina, 2013). This led to a total domestic sale of 117 million tonnes of the refined products (Ibid). In fact if we go further back it can be seen that despite acute recession and surging oil prices PetroChina received the rewards of its good work done in the previous years (with increasing assets and turnover) and managed with only a slight dip in its net profits. The surprising fact is that despite lower profits, PetroChina managed to pay a higher remuneration in the form of taxes (See Table 3.7).

Table 3.7: Economic Parameters of PetroChina (2007-09)

Item	2007	2008 2009
Total assets	10,696	11,962 14,503
Turnover	8,375	10,726 10,193
Taxes	1,722	2,227 2,095
Net profit	1,468	1,145 1,034

Unit: 100 million Yuan
Source Annual Report of PetroChina 2009

No wonder it has been expanding its network of laying down crude pipelines (km). in 2013 the Group had invested a total capital of 57,439 million yuan for the projects of Tangshan LNG Projects, the Third and the Fourth Daqing Tieling Crude Oil Pipeline, Zhongwei-Guiying Gas Pipeline etc.

Table 3.8: Economic Parameters of Sinopec.

The oil and gas domestic production of Sinopec have been no less impressive.

Year	Domestic oil production (mmbbls)	Domestic gas production (bcf)
2013	332.54	660.18
2012	328.28	598.01
2011	321.73	517.07

Source : Annual Report of Sinopec, 2013

A trajectory of turnover and profits and change compared to previous year from 2001-11 for Sinopec:

Year	Turnover (million yuan)	Profit for the given year (million yuan)	Change in turnover (per cent)	Change in profit (per cent)
2011	2,505,683	78,445	31	0.6
2010	1,913,182	78,004	42.2	16.4
2009	1,345,052	64,484	10	158.4
2008	1,502,443	26,200	24.2	55.4
2007	1,209,706	58,743	13.4	6.7
2006	1,076,402	55,408	29.3	23.7
2005	823,117	43,840	n.a	n.a
2004	597,197	41,791	n.a	n.a
2003	447,292	n.a	28.4	n.a
2002	345,145	n.a	6.8	n.a
2001	323,629	n.a	5.7	n.a

Source: Annual Report of Sinopec for various years

The growth chart of Sinopec's business structure is a revelation of its expanding business operations and rising operations albeit with some fluctuations in and around the period of recession. No wonder its domestic oil and gas production has been escalating steadily .

The energy companies, especially those of oil and gas, are generally the "proud prodigies" of the Chinese government on whom it relies on its aim of "China rise." They guarantee an assured future not only with their domestic production, sales and profits but also through their aggressive pursuance of overseas resources. The comparison of CNPC, Sinopec and CNOOC is like the comparison of three strong brothers who are vying for the ancestral property. Each has a glorious list of merits reflecting the judicious mix of business acumen and socialist viewpoint. CNPC as the largest oil and gas producer and supplier, Sinopec as the largest producer and marketer of petroleum products and CNOOC as the "overseas cousin" have also divided the territory of China amongst themselves as their production base. While CNPC operates in the north and the west, Sinopec works in the south and CNOOC works offshore. During their initiation, CNPC worked upstream and Sinopec operated in the downstream areas (Zhao, 2001:14). However in 1998, in a masterstroke by the Chinese government, CNPC and Sinopec were asked to exchange their refineries and oilfields so that they could become "vertically integrated companies." (Lewis, 2007:4)

Table 3.9: Energy Sectors and Their Corporations

Sector	Energy corporations
Oil and gas	CNPC (north and west oil exploration and production), Sinopec (east and south oil exploration and production), CNOOC (offshore oil and gas), Sinochem (imports and exports), Unipeck and China Oil
Coal	CNLCMDC (exploration and production), NIMUCIC, CNCIEC (imports and exports)
Electricity	State Power Corporation, Huaneng Group Inc., China National Power Industry Corporation, Regional Electric Power Corporations
Hydropower	China International Water and Electric Corporation
Nuclear	CNNC
Renewable energy	CREIA
Investment	State Energy Investment Corporation

Source: Zhao Jimin (November 2001:13).

Strategic Petroleum Reserves

Energy (especially oil) is not only an economic but also a political commodity. It is said that from the 1990s energy exploration and exploitation has entered the third phase of technology upgradation in China. Sixty years of liberation has expanded the base of technological progress in the exploration of fossil fuels in China. Yet it is also true that this is nowhere near to developed nations who on a rough estimate are at least ten years ahead by the technical aspect (Wang Xiaozong, 2011: 40-42). On the other hand, macroeconomic rise of international crude price has set off a reduction chain in investment, production, supply and a subtle tightening of residential consumption of fossil fuels. With every one dollar rise in international price of crude, China shells out an extra 1-1.5 billion Yuan for the same amount (Wang Xiaozong, 2011:

40-42). Every ten dollar rise in price is a GDP decline of 0.5 per cent, affecting the GDP growth rate and the income decline. In comparison of a decade (Wang Xiaozong, 2011: 40-42), it has been seen that China's oil imports have been increasing in tandem with increase in price of crude (Mr. Adam Smith must be rolling in his grave), affecting nearly 50 per cent of the exchequer.

Table 3.11: China's Petroleum Imports

Year	Imports (tonnes)
2000	60 million
2002	80 million
2004	120 million
2007	150 million
2009	200 million

Source: Wang Xiaozong (2011: 40-42).

Figure 3.4 : An Analysis of China's oil production and consumption by the EIA

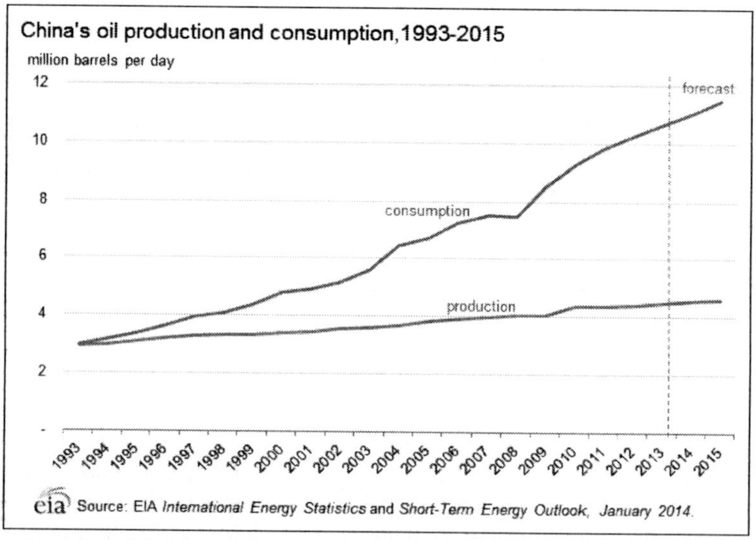

Source: Energy Information Administration (2014)

EIA claims that China's oil production, reached to a level of 4.5 million bbl/d, which was fifty percent higher, than the previous two decades, out of which 81 per cent was on-shore production. However, since most of its onshore oilfields are mature and have peaked their ouput, China is investing in innovative techniques such as Enhanced Oil Recovery Technique (EOR) etc. to retain its production status (*EIA website*) On December 18, 2007

NDRC gave its nod to the establishment of strategic petroleum reserves in China. With government investment, foundation was laid at Zhejiang, Liaoning, Zhoushan and Zhenhai (Wang, 2011:40-42). By 2008, reserves had totaled 16,400,000 cubic meters or 14 million tonnes (1 cubic meter of crude = 0.8551 tonnes) (Ibid). China has eleven major strategic reserves which are under the jurisdiction of various companies (Ibid).

Table 3.12: China's Strategic Petroleum Reserves

Strategic reserve	Company	Capacity
Tianjin strategic reserve	Sinopec group	10 million cubic metres
Zhoushan petroleum reserve	Sinochem group	5 million cubic metres
Dushanzi reserve	CNPC	5.4 million cubic metres
Zhenhai reserve	Sinopec	5.2 million cubic metres
Huangdao petroleum reserve	Sinopec	3.2 million cubic metres
Dalian petroleum reserve	CNPC	3 million cubic metres
Huizhou petroleum reserve	CNOOC	5 million cubic metres
Shanshan reserve	Xinjiang oilfields company under China Petroleum Enterprise	8 million cubic metres

Source: Wang Xiaozong (2011: 40-42).

Out of these Zhenhai, Zhoushan, Huangdao and Dalian reserves are enthusiastic in their target to enhance capacity with a massive dose (sometimes overdose) of government investment (Ibid).

Table 3.13: Investments and Capacities of four major reserves of China

Petroleum reserve	Reserve capacity (million cubic metres)	Occupied area (square kilometres)	Total investment (billion yuan)
Zhenhai	5.2	1.12	3.7
Zhoushan	5	1.42	4
Huangdao	3.2	0.63	2.4
Dalian	3	0.73	2.5

Source: Wang Xiaozong (2011: 40-42).

Given the present scenario, China should not only pump in investment in strategic petroleum reserves but also make big use of market demand by cultivating market structure and accelerating innovation.

Gas Guzzlers

With dwindling petroleum reserves China has taken the "journey towards the west." It has plenty of gas reserves in its farfetched and impoverished areas of northern and western China which have been unexplored due to technical deficiencies. The "Sichuan experiment,"[1] has been a big failure primarily due to this reason (Woetzel, 2003:105). Gas was discovered in both offshore regions of South China Sea (long before it became an international issue) and in Tarim and Ordos regions within the Chinese territory (Ibid). Both these regions were evaluated as "important drivers of economic growth" by none other than Premier Zhu Rongji (Woetzel, 2003:105). However the market lags behind demand primarily due to infrastructure bottlenecks of this region though PetroChina has tried to narrow down this divide. Yet infrastructure is just a part of the problem as the major problem lies in lack of pump priming in the gas market (ibid.106). Most of the gas ready for supply has to wait for almost a decade as negotiations go through the rigamarole process of government handling and negotiations regarding supply chains that costs keep on escalating (Ibid). An added pressure is that of the State Council which argues for reduced prices due to reasons of "public welfare." Woetzel (2003:106) has argued that local politics and lack of government support has kept investors away from China's gas market which could be more profitable than the already flourishing coal market. In fact in this context PetroChina's efforts should be lauded as it has attracted a number of international pipeline companies through persistent efforts of writing letters of intent and offering some "early bird profits." (Ibid:106)

Coal and Power Companies

China accounts for 13 per cent of global coal reserves, yet lacks a coordinated supply from its companies (Chen, 2008). It is an irony of sorts that some of its star players in the international coalfields (like the Shenhua group) fare miserably on the domestic front (Shenhua accounts for just 9 per cent of the total domestic supply) (Nicholas Chen, 2008).

1. Domestically gas development began in Sichuan fifty years ago, however conditions of an apathetic market (which was more in favour of fertilisers), technical bottlenecks of penetrating into granite based structures led to high costs and economic impracticality (Woetzel, 2003).

Figure 3.5: An Analysis of Total Coal Consumption in Relation to Thermal Power and Electricity Generation in China

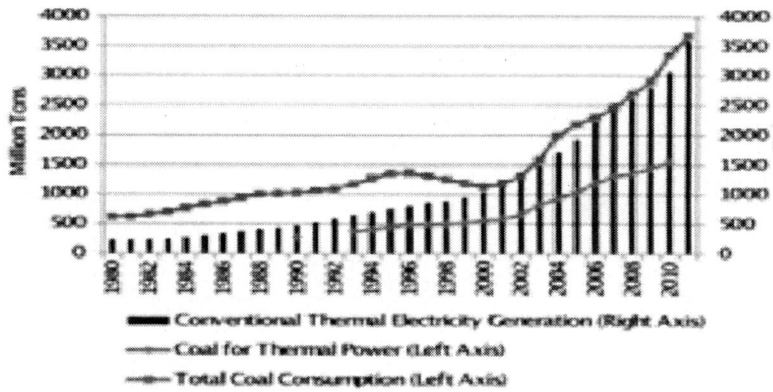

Source: ***Mathews and Tan* (2012).**

The above table shows that fluctuating coal consumption has witnessed a steady rise since 2000, doubling in just six years by 2010 to consume 3.4 billion tonnes with 46 per cent of it being utilised in power generation (Ibid). In any case, the workshop of the world is harnessing its coal energy almost to the extent of installing one gigawatt of thermal power station every week (Ibid).

The electricity sector has undergone a major process of overhauling since the 1990s. An electric power law was launched in 1995, which gave legal protection to investors, managers and consumers and regulated the generation and distribution of consumption of electricity (Xin Qiu and Li, 2012 : 10680).

As one of the largest consumers of electricity in the world, China faces transportation bottlenecks due to mismatch of reserves and market of electricity. It also has an immediate need of improvement in communications and infrastructure.

Table 3.14: China's Electricity Production from Coal over a Certain Period

Year	Coal electricity	Total	Per cent
2004	1,713	2,200	78
2007	2,656	3,279	81
2008	2,733	3,457	79
2009	2,913	3,696	79
2010	3,273	4,208	78
2011	3,724	4,715	79
2012	3,850	4,937	78
2013	4,200	5,398	78

Source: IEA Key World Energy Statistics

It can be seen that increasing production of coal has only resulted in its increasing utilisation of electricity production. Before 2002, State Power Corporation was the emperor of the electricity department whose throne was abdicated (at the obvious orders of the State Council) in favour of the companies which were set up to separate power plants from power supply networks (Ibid). China's electricity transmission system owns no national grid but an integration of six grids, five under State Grid Corporation and one under State China South Grid Corporation (Xin Qiu and Li, 2012:10682).

Figure 3.7: Electricity Sector of China

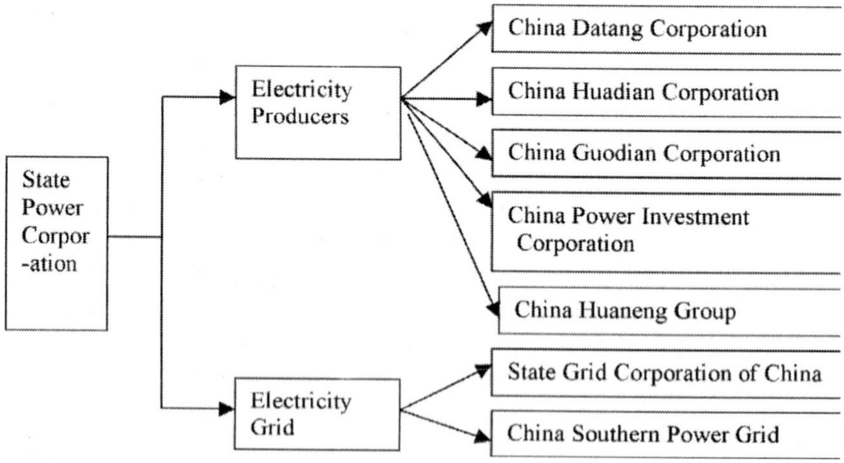

Source: Xin Qiu and Honglin Li (July 2012:10682).

Figure 3.7 above gives a thematic description of the hierarchy of electricity sector in China. It clearly identifies that both the electricity producers and the electricity grid are under the supervision of State Power Corporation. The chart also identifies two main power grids of China, namely, State Grid Corporation of China and China Southern Power Grid. It also identifies various electricity producers of China which are discussed below.

China National Coal Group Corporation (hereafter ChinaCoal): A descendant of China National Coal Import and Export Corporation (established in 1982), ChinaCoal is the second largest coal producer of China with a production capacity of 226 million tonnes and washing capacity of 246 million tonnes. As a state owned enterprise operating under the aegis of State Owned Assets Supervision and Administration Commission of State Council (SASAC), the company has a far lead in coking, coal based chemicals like ether and olefin, coke production and coal mining equipment (which are known for their technical sophistication and large domestic market share). Complying with economies of scale in production, informatisation of management, modernisation of technology, engagement in numerous mergers and acquisitions (M&A), ChinaCoal's latest statistics boast a robust health and growth potential of the country in the coal market. (The above section is based on Annual Report of China Coal 2013)

Table 3.15: Economic Parameters of China Coal

Item (yuan)	2009	2010	2011	2012	2013
Revenue	53,187,027	70,302,637	87,773,054	87,291,670	82,316,482
Profit	7,920,171	8,151,019	10,659,038	9,574,854	4,620114
Net Assets	78,195,702	86,338,550	95,964,789	101,431,367	103,093,140

Unit: thousand Yuan
Source: Annual Report of ChinaCoal 2013

Implementing its strategy of "transformation and upgrading, technological innovation, talent thriving and safety development," ChinaCoal operates in five area bases of Shanxi, Inner Mongolia-Shaanxi, Jiangsu, Heilongjiang and Xinjiang. Going by the paradigm of the 11th five year plan to "recover ecosystems and comprehensively utilise resources" ChinaCoal invested 790 million Yuan on 64 projects to stimulate the "green coal cover" and has contributed its share to conserve the environment. (The above section is based on Annual Report of ChinaCoal 2013)

China Shenhua Energy Company Limited (hereafter Shenhua): A joint-stock company with limited liability, the Shenhua group ventures into five business fields, namely, coal, power, railway, port and shipping (Website of

Shenhua, 2013). However for the purpose of this section we shall stick to its operations in the coal and power sector. Shenhua claims to have largest coal reserves in China and is also its largest domestic supplier (Ibid). Obviously the rising production, rising prices and therefore rising earnings in the stock exchange have meant rising mirth both for the company and its investors.

Table 3.16: Economic Parameters of Shenhua Group

Year	Commercial coal production (million tonnes)	Total power output dispatch (billion kilowatt-hour)	Average coal sales price (yuan/ tonne)	Earnings per share (yuan/ share)
2006	136.6	53.91	308.1	0.975
2007	158	74.35	312.9	1.110
2008	185.7	90.29	378.6	1.339
2009	210.3	97.72	387.9	1.594
2010	224.8	131.41	426.8	1,917
2011	281.9	167.61	n.a	n,a
2012	304	193.46	n.a	n.a
2013	318.9	210.18	n.a	n.a

Source: Website of Shenhua.

With sales volume of coal reaching to 292.6 million tonnes, installed capacity of power plants burgeoning to 27,433 megawatts, Shenhua's revenues have been increasing at a yearly basis of 25.3 per cent (152.063 billion as of 2010) and profits to 20.3 per cent (Annual Report of Shenhua, 2010). Obviously with the possession of own railway network and shipping companies, Shenhua has escaped the transportation bottlenecks and the costs associated with the rise in delays due to reliance on public transport in a Third World nation. The company has possession of three major mines: Shendong mines, Zhunge'er mines and Shengli mines dealing in production of long flame coal, non-coking coal and lignite (Ibid). The company is not an independent entity and has a hierarchy of working under a de facto controller. SASAC holds 100 per cent equity over the Shenhua Group Corporation Limited which holds 72.96 per cent of stakes at the China Shenhua Energy Company Limited (Ibid).

China Guodian Corporation: It was established on December 29, 2002 acquiring partial assets of former State Power Corporation of China and engages in investment, construction, management and sales of power (and heat). It owns GD Power Development Company Ltd., Guodian Changyuan Power Company Ltd., Inner Mongolia Pingzhuang Energy Resources

Company Limited, Ningxia Younglight Chemicals Company Ltd. (all in China), and China Longyuan Power Group Corporation Ltd. (in Hong Kong). Its wind installed capacity ranks fifth in the world and first in Asia. (The above section is based on Annual Report of China Guodian Corporation 2011.)

Figure 3.8: Branches of Guodian Corporation

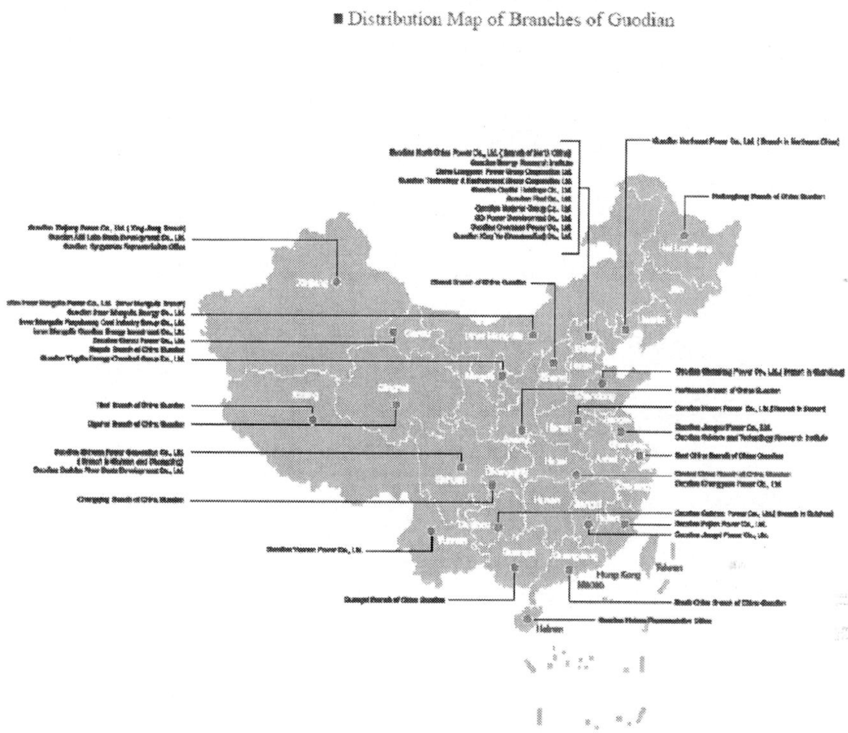

Source: Annual Report of China Guodian Corporation 2011.

It raised 17.7 billion yuan in the Hong Kong stock exchange and has become the third largest IPO (Initial Public Offering) raised by renewable enterprises since 1999 (Ibid).

Figure 3.9: Installed Capacity of China Guodian Corporation

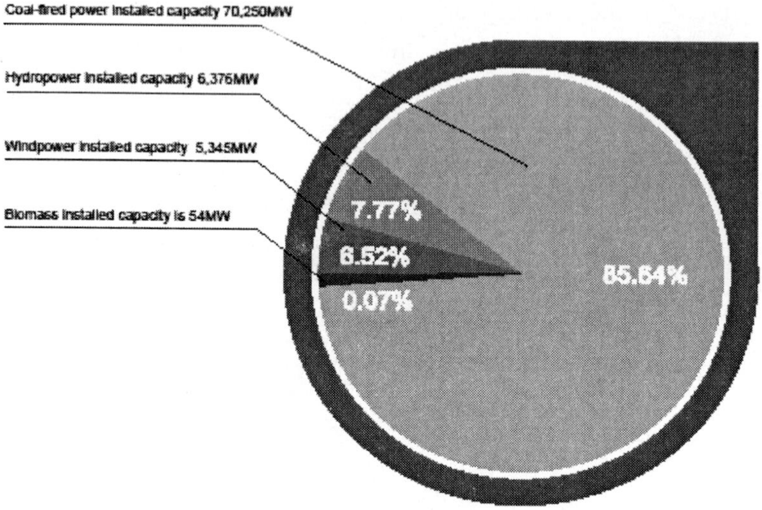

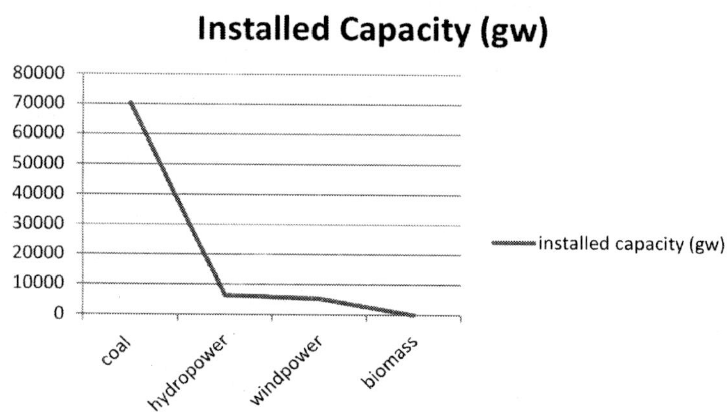

Source: Annual Report of China Guodian Corporation 2011.

The above figures are till December 2009. While China Guodian Corporation's wind power installed capacity is fifth in the world and first in Asia, its tidal power installed capacity is third in the world and first in Asia. In its coal power its trump card is the Guodian Beilun power plant which has an installed capacity of 5,000 MW and is also the largest coal plant of China. It works with all kinds of large, medium and small hydropower stations on Kaiduhe River, Akesu River and Jinghe River (Xinjiang) and Amojiang River (Yunan). Its wind power operations are in Jiangsu and Zhejiang (The above section is based on Annual Report of China Guodian Corporation 2011).

As its major focus lies in building up new energy technology its continuous painstaking efforts have laid fruit in the form of seawater desulphurisation project, plasma ignition technology and air cooling system which have been indigenously built by China Guodian (The above section is based on Annual Report of China Guodian Corporation 2011).

As a company of international ranking dealing with the most abundant resource of the fastest developing nation, China Guodian owns 13.2 billion tonnes of coal reserves with 32 million annual output with its largest players being the Pingzhuang coal group (coal reserve: 2.4 billion tonnes, annual output: 18 million tonnes), Ningxia Younglight Chemicals, Qinghuangdao port etc. (The above section is based on Annual Report of China Guodian Corporation 2011).

Obviously with China's "go out" (*zou chuqu*) policy, the scope of expansion of any foreign company lies outside the domestic boundary and so is true for Guodian Corp. The president of the company is in regular contact with foreign and energy ministries who are increasingly working in consonance with each other (Ibid). It is also believed that aggressive pursuance of international expansion is a logical outcome with escalating prices of all fossil fuels. Being a private company, China's Guodian Corporation aggressively pursues strategic cooperation agreement with other state owned companies (the latest being with CNPC on April 5, 2012) to grant more legitimacy and girth to its operations (CNPC website 2012).

China Huaneng Group (hereafter CHNG): A key state owned company with a registered capital of 20 billion yuan, CHNG was formed in 1985 and (unlike others) aims to abide by Huaneng characteristics. It has a three-colour corporate mission, red, green and blue, each for serving socialism, environment, innovation and internationalisation respectively. One of the first power producers of China in the Fortune Group (276th in 2011), CHNG charter has huge overtones of "Deng Xiaoping Theory" and "The Three Represents" as its guiding light. No wonder the president of the company and the secretary of CPC Huaneng Committee share equal position and power (in fact, the president of the company is actually the vice secretary of the CPC Huaneng committee and the secretary of the committee is the vice-president of the company) in the company's organisational structure. In its early days CHNG made great strides in becoming China's many firsts: the first to import 350 MW coal generating units and construction at Dalian, Shangan, Fuzhou and Nantong. By 1992 the 35 MW unit had become an import of 600 MW unit and was utilised at Shanghai power plant, which speaks of the burgeoning trade in a matter of just seven years. The turn of the century marked the turn of strategy from import to indigenous and

2004 was the first year when domestically generated coal units were put into use. Not only coal but Huaneng has won some early bird prizes in hydro and wind power energy, thanks to the support of both the central and local governments. In 1985, the Ministry of Water Resources and the provincial government joined hands to form a large-scale water plant. The year 1996 fulfilled a major target of the Eighth Five Year Plan, the Huaneng Taipingyi hydropower plant. In 2004 China's first wind-solar power generation system began to work and 2009 brought in biomass power plants. Since 2007 it has launched "developing large generation units and retiring small ones" as the major project to reduce environment degradation. Hence it has engaged in strategic alliances of thermal-power industry, wind generation industry and coal chemical industry with Ministry of Science and Technology (MOST). A deep blue logo formed with morphed letters of "h" and "n" connected by three radials (like a lightning), the company claims to have an installed capacity which is first in Asia and second in the world (The above section is based on the website of China Huaneng).

Table 3.17: Various Subsidiary Plants of Huaneng Corporation

Huaneng plant	As a pioneer of the 'firsts'
Nan'ao wind farm	China's first commercial wind and solar hybrid power generation system
Huaneng Yuhuan power plant	China's first domestic 1000 mw ultra-supercritical coal-fire power unit
Huaneng Shidongkou power plant 2	World's largest carbon capture facility
Xiaowan hydropower station	World's highest double curvature arch dam
Tianjin IGCC demonstration power plant	China's first IGCC demonstration power project
Yimin coal and electricity company	China's first large scale integrated coal and electricity enterprise

Source: Annual Report of Huaneng 2005

China Datang Corporation Power Company Limited (hereafter CDT): CDT was established as a large-scale power generation enterprise group on December 29, 2002 with a registered capital of 15.39 billion Yuan from the assets of the former state power corporation of China. A wholly state owned enterprise managed by CPC Central Committee, it engages in management of state owned assets, development, construction, maintenance, distribution and sales of thermal energy and electricity. It also deals with application and promotion of low carbon technology, maintenance, testing, sale and research of renewable energy related equipment, generation, engineering, construction, installation, repair and maintenance of power projects both at home and abroad, construction of feed water piping, renewable related training and consultation services and also lease of property. With seven funded subsidiaries and eight branch companies, the company operates, on a hierarchical basis, whose subsidiaries and enterprises are a notch higher than grassroots enterprises but are answerable to the CDT headquarters. Ex-president Hu Jintao has visited the edifice of CDT, twice, to personally "oversee and encourage" the work of the company. The company has also been instrumental in establishing the largest wind farm of the world. (The above section is based on the website of China Datang Corporation).

China Huadian Corporation (hereafter CHD): A state owned enterprise with a registered capital of 12 billion Yuan (till 2002), CHD supplies heat and electricity (relying on coal combustion as the main source) to China. The company claims to follow the "outlook of scientific development" (as directed by the Third and Fourth Plenum of the Seventeenth Party Congress). It set up its subsidiary in Hong Kong on June 14, 2006 looking over overseas projects. Its three major companies for overseas business are China Huadian Hong Kong Company Limited, Huadian Engineering Company Limited and CHD Power Plant Operation Company Limited. As per the direction of the "11th five year plan" it has aggressively pursued investments in its neighbouring countries. Its five major listed companies are: Huadian Power International Company Limited, Huadian Power Company Limited, State Power Nanjing Automation Company Limited, Huadian Jinshan Power Company Limited and Guizhou Qianyuan Power Company (The above section is based on the website of China Huadian Corporation).

Figure 3.11: Business Activities of China Huadian Corporation

Business Scope

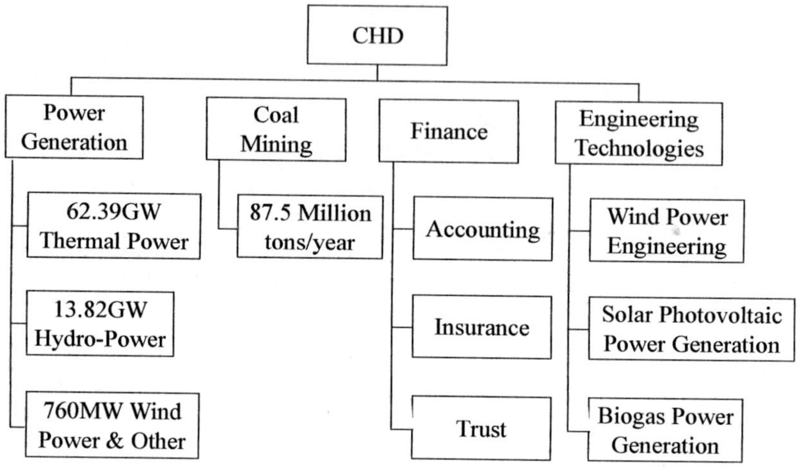

Source: Website of China Huadian Corporation

China Power Investment Corporation (hereafter CPI): This company's unique selling point lies in establishing a circular economic structure in east inner Mongolia, east Ningxia, Guizhou and Heilongjiang as the industrial chain of coal-electricity-non ferrous metals and coal-electricity-chemicals aiming to achieve a "comprehensive resource efficiency" and "rational resource utilization." CPI has been very active in the recent years in promoting the development of clean energies in China. In its aim of "providing green energy," it entered into lots of contracts and agreements (both domestic and abroad) with various public and private enterprises (The above section is based on the website of China Power Investment Corporation).

Figure 3.12: The Installed Capacity of China Power Investment Corporation from Clean Energy Resources

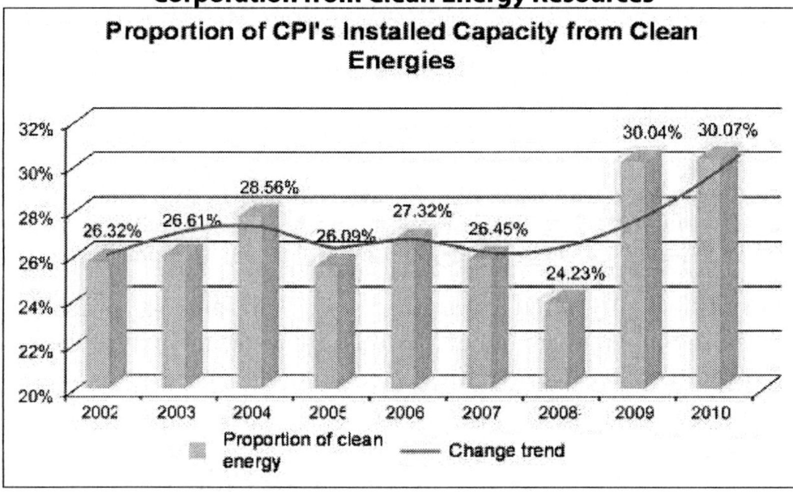

Source: Annual Report of CPI. 2011

From the above figure it can be derived that CPI has played its part well in building up installed capacity from clean energies (read, renewable). In the span of a decade CPI has been expanding its installed capacity while restricting to clean energy resources, and despite fluctuations in consecutive years from 2005-8 (Ibid). However, not all companies can build up all of their capacities relying only on clean energies. Given below is the analysis of the major power companies of China under economic parameters.

Table 3.19: Business Conditions and Economic Parameters of Other Major Power Companies of China over a Period of Time

Installed Capacities

Year	Huaneng Corporation (MW)	China Guodian corporation (MW)	China Datang corporation (MW)
2002	n.a.	22,129	23,847.5
2003	n.a.	25,343	27,455.5
2004	n.a.	29,303.9	33,534
2005	n.a.	35,060	41,655.5
2006	n.a.	44,452.5	54,059.5
2007	n.a.	60,060	64,823.4
2008	n.a.	70,235	82,420.3

2009	45,340	82,030	100,172.3
2010	46,512	n.a.	105,895.9
2011	53,687	n.a.	111,060
2012	56,572	n.a.	113,800
2013	59,625	122,790	115,430

Unit: Megawatt
Source: Annual Report of Huaneng Power International Inc. 2013, Annual Report of China Guodian Corporation 2011, Website of China Guodian Corporation, Corporate Social Responsibility Report of China Datang Corporation of 2013 and 2008

Given their installed capacities which are almost in complete synchronisation with each other, it would be better to analyse their coal and power outputs, in order to determine their success for optimum utilisation.

Annual Power Generation Volume (GWH)

Year	Huaneng	Guodian	Datang
2002	n.a	121,930	117,447
2003	n.a	137,100	142,753
2004	n.a	168,100	173,370
2005	n.a.	190,400	209,770
2006	n.a.	225,912	251,621
2007	n.a.	264,000	304,757
2008	n.a.	297,800	352,956
2009	203,520	353,200	389,854
2010	256,950	n.a	472,575
2011	313,554	n.a.	508,0
2012	302,433	n.a.	506,0
2013	317,481	n.a.	494,0

Source: Annual Report of Huaneng Power International Inc. 2013, Annual Report of China Guodian Corporation 2011, Website of China Guodian Corporation, Corporate Social Responsibility Report of China Datang Corporation of 2013 and 2008

Comparing the installed capacities and power output of the above three companies we can see that all the companies have been fluctuating in their installed capacity and output and have been maintaining this trend for the last decade. However, a company's work does not end up as a producer but has to consider all other costs and escalations before finally earning the seller's share.

The next three tables shall compare the assets, sales and profits on a yearly basis in determining the economic forte of the companies.

Total Assets (100 million yuan)

Year	Huaneng	Guodian	Datang
2009	1,978.87	4,188.6	4,778.45
2010	2,279.3	n.a.	5,205.82
2011	2,574.1	n.a.	6,055
2012	2,591	n.a.	6,559
2013	2,622.3	1,183.6	6,980

Total Revenue (100 million yuan)

Year	Huaneng	Datang
2009	7,68.62	1,466
2010	1,043.1	1,754
2011	1,334	1,912
2012	1,339.6	1,916
2013	1,338	1,903

Total Profits (100 million yuan)

Year	Huaneng	Datang
2009	49.3	22.91
2010	33.48	15.22
2011	11.81	16.06
2012	55.12	60.28
2013	104.12	109.61

Source: Annual Reports of China Huaneng Power International Inc. 2013, Corporate Social Responsibility Report of China Datang Corporation 2013, Annual Report of China Guodian Corporation 2011, Website of China Guodian Corporation

The growth and expansion of the energy companies seem to vitiate CCP's claim of "green cover expansion" in the near future. Yet coal is reducing its pivotal position in the power sector, no matter how much longer it can stand to dominate. Intelligentsia and energy experts (both in and outside China) believe that China has reached its peak coal position (a phenomenon discussed in detail in the market section) and shall soon be retracing its steps from fuelling its other sectors with sole reliance on coal (Mathews and Tan, 2012). This, they believe, should not be judged as a mere platitude but as an imperative stance. China in its "green plan" (read, the Twelfth Five Year Plan) could not resist in targeting an addition of 223 GW of coal fired power in four years (2011-2015), i.e., 55 GW per year, or

1 GW per week!(Mathew and Tan, 2012). However the China Electricity Council in its report of March 2012 seems placid in assuring that given the present conditions China shall be reversing its trend of coal consumption to pre-2011 levels by 2015. If this can happen or not is for the future to tell (Mathews and Tan, 2012).

Consumers of China

The US department of energy divides the consumers of energy into three kinds: residential or commercial consumers, industrial consumers and transportation consumers. *(Conserve Energy Future n.a)* While residential and commercial usage is restricted to the primary needs of lighting, heating and cooling, Industrial usage is mainly for production purposes and running of machinery. The transportation sector relying almost entirely on oil and gas is involved with "uploading and downloading of goods from one part of the country to another." (*Conserve Energy Future n.a*)

China's Communist Party (CCP) draws legitimacy to its authority from China's transformation from being a "Sick Man of Asia" to an economic powerhouse. It also aims to achieve the status of a "well-off society" by 2020, of which energy is the main ingredient. However rising living standards have invariably shifted household consumption of energy from organic energy to commercial energy products, adding further strain on the already burdened energy resources. China's energy products hold the intrinsic characteristic of being a "supply product." This has gained evidence from the government practice of subsidising the necessary energy products for the poor and the ultra poor. Even the governments of developed nations which have undergone complete marketisation of their energy structure have earmarked a certain proportion of subsidy to fulfil the least consumption unit of the poor of their country. However the problem in China is that not only are there poor people in substantial numbers but also the vast "income inequality" divide between the rich and the poor has raised the living standards of the rich to such an extent that their gluttonous consumption and wasteful draining of energy resources is viewed as an epitome of "lifestyle" rather than a practice to be "shunned." Hence the question of energy supply is not just limited to "security" but also to "morality." While the government cannot tame the rising living standards as well as the burgeoning demands of the nouveau riche it can also not ask the rest of the poor to sacrifice their basic energy consumption for the comfort of the few individuals or for its new "rising China" image. Another major problem faced by China is not just in its domestic consumption but also implicit export of energy through its energy intensive low value added products. These products are high yielding per unit cost of consumption, but a great strain on energy equilibrium of China (CASS, 2008). Adding insult to the injury of China's energy woes is the small scale and market for renewable which eventually leads to high cost of unit source output. In fact it has largely been analysed that China should resort to economic incentives rather than coercive administrative actions to build up a market for renewable sources. Advocates of market economy, and subsequently the marketisation of all energy sectors in China, believe that such a move would enhance the accountability of the energy sector thereby curbing wasteful consumption (Churchill, 1993). The lure of gaining "windfall profits" would subsequently lead to enhanced private investment in eco-friendly technologies which would usher in a matured development in China. In fact owing to problems of burgeoning demand ad transportation bottlenecks China is fast emerging as the largest investor in renewable technologies. Buijs (2012:19) has identified that Chinese policy makers are investing in the renewable sector, not only because of the push of demand from the consumers but also because of its independence from any international binding of a global treaty or any financial constraint (Bujis, 2012: 19). While in the former case it is not dependent on commitmments by other countries to pursue its renewable targets, in the latter case China's internal financial structure which involves extensive government funding in the state owned companies by the state owned banks insulates it from global or regional 'economic meltdowns'(Ibid). However, it should not be forgotten that no matter how fast a country's economy grows the average Third World consumer, even if she/he turns into a producer of energy, cannot shy away from the issue of price, both domestic and international. From the perspective of the sensitivity of price issue it is seen that individuals or enterprises at the higher income group are less sensitive to the issue of energy scarcity because of their high consumption affordability and capacity (Churchill, 1993). Similar is the condition of various financial institutions of the government who advocate the insulation of energy consumption from the market prices but are not much bothered about it in concrete terms. Thus it can be safely concluded that China is not only an energy dependent economy but also a driving energy consumption economy.

Demand and Consumers

Demand Side Management came to China in the 1990s in the electricity sector, to monitor the mechanisms of regulations as well as the technologies used in the energy sector (Xin Qiu and Li, 2012:10687). Demand Side Management is a two pronged process where the consumers demand is controlled by energy efficiency. Energy efficiency in turn is stimulated by changing the consumers demand through manipulation of the prices and the enterprises demand is manipulated through the process of integrated resource planning (IRP) by evaluation of costs and feasibility of the power plant through its installation (Ibid). In fact the main aim of DSM is to have an elaborate price structure so that the actual costs are covered from both the residential consumers and the commercial enterprises (Xin Qiu and Li, 2012:10687). The 2001 regulation on electricity conservation and the 2005 interim provisions for the administration of the power selling prices (2005 provision) are related to DSM (ibid). However DSM is not much effective in the electricity sector because while DSM requires SERC to monitor the prices the actual electricity prices are decided by the NDRC (Ibid). DSM is still an unexplored area in China due to high economic targets, rigid competition laws and lack of incentives for investment in DSM projects (Ibid). It would be beneficial for the future of China's energy resources to enhance the presence of DSM projects in the energy sector in a big way and diversify the price structure so that the true costs of production are reflected and judicious consumption and energy efficiency is promoted among the energy consumers (Ibid).

The drive for urbanisation is expanding at cataclysmic speed in China. With the construction industry mushrooming at breakneck speed the building energy consumption is 20-30 per cent of the general commodity consumption in China, out of which the residential consumption is 60 per cent of the total construction energy consumption (Ling et. al., 2010: 35). This is the national average, and metropolitan cities like Beijing and others are far above the general standards. With the economies of these areas also being far more prosperous than the national average an obvious impact has been on their rising living standards and the increased electric consumption of the consumers spiralling up to an unsatisfied energy demand of the consumers.

A case study of Beijing was done for the period of five months spanning from January 2009 to May 2009 (Ling et. al., 2010: 35). The aim of the survey was to investigate the impact of changing living standards on the residential energy consumption and the individual measures adopted by an average citizen for energy conservation. The area covered was 23 residential communities in seven districts of Beijing and two agricultural markets. The area was spread over second ring road to the sixth ring road which covered the 8 communities and one market of Chaoyang district, 8 from Haidian district, 2 from Fengtai, 2 from Chongwen, 1 from Xuanwu, 1 from Shijing and 1 district and 1 market from Xicheng. The total questionnaires were 3,000 out of which 1,692 were valid. The district-wise break-up of responses was 251 from Fengtai, 725 from Chaoyang, 110 from Xuanwu, 186 from Chongwen,

225 from Xicheng, 45 from Shijing and 482 from Haidian. This study has kept in mind the growing relevance of the construction industry in China in general and the booming real estate industry in Beijing in particular since the reform era. It was calculated that before 1980 the construction in Beijing was merely 1 per cent which rose to 13 per cent in the decade of the 1980s. The steepest rise was in the 1990s when construction rose to 38 per cent and then to 40 per cent by 2004 (ibid, 36-37). It has been observed that while the developed countries like Japan, Sweden and Germany have their residential compounds built within the range of 85 to 99 square metres, in China it has a wide range from 50 to 110 square metres (Ibid). Obviously rising income inequalities and conspicuous consumption is inherent in almost every feature of the demonstration effect of rising incomes and living standards, especially housing. The energy consumption is not only determined by the brick-and-mortar but also the kind of doors and windows used. It has been seen that 40 to 50 per cent of the total energy consumption of the residential housing has been through the material of doors and windows used (Ibid). This increases to 75 per cent if the windows and doors are made of glass (Ibid). Hence the material chosen for the building is an extremely important component for the analysis of the energy consumption of a particular building. Beijing consumers are big customers of vinyl coated steel (65 per cent), aluminium alloy (23 per cent), iron (9 per cent), wood (2 per cent) and others (1 per cent). (The above case study has been taken from Ling et. al., 2010).

Air conditioners are another electricity guzzling device which are soon becoming a necessity for Beijing residents rather than a luxury (Ibid). With rising summer temperatures as well as living standards the predominance of air conditioners is shifting from one per house to each per room. Statistics reveal that per capita consumption of Beijing families is two or more air conditioners while merely 5 per cent of the families do not use air conditioners (Ibid). Obviously the low and middle-income groups are also caught in this swirl of air conditioners' contribution to the upward spiral of energy consumption.

Figure 3.13: Air Conditioners and Energy Consumption

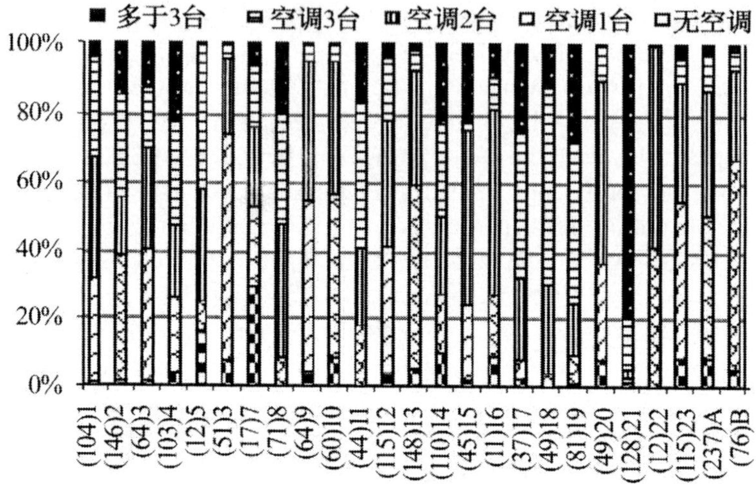

Source: Ling Haoshu et. al. (2010:35-37)

The above statistics give details about the number of air conditioners used per household in Beijing. The data given here is based on the amount of usage of the air conditioners.

Table 3.21: Percentage of Usage of the Air Conditioners

Usage of air conditioners (category)	Number of households (per cent)
Not used	5
Least used	15
Infrequently used	45
Frequently used	35

Source: Ling Haoshu et. al. (2010:35-37).

Thus it can be seen that the maximum number of residents of Beijing use air conditioners either sometimes or frequently. This is a major strain on the already scarce electricity supply of Beijing which gets more acute during summers. The issue of temperature settings of air conditioners also contributes to the greater electric consumption of the air conditioners. While only 1 per cent of Beijing residents adjust their temperatures above 28 degrees Celsius, the rest 99 per cent adjust their temperatures to below 28 degrees Celsius (up to 20 degrees Celsius, 21 per cent; 21 to 24 degrees, 23 per cent; and 25 to 28 degrees, 55 per cent) (Ibid). While low temperatures of the air conditioners cool the immediate vicinity of the room, they definitely heat up the electricity supply unit (Ibid).

When a consumer is discussed an invariant focus is not just on how much she/he consumes but also how much she/he pays for this consumption. Despite electricity being a state funded and subsidised commodity, it is not a hidden fact that the electricity bills flare up faster than the temperatures of Beijing.

Figure 3.14: Households and Electricity Bills

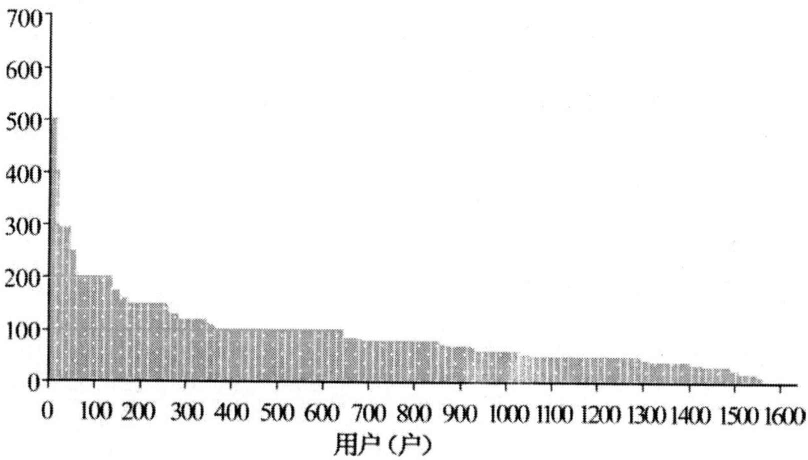

Axis X number of households
Axis Y electricity bills in Yuan
Source: Ling Haoshu et. al. (2010:35-37).

While the maximum record of a bill has touched 600 Yuan, three-fourths of the electricity bills stay within the limits of 50 to 200 Yuan (Ibid). On an average a residential bill is 93 Yuan per month which is equivalent to consuming 68.1 kg of standard coal (Ibid). Similarly the data for fuel consumption was analysed for 908 households and it was found that 60 per cent of the households paid 30 to 70 Yuan per month for their gas cylinders while the average of total households was 51 Yuan, which is equivalent 33.9 kg of standard coal (Ibid). This conversion has been derived taking 1 cubic metre of gas as equal to 1.33 kgce and 1 kilowatt hour of electricity as equivalent to 0.366 kgce (Ibid). Thus it can be seen that the fuel consumption is 1.48 times more than the electric consumption of average Beijing households (Ibid).

Figure 3.15: Total Amount of Energy Consumption by Households

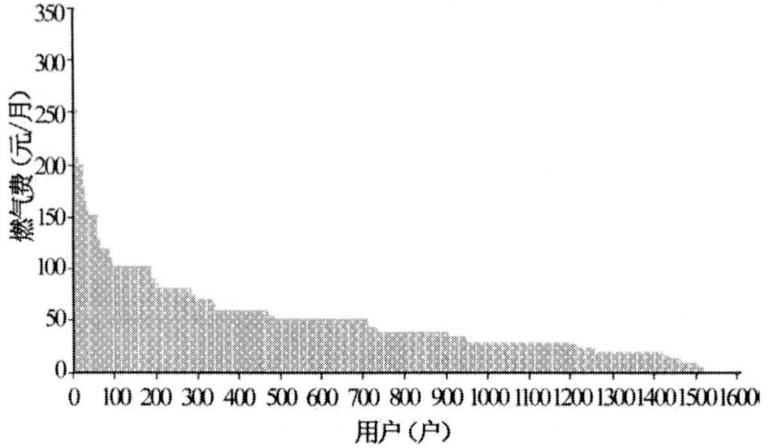

Axis X number of households
Axis Y amount spent on energy consumption
Source: Ling Haoshu et. al. (2010: 37).

In an individual analysis of the seven districts of Beijing it has been observed that individual energy consumption and household consumption in Haidian district has been a notch higher than the other districts of Beijing (Ibid). While Shijing district consumes the least, the rest of the districts have almost similar consumption patterns, which is, however, half of the Haidian district (Ibid). This undulating pattern of energy is an evidence of differences in the economic development of the various districts. They too are in synch with the theory of "more the development, more the consumption."

The study had revealed that while most of the Beijing residents were aware of the growing menace and energy shortage, they have not been able to apply energy conservation methods in their daily household work. An attitude of "let others do the conservation" does not augur well for the future of the Chinese consumer of energy (ibid., 38-39). Yet it cannot be denied that the consumer of today's China is a tech savvy, ecologically conscious citizen who believes in making an individual contribution to alleviate China's deteriorating air and water quality which has started to affect its health and its pocket over the medicines and treatment. Following the dictum of "prevention is better than cure" China's shoppers take initiatives in buying products with "energy saving" *(jieneng shangpin)* labels (M. Diana, 2013). In fact many international organisations have gathered a strong foothold in China's market, and social networking websites advocate the energy saving products available in China. One such organisation is the Top Ten China Network which began in Switzerland and now has a large number of Chinese visiting its website regularly to check for the latest cheap and energy efficient products in the nearby stores before going shopping (Ibid). The website claims to provide transparent data to its consumers and provides free advertising for producers of energy saving products (M. Diana, 2013). However, sceptics believe that this Swiss funded company does not operate without lots of "*guanxi*" (connections) in the government sector and its transparency is all a smokescreen (Ibid).

Conclusion

This chapter was an identification of the domestic actors of energy policies in China. It tried to explore the idea of not only how they influence the energy policies, but also what influences them into forming a certain kind of interests. At a time when China had just begun its journey as a liberalised state, the larger role lay in the hands of only one determinant—the government and the bureaucracy. With a centralised administrative system operating under one-party rule, the other determinants were mere passive receivers of the orders from the government and had little influence over leadership psyche and political ideology. Yet development and self-sufficiency was the main theme and anything which favoured these two targets could result as an influencing factor in determining or perhaps channelising the course of the energy policies. Hence in the socialist set-up, if there was any other determinant which had some form of influence apart from the bureaucracy, it was the state owned companies which marked the onset of intensive exploration and exploitation of the fossil fuels. However now with the reforms serving as a backdrop of the changed and economically charged political landscape and with the growth rate spiral escalating upwards, the heads of these various energy companies, which were officially the state owned companies, could gather more weight in their opinions as they shared tables with the government on the decision-making level. Yet it could not be neglected that the ground realities were disintegrated with the euphoria of the air conditioned rooms of the government officials and executive officers of these companies. Despite a continuous target China was no longer self-sufficient in energy resources, and in fact was fast accelerating towards the phase of "economic scarcity" due to its economic development and consumer demand. The consumers now were large enough in number to be able to influence the market demand patterns, forming an intrusion or influence of their own kind on the energy policies.

The recent spate of corruption investigations which have dominated the first year of Xi Jinping's regime have perhaps laid a perfect example of the influence of bureaucracy, energy companies and consumers (who are getting their opinions increasingly noticed through the internet platforms). The crackdown on Zhou Yongkang (a top echelon of CNPC) soon after Bo Xilai has drawn massive attention of the netizens to the connections shared between the two. Reports by Wall Street Journal and other Western media have quoted the "industry insiders" highlighting this crackdown as a move to "weaken the vested interests." However it is true that no matter how much euphoria is displayed over the government's commitment to "root out corruption and inefficiency," or how much rhetoric is applied in speeches as to "no tigers and flies will be spared," there are also certain sceptics who believe that all this is a mere move to "eliminate opposition" or "protest against monopolisation of the energy economy of China by the energy companies." This power struggle between the energy companies and the bureaucracy has given a forum to consumers (who are usually at the receiving end of government diktat and companies' policies) who played a delightful role of informed and opinioned citizens protesting against all forms of show and glamour of merging with the public or corruption and embezzlement being the cause of burning holes in their pocket. Whether the consumers are able to utilise this power of unity even in matters of political stringency is a saga to wait and watch for.

4. The Domestic Determinants of China's Energy Policies: The Factors Involved

Despite a dominant one-party system China could never eschew the causes or forces which, though intangible, held a bearing effect on its energy decisions. Yang and Qu (2009:24) in their paper on energy mix optimisation have highlighted the changing trend of coal dominance and advocate changes in market mechanism, harnessing of advanced technology and incorporation of ecological sensitivities as not only the ideal but also the only path for energy optimisation. The market of China has survived on its manufacturing sector and thrived on investment and growth. Negatively, market has dominated the psyche of China to such an extent that it has completely marginalised factors of environment sustainability which has been the breeding ground of its 'energy' (pun unintended) a.k.a fossil fuels and now the potentially vibrant renewable sector. However it should not be forgotten that it is the same market which can turn around the fate of ecological degradation by merely redirecting its sources of investment and supply to cleaner energy resources and investments in advanced technology options which are not only viable but also durable for a long time. Hence economy and environment along with energy share the bond of inseparable trinity whose holistic viewing is indispensable in understanding the domestic energy sector of China. The domestic factors determining China's energy policies are market mechanism, environment and advanced technology.

Market mechanism- The market mechanism incorporates security of supply, economic efficiency and social equity. Market carries a different meaning and implication in different economic systems. With China's transformation into a socialist market economy the definition of market too changed in the dictionaries. While market economies bring price and other economic variables into determining production and distribution, a socialist market economy too operates in a similar pattern but under national macro control (*Modern Chinese Dictionary Xiandai Hanyu Cidian* 现代汉语词典, 2009: 1244). This phenomenon is well exhibited in the energy market. The demand and supply meet converges on security issues and fuel mix choices.

Prices are linked to economic efficiency in production and in allocation to the market with effective application of market signals and government control. Talking about social equity brings us to the problem of distribution between rich and poor urban and rural sectors. It is unrealistic for China to build a uniform energy policy for its different provinces and strata of people. Tax rates for oil products, fertilisers and electricity to be subjected to corrective measures timed according to market conditions. Issues related to China's fossil fuel market, production, distribution as well as impact of domestic price reforms and rising international crude price in the domestic sphere shall be discussed.

Harnessing of advanced technology to realise optimisation-Advanced technology is an amalgamation of scientific concept and technological aspects. Hence the Chinese term it as *keji,* i.e. science and technology. This involves prioritising the conservation of energy, promoting the development of renewable energy sources, especially wind and nuclear, and curbing headlong momentum of coal to oil projects. This also involves a gradual transition from high carbon economy to low carbon economy. Simply put, it involves low energy consumption, emission and pollution involving various industries on clean energy, industrial energy conservation, high efficient energy conversion, energy storage devices. Acquiring advanced technology is a big issue in China especially as policy-makers avidly advocate large-scale development of renewable resources. Moreover as issues of energy conservation gain greater momentum all in China, be it producers or consumers, are encouraged to adopt 'green products' which are made by technology promoting energy conservation.

Environment – Environment primarily evolves ecology and its protection. The Chinese usually define 'environment protection' where the environment needs to be improved to be made suitable for human labour and life's work. (*Modern Chinese Dictionary, Xiandai Hanyu Cidian,* 2009:594). Hence the concept of environment being subservient to man has been a reasonable dictum maintained in the Chinese psyche for a long time. However with international spotlight shifting towards 'sustainable development' the building up of new energy resources has become an imperative issue finding serious advocates even in policy circles of the government. Moreover with China already having gained the experience of energy conservation in the 1980s, more voices are heard to pick up the trails of a lost path and bring in energy efficiency not as an option but as the only choice. Most Chinese authors too argue on the same lines demanding inclusion of sustainability of development with local characteristics (and not with Chinese characteristics as a whole per se). Greater role of local products and population (especially with rural areas) not only assures greater energy efficiency, but also assures more economic autonomy and environmental accountability (Byrne et. al.., 1996). It is no assumption that energy optimisation is affected by an amalgamation of energy policies, economic growth and environmental degradation. Efficiency in energy can be maintained by efficiently utilising energy investment and production of renewable energy sources. However how much of that has happened and will happen in China is still a question to be researched.

Market Mechanism

"China's energy profile is a window into its economic soul" (Rosen and Houser, 2007b:25).When we talk of market in the energy context, two kinds of market need to be discussed. One, market for energy resources i.e. direct consumption of fossil and non-fossil fuels where energy is the end product and secondly, a market existing because of energy resources through indirect consumption i.e. where energy is the raw material.

Market of Energy

> The energy profile of China is in a state of flux, changing quickly in a constant effort to keep up with the rest of the economy. It is a fusion of plan and market forces, formal regulation and seat-of-the-pants fixes, central plans and local interests. In energy many key metrics are obscured by national security considerations or habits of secrecy at state-owned enterprises (Rosen and Houser, 2007a:4).

The energy market involves two concepts: rate of energy consumption and change in energy intensity (which is consumption per unit of GDP) (Crompton and Wu, 2012:5). In a period analysis of China's energy structure from the liberation to the turn of the century has revealed that while energy consumption has risen to stupendous proportions, a welcome respite has been the decline in energy intensity due to technological advancements and structural changes in consumption pattern (Ibid).

Figure 4.1: Total Energy Consumption and Energy Intensity of China from 1953 to 2003

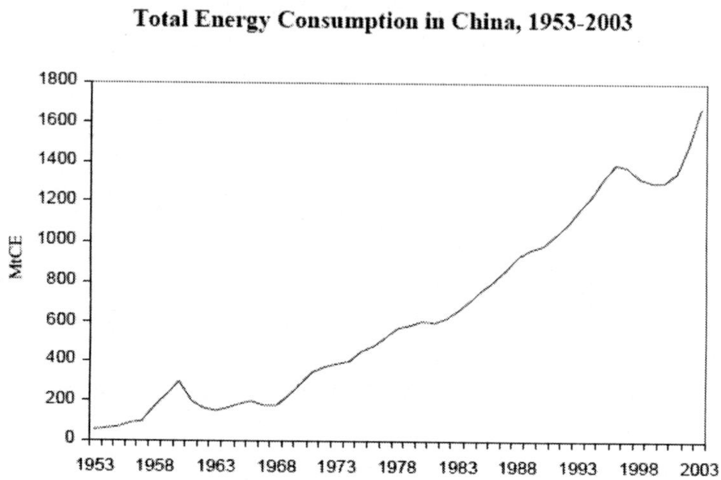

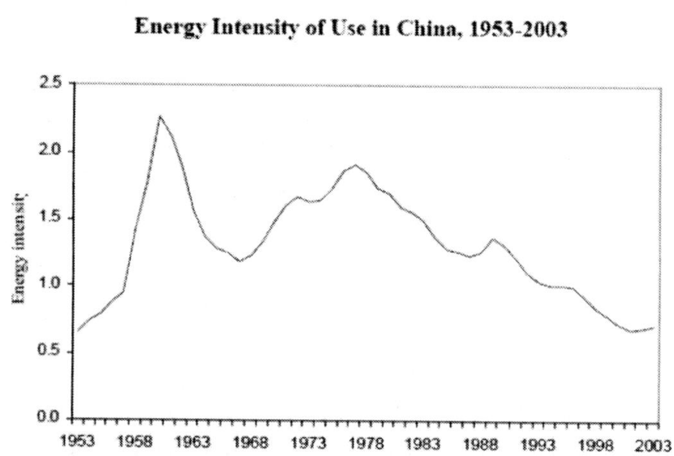

Source: Crompton and Wu (2012:5).

The above figures show that while energy consumption has been steadily climbing since 1978 with a slight dip in 1997-1999, energy intensity has been steadily declining with a peak of 1978. This speaks volumes about the reform period to ardently restore the wrongs of the Cultural Revolution and reinstate not just the economy but also (albeit very subtly) the environment (Crompton and Wu, 2012: 4). Variations in China's energy consumption are not just between times but also between geography as its developed provinces are great power guzzlers while resource rich areas are deficient of development. This sparks an issue of proximity towards transportation and historical importance versus proximity towards resources as the carrier of development. Was 'nearness to coastal areas' (Shanghai) and 'historical eminence' (Beijing) a reason for speedier development in these areas than 'resource possessors' (Shaanxi). This urban- rural divide and east-west divide has sparked a greater controversy of; energy ruling the market or market ruling the energy. Obviously, coal as the copious and the cheapest fuel has never lost its gleam in the last twenty years no matter how much of oil and other resources have tried to seek attention (See Table 4.1).

Table 4.1: Primary energy consumption of China from 1990 to 2013

Year	Coal	Oil	Gas	Hydro	Total
1990	752.1	163.8	20.7	50.3	987
1991	789.8	177.5	20.8	49.8	1,037.8
1992	826.4	191	20.7	53.5	1,091.7
1993	866.5	211.1	22	60.3	1,159.9
1994	920.5	213.6	23.3	70	1,227.4
1995	978.6	229.6	23.6	80	1,311.8
1996	1,037.9	250.1	25	76.4	1,389.5
1997	985.3	281.1	23.4	85.4	1,378
1998	920.2	284.3	29.1	88.6	1,303
1999	884.8	301.9	28.6	85.9	1,301.2
2000	861.3	320.5	32.6	88.6	1,322.1
2001	881	327.8	36.4	103.9	1,349.1
2002	972.3	355.7	38.5	115.6	1,482.2
2003	1,125.9	380.9	47	124.2	1,678
2004	1,176.8	391	50.5	128.8	1,747
2005	1,215.9	402.9	54.1	133.4	1,806.3
2006	1,245.1	417.5	57.8	138.2	1,858.3
2007	1,274.1	435.4	61.6	143.2	1,914.3
2008	1,311.1	457.6	65.5	148.4	1,982.6
2009	1,359.7	485.4	69.4	154	2,068.5
2010	1,421.1	519.5	73.3	159.7	2,173.5
*2011	1760.8	459.4	117.5	158.2	2,540.8
*2012	1,856.4	490.1	131.7	197.3	2,731.1
*2013	1,925.3	507.4	145.5	206.3	2,852.4

Unit: million tonnes coal equivalent
* Unit: million tonnes oil equivalent
Source: Crompton and Wu (2012:15). *BP Statistical Review of World Energy (2013 and 2014)

From the above table it can be deduced that there has been a slight dip in growth rate of coal consumption from 2004, and other resources have seen a gradual rise in their share of energy consumption especially oil, albeit with stifling intensity. Rising focus on cleaner energy and reducing energy intensity industries reflect a different future for China's energy consumption in the years to come.

An Accenture survey has revealed that China, despite being the number one attraction for investors is also considered the country with maximum risks because of the rising prices and paucity of fossil fuels (Austin, 2005). China's regulatory institutions refuse to raise the price of electricity despite regular power cuts and receding coal reserves (Ibid). Experts believe that price rise would not only motivate (albeit forcefully) the industries to enhance capacity generation and transmission but also the customers for taking a step forward towards energy conservation and efficiency (Ibid). This is more important especially when China is consuming more than the USA by almost five times per unit of GDP which speaks volumes about the undone work potential (Ibid). The current energy system of China is plagued with feeble prices, weak institutions and limited transmission capacity. Energy shortage has been considered a regular threat in the party reports and government reports of the CCP (Wen Jiabao's 2005 party report declared energy shortage as one of the five major threats to China) (Ibid:1). He also promulgated regulations on electricity management (15 February 2005) and regulation on electricity supervision and control (25 February 2005) (Ibid). These two regulations were moved to promote competition in the energy market (Ibid). A market for a commodity is viewed in terms of its income elasticity in relation to GDP and regulations imposed on its market (Ibid). Many people think differently about difference in income elasticity of energy demand (corresponding rise of energy demand with every one percent rise in GDP) (Ibid). Variations in reports ranging from 0.5 to 1.5 have been caused by the decoupling of power consumption in relation to economic growth due to lacuna in energy efficiency, technological breakthroughs and capital limitations (Ibid:3). It is a given fact that the bulk of energy demand in China comes from industrial production of various goods catering to domestic and global demand at lower prices. Yet International Energy Agency (IEA) predicts a different demand curve where the end-user continues to demand more and more (as his lifestyle improves) with voracious industrial demand too growing unabated in the coming two or so decades. IEA predicts that by 2030 (Austin 2005: 5):

- China will be responsible for 20 percent increase in energy demand, and be using half of the world's coal.(Ibid)

- China's oil imports would be catering to 80 percent of its domestic oil demand (Ibid).
- Despite a gradual shift from coal and oil-fed energy structure to gas production, China would still need to heavily import to sustain its demand (Ibid).
- An investment of 4 billion dollars per year is required in coal not only in enhanced production but also in meeting safety standards (Ibid).
- A perennial shortage of electricity requires a perennial investment in the power sector especially in transmission and distribution (Ibid).

With high rate of volatility in the domestic energy consumption market of China which sometimes is reflected in its peculiar characteristics (many Western scholars tend to consider those peculiar characteristics as irrational, Austin 2005: 5), we shall take an individual analysis of each energy resource and its market followed by its implications on the general goods and services market.

Coal and Its Market

Coal has a special place in the Chinese economy. It is the cheapest source of producing electricity as it is almost wholly domestically produced (with only 10 percent accounting from its imports) and its price changes are one of the most pure indicators of changes in domestic demand structure of China (Ibid:6). It is increasingly being recognised that ecological costs of power production from coal has off set (and sometimes even goes into the negative) the economical benefits of coal (Ibid). Hence the governments' right from the central government to the provincial government and down to local government has been investing in renewable technology (Ibid). Renewable technology is given direct subsidies by the central government, funding is also made by State Science and Technology Commission (SSTC) and various other tax holidays by the local governments (Ibid:7). Differential pricing is also done during peak and off peak season and on six high consumption industries such as aluminium, ferroalloy, calcium carbide, caustic soda, steel and cement production (Ibid). Also, power discounts in remote areas have been removed for such industries (Austin 2005: 7). Household consumption patterns reflect an inelastic demand curve where rising prices have not reduced the demand for electricity. Differential pricing was observed in urban-rural divide where farmers (till the late 1990's) paid one-fourth the cost of their industrial neighbours (Ibid:8). Huaneng Power International in its Annual Report of 2004-5 discussed extensively the proposal of 'marketised' prices for the east and north-east electricity grid by the State Council. The following were the salient points:

- To establish an appropriate on-grid price setting mechanism
- To accommodate a reasonable level of competition in power generation
- To establish a preliminary pricing mechanism for transmission and distribution to facilitate the healthy development of the power grids
- To link the retail prices with the on-grid prices
- To optimise the structure of the retail price
- To pilot run the practice for high-voltage users to directly make purchases from the power generation companies based on a reasonable price for transmission and distribution.

> We believe China's government is hoping to establish a standardised and transparent price setting mechanism, classifying the electricity prices into the on–grid price, the transmission price, the distribution price, and the end user retail price and to allow them to be determined through market competition (Annual Report of Huaneng Power International Inc., 2005).

China's state-owned enterprises catering to common, essential public goods like power are increasingly voicing their opinion in favour of market determined prices, a trend which was nurtured in 1978 where talking of profit is not a luxury but a necessity. However how much of that profit caters to the larger goals of 'well-off society' and 'sustainable development' is a question of great scrutiny and debate.

Oil and the Market

China's entry into the World Trade Organisation (WTO) meant an import surge and reduced tariff barriers especially for automobile makers (Ibid, 10). This led to a price war between the local auto dealers and foreign manufacturers leading to an escalation of demand (almost to a situation of explosion) in 2002 (Angie, 2005:11). This was more viable as the fruits of the reform era had begun to be harvested and a generation lay prepared with repressed desires of materialistic consumerism making a heady situation of demand influx. Why does China account for at least one third of global oil demand? Clearly the per capita rise of power consumption and motor vehicles are the primary reasons. China does not have the luxury of oil, however its domestic prices do not reflect so as the government seals it from fluctuations in international crude price analysed and revised every month (Ibid). The profit margins of big oil conglomerates like PetroChina and Sinopec do not reflect this imbalance as retail prices at pump are maintained by wringing wholesale profits (Ibid). IEA reports that administered price policy of

China is an economic shield sacrificing the profit margins of refining (Ibid). However while petroleum is under 'administered price' policy, petroleum products are sold above the administered price due to which consumer stockpiling takes place creating an artificial scarcity (Austin 2005: 11). An oligopolistic culture exists in the oil market of China with four large players. Out of which two, PetroChina and Sinopec, dominate the domestic scenario. These two live like two large friendly kingdoms with CNPC supply dominating the north and west and Sinopec the south and east (Burke et. al., 2009:15).

Gas and Its Market

Liquefied natural gas projects are the most sought after projects for investment despite being expensive. A general LNG project's expenses are roughly divided into the following: gas production 15 to 20 percent, plant set up 30 to 45 percent, shipping 10 to 30 percent and receiving terminal 15 to 20 percent (Austin, 2005:13). China's regulatory sector especially SERC has been blamed for being subservient to NDRC even in matters of investment in the power sector (Austin, 2005:13-15). An integration of electricity grid has been a suggestion put forth to reduce the creation of artificial scarcity and allowing of market based bidding for such projects (Ibid).

Renewable Energy and Market

China's technological hindrance has prevented it from meeting better energy efficiency and still relies on technology imports or rudimentary innovations to reduce costs. A number of policy options are brought onto the table, such as bringing in ecological costs into the balance sheet under the liabilities by the producer and increased prices by the consumer instead of unsolicited cost payment by the general public (Ibid). This can be done through implementation of pollution tax or changes in industry norms (Ibid).

When it comes to energy market, an 'avoidance-avoidance' conflict emerges. In the situation of acute scarcity and voraciously growing demand which devil is the easier of the two? State controlled trading or open competitive bidding? Repressed prices with depressed gains or market prices with reduced demand? Would the second option give rise to situation of monopolistic market? China with its political structure is a natural ally of the first option but how long can it sustain the pressure? And even if it does so, is sustaining of such volatile pressure a feasible choice or a mere 'calm before the storm' to gain time.

The biggest consumer of energy in China is its heavy industry and not its industrial consumer (Rosen and Houser, 2007a:4). Since 1978 the government focused on reducing energy intensity but the trend got reversed coinciding with China's entry into WTO undoing the good work done in the previous years. This is not to say that new plants set up were pollution makers, in fact they were more energy efficient but the nature of their production made them more villains than heroes (Ibid). The table below shows the energy intensity and industry value added as a share of economic output of different energy intensive industries.

Figure 4.2: Energy Intensity of an Industry and Its Share in Economic Output

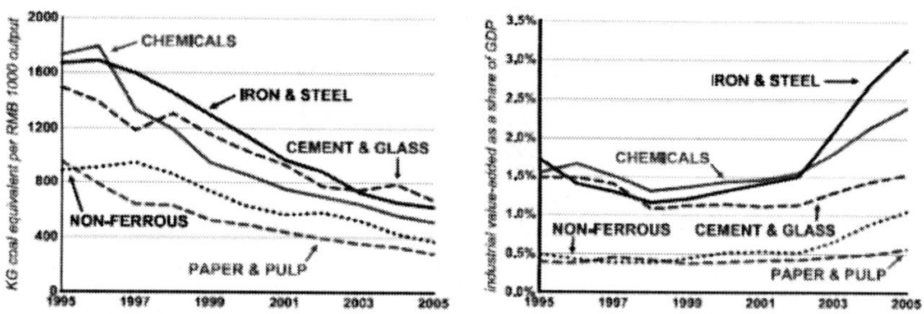

Source: Rosen and Houser (2007a:8).

The above graph reveals that the two industries, iron and steel and chemicals, are the largest contributors to economic output but at the same time are the worst perpetrators of energy intensity indicators. China today accounts for almost half of the world production but also imports the energy intensity problems of other nations by producing for them (Ibid). The economic gains it earns come at a price of ecological cost. Being the most attractive destination for foreign investment China today has investments in most of the energy guzzling industries (Ibid). China had witnessed a surge in industrial production even in the late 1970s and early 1990s, yet has never before witnessed an unprecedented increase in industrial production of industries which are exclusively oriented towards high energy consumption (Ibid). Has the aggressive investment in infrastructure obscured the rising threat of scarcity (and perhaps a hidden insanity) of energy sources. Does China feel equipped to invest in capital intensive industries when the bulk of its strength lies in its population and cheap labour? Does China want to control the future before tackling with its present?

Figure 4.3: China's Major Producing Industries

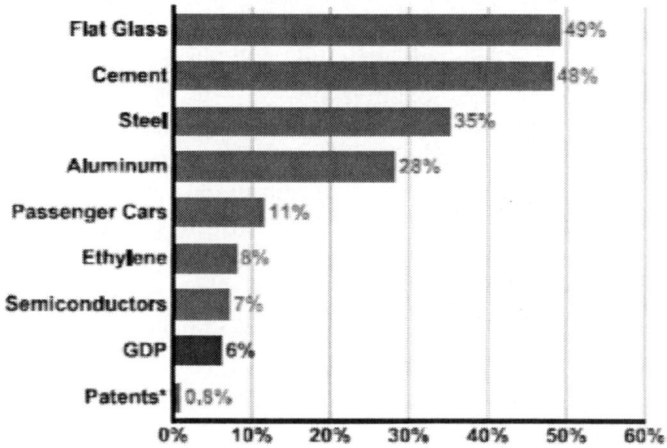

Source: Rosen and Houser (2007a:10).

The above figures are of China's share in global production in 2006. The glass and the cement industry account for almost half of the world production (49 percent and 48 percent) respectively while its patents are a miniscule 0.8 percent (innovation, perhaps is still meant only for glorified speeches of the party congresses). The other components of production in which China plays the lion's part (like steel aluminium, passenger cars, ethylene and semiconductors) do not reveal any signs of reduced energy utilisation as their inherent characteristics (Rosen and Houser, 2007a:10).

Why can China produce?

The thumb rule of economics is factors of production and their synthesis to make a market. Economics begins with a claim that the success of an entrepreneur lies in the comparative cost advantage of these factors namely: land, labour and capital. Labour obviously is the USP of China. Land, unlike most other nations is the property of the government which can only be leased but never owned (Ibid, 11). Urban real estate agents behave professionally and do not (or perhaps cannot) draw larger difference in market value and state determined price (Ibid). However, this is not so with the farm land. China does not ban agriculturally productive land for being utilised for industrial or non-agricultural purposes (Ibid). The result is that the land is bought underpriced as the valuation is done on agricultural basis and then sold while accounting for the industrial value of the same land (Ibid). Moreover, land is sometimes even sold at a discount as 'industrialists would pay taxes in the future but a farmer would not'(Rosen and Houser,

2007a:11). In the question of capital it has been amply discussed that state owned enterprises enjoy a comparative advantage with respect to private enterprises with respect to subsidies, tax benefits and loans at lower cost rates. This makes us conclude that Beijing is perhaps still not sympathetic to the future imminent worries and is still focusing on shrewd numbers of GDP. However, this is indeed not true as all policies seem to start with the buzzer of the 'green'. Yet apart from the latest plans most of the capital till 2005 went to enhance capacities in energy consuming industries. There were strong financial reasons for it. One, operating costs of such industries is low; they can be exported without any strain on foreign exchequer. Also foreign enterprises are ready to invest for such products bringing in the much needed technology and back-linkages for the market. Again a 'balkanised' approach exists between firms of different provinces who avoid consolidation and sharing between firms of different provinces (Ibid:12).

Figure 4.4: Profit of Various Industries in China

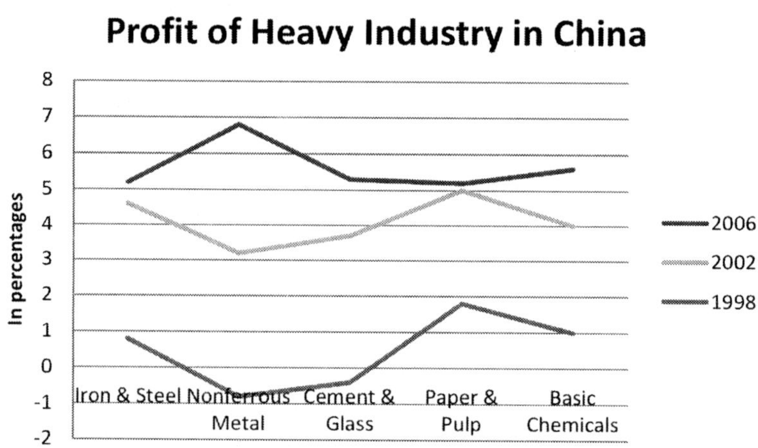

Profit of light industry in China (given below) and heavy industry in China (given above)

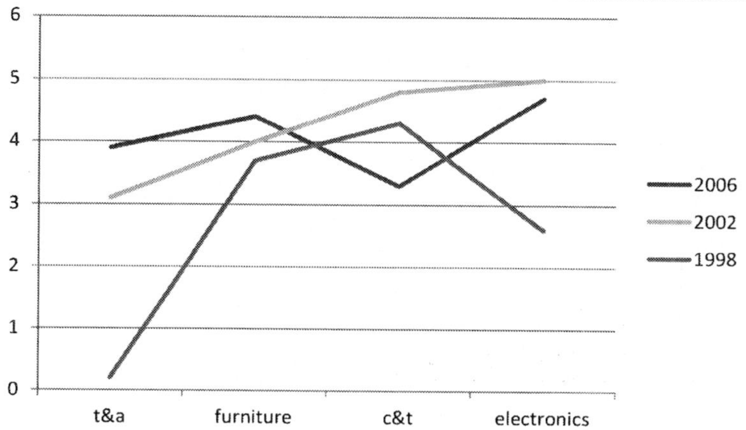

Industry	2006	2002	1998
Heavy Industry			
Iron & Steel	5.2	4.6	0.8
Nonferrous Metals	6.8	3.2	-0.8
Cement & Glass	5.3	3.7	-0.4
Paper & Pulp	5.2	5.0	1.8
Basic Chemicals	5.6	4.0	1.0
Light Industry			
Textiles & Apparel	3.9	3.1	0.2
Furniture Manufacturing	4.4	4.0	3.7
Computers & Telecom	3.3	4.8	4.3
Electronic Machinery	4.7	5.0	2.6

Unit: percent
Source: Rosen and Houser (2007a:12).

The above figures are the profit margins of all industries based on EBT (earnings before tax) basis. It can be seen that from near negative in 1998, heavy industries have made a dramatic comeback in terms of earning profits almost at par (and even exceeding) the light industry. Hence, the central government, despite its near everyday rhetoric of adherence to 'sustainable development,' has not been able to achieve its objective (Ibid). In fact China has been overproducing for the last two decades with its safety valve being its large sale outside the production gambit (Rosen and Houser, 2007a:13). A comparison of twenty years was made on energy demand for various sectors and it was identified that the household sector despite increasingly consuming more power intensive products is relatively consuming less (almost 10 percent of the whole energy demand) than the iron and steel industry which is expanding its appetite at break-neck speed (Rosen and Houser, 2007a:13).

Figure 4.5: Energy Demand of One Major Industry in Comparison to Households in China

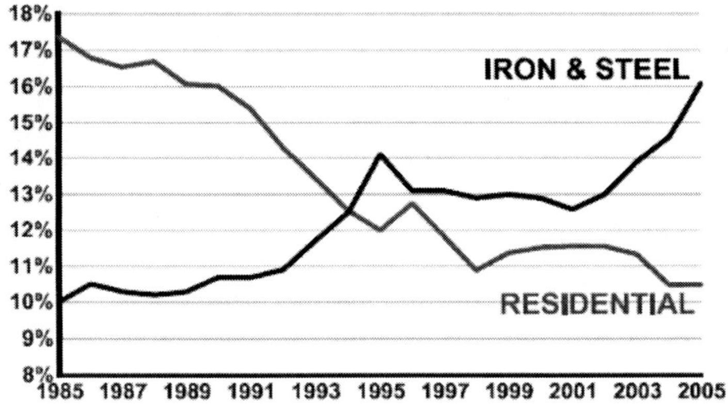

Source: Rosen and Houser (2007a:14)

The above figure shows that the iron and steel industry has witnessed a stupendous rise in its energy demand ratios from 13 to 17 percent over just a period of just five years (2001-2005) (Rosen and Houser, 2007a:14).

The 'workshop of the world' is fast foraying into the tertiary sector, especially its more developed areas like Beijing, Shanghai, Guangdong, etc. have an emerging middle class whose per capita incomes allow them to demand a lot more than basic iron and steel and glass (Ibid). China's current investment into infrastructure is proof enough of its production prowess; however she needs not just buildings but working conditions for lighting, cooling and heating to maintain it. Also, with expansion of cities, the number of vehicles plying the roads for commuting is no more a luxury for the office goers (Ibid).

Apart from income and price the energy market is affected by other economic factors like the capital-labour ratio, construction cost investment, investment in innovation and up gradation of R&D, etc. (Song and Zheng, 2012: 449-52). For a long time it has been debated among the economists whether the relationship of capital and energy is complementary in nature or whether they act as substitutes. The authors have analysed that 'energy and capital can first be complements and then be substitutes' (Song and Zheng,

2012: 449-52). The authors cite the analysis of Griffin who points out that while the above is true by holding economic activity as constant, it is not so when efficiency is held as a constant because then capital and energy always act as complements to each other. This can be because then the capital is used to buy energy-saving technology which helps to promote efficiency and conservation of efficiency on the other hand helps to keep more capital in hand (Ibid). The authors have also observed that when the economy accumulates capital stock the relationship shifts from being complementary to substitution in nature which helps to reduce energy intensity (Ibid).

Price Reforms and Energy Policies

Determining the prices of energy products is like walking on a 'double-edged sword'. Setting too low a price (which was the situation before the 1980s) was a deterrent to energy efficiency. However, demanding market prices of energy from the average consumer means segregating a large chunk of population who would not be able to afford the energy resources. Hence the 1980's saw the introduction of a 'tiered' price structure in the coal and petroleum sectors (Zhao, 2001:18). Beyond a certain quota, prices of coal and petroleum were allowed to operate at the market rate. While market prices were at first given some restriction to limit themselves to the plan prices (called the indicative prices), these prices were allowed to operate at floating rate (Zhao, 2001:18). In China, despite the trend of increasing price of the 1980s the entire cost of coal production has not been covered.

> The artificial difference in price between the outputs of state owned rural mines led to unfair competition among coal mines of different ownership types. Struggling under the price ceilings state owned mines did not have the capital to invest in increasing output. Relatively high prices for the low quality products of rural mines, which typically have very low capital requirements, encouraged proliferation of such mines. (Zhao, 2001: 18)

This dual price system continued in China till 1994 (Ibid). Planned prices for state mines and market prices for inefficient rural and small township mines meant that inefficiency existed not only in all stages of production but also in allocation of coal blocks between village and town enterprises which were obviously producing more despite the poor quality than the state-owned mines (Ibid:18). Yet sudden liberalisation was not the solution especially when prices of coal used for producing electricity were still government regulated. However this is precisely what China did after 1994 leading to a frenzy of over-production by cost-intensive coal mines specially those who were unceremoniously and almost overnight thrown out of the government shield of price rise (Ibid:18).

In the case of oil, the same 'contractual' approach of production and price was introduced in 1981(Ibid:19). Although this was done to encourage production yet 'the increase was much less than production potential during the same period', says Zhao (2001), citing Yang and other Chinese authors. The oil sector was not just plagued by the issue of producing at a loss, but also by the differences in prices of upstream and downstream production due to which the losses incurred by the refineries were transferred to the oil-fields (Ibid). This 'price distortion' and 'production at loss' also spread over to areas of diesel which was heavily consumed in rural areas resulting in shift to pollution-inducing gasoline engines (Ibid). By the turn of the last decade of the century when China had already turned into an importer of oil it had no choice but to pay international prices to all its offshore activities (Ibid, 23). This meant that prices of all oil, petrol and diesel products were rising unabated. This raised a clamour and the government had to re-strategise its fuel price policy to outwit the market diktats.

> The government controlled the prices of all onshore oil, increased the crude oil price and formulated prices for different categories of crude oil. The increased oil prices raised enterprises capability to collect funds, although prices remained lower than the international price. (Zhao, 2001: 24)

The masterstroke came in June 1998 when the government decided that the domestic oil prices should be fixed in tandem with Singapore prices (Ibid). In fact the low price system of the late 1990's meant that it was more profitable to import rather than to explore domestic options (Ibid). Moreover smuggling was another threat that almost all world governments were unanimously badgered by (Ibid).

Gas till date is a small item in the itinerary of China's energy system. The reason is cited in historical tradition when gas was used to subsidise fertilizers and industrial production (Ibid, 19). Despite a 'two track price system' introduced in 1987, production of gas was never given its due importance as the limelight had always been hogged by oil and hence it could never unleash its full contribution to China's energy consumption pattern (Zhao, 2001:19). In fact till date gas prices have received a step motherly treatment by having differential prices for different consumers and since most of its consumers are poor farmers using fertilizers, any increase in price is off-settled by large volume of sales at low prices (Ibid:19).

In the case of electricity China had never grown out of acute shortages and the government was always planning of some 'administrative innovations' which could act as a valuable pill against this chronic headache. Chinese government was extremely liberal to the independent power producers setting their prices higher than the state producers (Ibid). Even the state producers were given many concessions which were not available for any other energy producers of the state (Ibid). A 50 percent increment on the plan price was allowed for even one percent production over and above the contractual level (Ibid). Two years later in 1987 peak load pricing had also begun to foray in the electricity sector. Zhao (2001:20) believes that the electricity sector has been one of the few lucky sectors of China where production has almost always been in a profitable position. Apart from government generosity Zhao (2001:20) says that this was also because the losses were partly redirected to the coal sector and also because the government was less than the stringent in regulating prices and allowed market rates to dominate (Ibid). Protracted and partial behavior in the energy reforms not only sent wrong market signals but also distorted the growth of energy enterprises who had to make room for certain preferred customers even at the cost of their own development (Ibid). By the early 1990's the government had realised that arbitrariness of prices had not only confused the producers and consumers alike but had also become a convenient way for local government officials to pocket the profits of the enterprises and the tax payers money by introducing any sudden breach of rules and regulations as the reason (Ibid:22). Hence all operations which began to operate after 1992 were given the formula of rate of return on investment as the basis for the price determination (Ibid). This measure was introduced partly to encourage investment and partly to regulate demand and unfortunately it could not each either of its objectives (Ibid). While the folly did not lay in the contents of its intention it definitely did not go down well with the urgency of implementation even in economically advanced coastal areas. For example peak load pricing had been introduced as early as 1987 yet could not even make a dent in the pricing anomalies of the electricity sector (Ibid). Obviously implementation factor also had its own limitations as the equipment required for load management was not readily available with the local officials (Ibid). Load management, Zhao (2001:24) defines as 'agreements between utilities and customers e.g. for large industrial uses to shift electricity intensive operations to night hours during the summer months when cooling loads are high or to shut down during periods when agricultural use is high. The end of the twentieth century also saw the dissolving of various illegal fees which led to a drastic reduction in price (Ibid).

Figure 4.6 Relations of Investment, Economy and Energy in China from Period 1993-2005

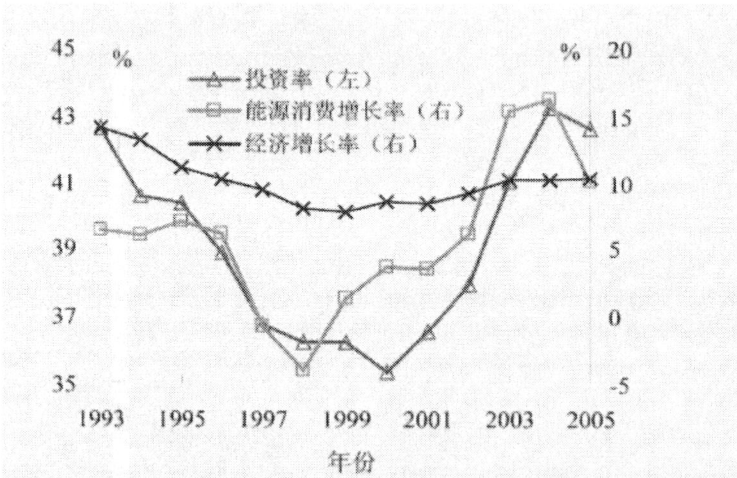

图 1 1993–2005 年我国的投资率、经济和能源消费增长率

（数据来源：《中国统计年鉴 2006》）

Line 1 investment rate (triangle line)
Line 2 energy consumption growth rate (square line)
Line 3 economic growth rate (crossed line)
Source: Yi et. al. (2007:21)

The above table shows a trend analysis of investment rate, rate of energy consumption growth and economic growth rate from the period of it turning to a net importer of energy (1993) till it passed the Renewable Energy Law (2005). It has been seen that rising investment has been directly proportional not only to economic growth but also to energy consumption rate. This means that major investment whether it is governmental or private has been in high consumption industries which have also been the major forces triggering the 'double digit growth decade'. It was also found that with every one percent rise in investment for economic activities, energy consumption rate and henceforth energy demand grew by 1.03 percent (Yi et. al., 2007:21). In the midst of rapid industrialisation and urbanisation process high investment levels is a necessary prerequisite to not only maintain economic growth rate but also employment opportunities. However the main question is what determines the investment growth. Yi et. al. (2007) identify two types of incomes which fuel the investment levels: profits of the domestic enterprises and residential income especially from the rural areas. In its pursuit of economic growth and enhanced financial income the government too has been providing various economic assets like land, credit and energy prices at preferential rates to encourage investment. Energy consumption and prices of various commodities bear the relationship of elasticity with each other. While their short term elasticity is 0.015, their long term elasticity is 0.122 (Yi et. al., 2007:21). Since 1993, the prices of commodities have been reflective of cost of energy consumption in the production process. This has led to overall domestic economic inflation and has escalated the prices of even essential commodities manifold. Although this has also had a positive effect in promotion of almost an entire gauntlet of energy saving products and has reduced the demand of energy by the enterprises. However, for (Yi.et. al. 2007:22) this relationship has had a flipside as the elasticity between energy consumption and prices of commodities is quite low thus the elasticity of the entire economic system is also not quite high. Jia Haiyuan (cited from Yan et. al., 2009:7) also reiterates the findings of Yi et. al. calling the basis between economic investment and energy demand has a cause effect relationship. Traditional production theories have considered science and technology, administration and information as its major derivatives. However with the arrival of the 'emerging economies' and 'China rise' at a cataclysmic speed it has been seen that more and more people are debating to expand the production derivatives chart to include energy and infrastructure.

The phenomena of petrol price rise

Of all energy commodities petrol has commanded special attention both from domestic and international media. This even happened in nations (like China) where oil was not the basis of their energy structure and they had no shortage of their main existing supply (read coal). However, frequent oil crises and occasional rise in petroleum prices has not had a ubiquitous impact and has affected each nation in a different manner. What does an oil price rise result in a country? Yang Yuanhua (2005:26) describes it as an expansion of uncertainty, instability and rise of threat in the economy of a country. Obviously in this globalised world inflation in any one country causes ripples in other countries also especially when it is due to an international calamity like petrol price rise. General logic says that this inflation then spreads to socio economic upheavals and it is best to nip the price rise in its bud. However what causes this price rise is a matter of debate among most energy analysts of the world.

Environment as a determinant

The Twelfth Five Year Plan explicitly points out the promotion of 'new energy resources domestically'. New energy (*xin neng yuan*) or renewable energy is basically a composition of all non fossil fuels like solar, wind, biomass, geo thermal energy, hydropower and nuclear power (*China's Policies and Actions for Addressing Climate Change*, 2012).

The twentieth century can perhaps be called as an era for fossil fuel combustion. This fuel which was coal till the late seventies became oil despite the oil crisis in the immediately preceding years. However, all combustion alters the air quality around it and so did the fossil fuels raising a new threat of pollution bringing in a third new component, gas, overriding its other partners. Fossil fuels are exhaustible sources of energy and are soon depleting is a common knowledge (Liu, 2007:47). It is now increasingly sensed that our ancestors have cultivated the earth enough and now it is our chance to cultivate the sky. Hence the growing interest in renewable forms of energy which are non- polluting and non exhaustible.

> China's energy policy has shifted from maximising domestic energy self sufficiency to a more balanced set of objectives including increasing the efficiency of its energy sector, minimising energy waste and environmental costs. (Woetzel, 2003:103).

As an explosively populated, speedily developing economy every level of governance and every sector of every industry of China are concerned about energy. As one of the oldest civilisation China's traditional economy despite being based on ecology never considered the cost and benefit analysis of the environment on the economy. The ecological costs of these economic gains were not very detrimental at that time to be taken seriously. The combination of man and machine has brought in unprecedented growth and exploration of resources. Increased mechanisation has increased the productivity yet has also consistently reduced the green cover and area production. The globalisation of the economy has also brought in globalisation of the environment problems and the people's voices. The twenty first century has witnessed a constant silent war between environment sustainability and economic development. It has been constantly felt that China's frequent blackouts have led to a colossal loss on its exchequer as its energy efficiency is a mere 33 percent of its total energy consumption, comparatively China is at the rock bottom of energy efficiency charts maintaining just 10 percent of energy efficiency standards compared to other countries) (Liu, 2007:48). Energy efficiency is a juxtaposition of very many factors like natural conditions, status of economy, industrial structure etc. This has led to regional discrepancy in maintaining energy efficiency levels. Obviously the more developed the area the more conscious and hence more progressive towards maintaining energy efficiency levels. E.g. Guangdong topped the EE standards in 2006, domestically (Ibid). In fact it is not just the industrial structure but the synchronization between industrial and production system which matters. Industrial sector consumes 70.4 percent of China's total domestic energy consumption and high consumption energy industries consume 79.2 percent of total industrial consumption. (Ibid)

Hence a transition from high carbon based economy to low carbon based economy is imminent. However under different economic conditions energy policies have opted for different priorities. Zhou Hongchun (2012) elucidates that from the western perspective, low- carbon economy is the new saviour. From the domestic perspective China's wave of institutionalisation and urbanisation has not finished, hence it need not blindly follow the international outlook but capture the basic conditions and special characteristics of China's growth trajectory. This way it can guide the concept of *chaoqian xing* (looking forward) and give value to *kecaozuoxing* (operationality) (Zhou Hongchun, 2012:5-8).

Environment Enigma: The Gleam of the Green

Many researches have been done on measuring China's energy intensity (ratio of energy consumption over output) some comparing with other developing and developed nations and many others with China itself over a period of time (Wu, 2011:1). However there are a very few researches which have compared the regional efficiency of China. It has been found that the lowest energy efficiency has been found in the regions of central China (Ibid, 9). The regional energy efficiency was defined in the research as the ratio of gross regional product to that of the energy use (Ibid). Yanrui Wu (2011:8-10) has observed that the definition of measuring regional efficiency is completely reverse to that of the measurement of national or international energy efficiency. The research has cited economic reasons for the variations in regional energy efficiency and has pin pointed out that the developed coastal areas are the best at maintaining regional energy efficiency. It seems that this research is trying to justify the sentiments of various scholars and 'princelings' of China who still believe that economic growth should be at the top priority and the environmental adjustments can follow later- a reminiscent of Deng Xiaoping theory of 'let some people get rich first'. Wu also writes that none of the research has bothered to identify the sector differences in the territorial regions. It has been seen that when China was experiencing its 'growth spurt' between the decades of 1997 to 2007 it was also witnessing a decline in its energy intensity almost in all the provinces. A decline in energy intensity is a rise in energy efficiency which means that China was following 'a balanced approach' since the 1980's and it had not diverted from its tracks even during the 'rise period'. Yet international statistics and declining air quality have shown otherwise (Wu, 2011).

Table 4.2 Changing Energy Intensity in Various Provinces of China

Region	Energy intensity (1997)	Energy intensity (2007)	Absolute changes	Change in energy efficiency
Beijing	206.4	83.6	-122.7	-97.3
Tianjin	187.1	94.8	-92.4	-96.6
Hebei	246.8	225.5	-21.3	-31.1
Liaoning	310.0	284.4	-25.6	-32.7
Shanghai	170.6	82.9	-87.8	-83.2
Jiangsu	104.5	81.3	-23.2	-28.9
Zhejiang	78.9	60.1	-18.8	-17.1
Fujian	59.7	80.9	21.3	15.2
Shandong	98.2	98.6	0.3	-9.8
Guangdong	81.3	62.0	-19.3	-22.3
Shanxi	404.5	391.5	-12.9	-36.9
Jilin	328.5	181.4	39.9	13.2
Heilongjiang	186.9	112.3	-74.6	-67.5
Anhui	164.1	109.5	-54.6	-39.7
Jiangxi	141.6	181.4	39.9	13.2
Henan	161.5	132.6	28.9	-45.4
Hubei	170.2	124.4	-45.8	-34.7
Hunan	134.9	133.9	-1	-4.6
Inner Mongolia	435.3	224.8	-210.5	-261.5
Guangxi	111.4	140.6	29.2	22.9
Sichuan	154.6	90.0	-64.5	-66.5
Guizhou	384.5	226.5	-157.9	-175.6
Yunnan	192.5	187.9	-4.6	9.8
Shaanxi	196	102.1	-93.9	-109.6
Gansu	271.5	184.4	-87.1	-91.3
Qinghai	307.3	182.3	-125	-180.1
Xinjiang	284.2	174.9	-109.3	-139.4

Source: Wu Yanrui (2011:11)

In the above data research, income and price were taken as variables and based on the assumptions of this research they should appear negative.

Rising income implies rising economic development which is a precursor to energy efficiency (Ibid, 12). Similarly rise in prices also raises the cost of production and forces the producers to raise their contribution for energy efficiency (Ibid, 12). This means that both price and income should be negative. Wu says

> Some Chinese regions have already passed the turning point of the inverted U shaped curve. Energy intensity in those regions may be reduced due to the adoption of energy saving technology embodied in rapidly growing new capital. Thus while new technology may play a role in improving energy efficiency and hence reduce energy intensity, Growth in capital intensity alone would not bring the decline in energy consumption in China (Wu, 2011: 24).

Suisheng Zhao (year n.a.) believes that 'to meet China's quickly growing energy demands, Chinese leaders have struggled between a market oriented approach and a state centered approach'. While the market brings greater prospects of energy security by allowing greater integration of markets as well as a series of dissemination of information through multiple levels, the state centered approach Zhao cites as a 'neo mercantilists approach' where economic tools like investments of domestic companies are used to promote non economic interests by beefing up diplomacy with other oil producing states. He also observes that while China has avidly promoted itself as a 'socialist market economy' especially after the reforms, it did not feel convenient to apply that model in the ramifications of energy sector as it feared that the energy was 'too important to be left to market forces alone'. Zheng Bijian one of the senior analysts of ex president Hu Jintao believed that shortage of energy resources is one of the fundamental factors which could contain China's peaceful rise (Zhao Suisheng). Two Korean authors (Hyung and Seong, 2006:846-850) have identified that the response of China's policies towards the environment should be measured from the aspects of a typical structure of energy industry and market, the relationship between the state and the enterprise and administrative decentralisation. It has been largely seen that apart from the few conglomerates of energy companies there are also a large number of state-owned enterprises scattered across the country (Ibid). They are remnants of socialism in China as despite not contributing much to the exchequer they are the biggest employment generators in rural and semi urban China (Ibid). While closing them is a 'political blunder', maintaining them is an 'uneconomic energy' move. While any natural material that has economic value for humans is a resource, all others with indirect or physical value fell in to the domain of environment (Ibid). Hence energy was always a 'natural resource' whose exploration and production was always against the 'environment' (Ibid). To measure the energy intensity Song and Zheng (2012) have also introduced an energy gap variable which is 'measured by the ratio of energy production and consumption as a proxy variable of natural endowment'. The paper contends that energy intensity shall automatically increase in areas which are by virtue of their natural topography are rich in energy resources. In contrast the areas where energy gap is large will have a tendency to use the energy more judiciously and efficiently. The paper also made an analysis of intra trade of energy resources by comparing the energy prices of energy exporting provinces (Shaanxi, Shanxi, Inner Mongolia, Heilongjiang, Guizhou and Xinjiang) to that of energy importing provinces. It has been seen that fuel prices rose faster in the former areas to that of the latter areas.

Figure 4.7 Energy Intensity of China across time of both Energy Importing and Exporting Provinces

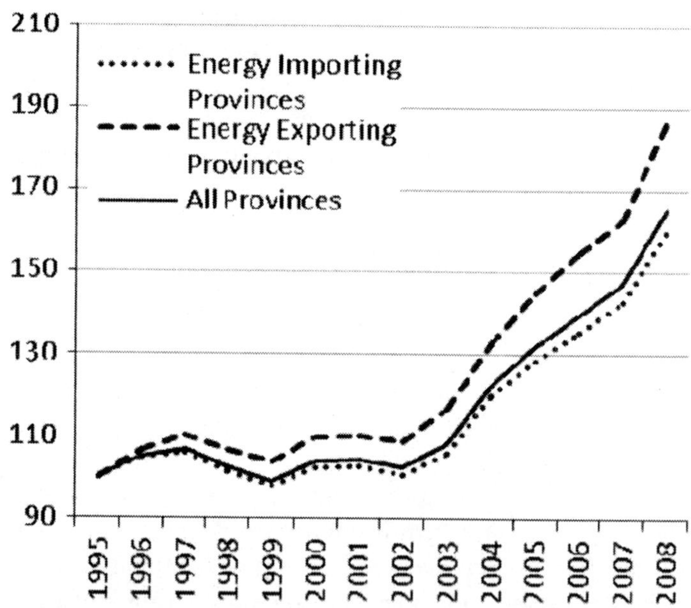

Source: Song and Zheng (2012:451)

The authors contend that the reason for this variation could be the withdrawal of subsidies from these areas faster than the rest of China (Ibid). Yet it cannot be denied that subsidies form a major chunk of the fuel prices to be in approachable limit of the people (Ibid). The issue of urbanisation has been fuelling up the coefficients of energy intensity (Ibid). An urbanised area demands energy consuming amenities and employment opportunities for industries (Ibid). A one percent rise in population pushes up the energy intensity figure by 0.14 percent (Song and Zheng, 2012:451).

Energy Companies and Environment

A nation which lights up with coal cannot be very sympathetic to the drudgery of pollution associated with it. China's coal prices are an abysmal low because they do not account for the ecological costs (Rosen and Houser 2007a:11). With 80 percent of electricity coming from coal plant almost less than 15 percent of coal plants have installed flu gas desulphurisation system, which removes sulphur dioxide from emissions and those who have installed them do not care for its maintenance (Rosen and Houser 2007a:11). Yet this should not be believed that the companies are bereft of their social responsibility, especially, towards the environment. In fact all companies seem to add a special section in their 'sustainability reports' about their contribution to the environment especially in the 'western development strategy' and exclusively in the volatile areas like Tibet and Xinjiang.

A company's responsibility towards conservation of the environment is reflected by its connivance with pollution makers and the energy savings it adds to the country's carbon account. All companies now publish a regular feature of 'sustainability reports' along with their annual reports. PetroChina has made a record of 100 percent replacement ratio of oil and gas reserves and has conserved 1.13 million tones of standard coal equivalent, 17.44 million cubic meters of water and reduction of COD and SO2 emission by 5.4 percent and 2.5 percent (till 2011) (Sustainability Report of PetroChina, 2012).

Table 4.3 Environment Parameters of PetroChina

Year	Oil discharged in waste water (tonnes)	Energy conserved (10,000 tonnes of coal equivalent)	Water conserved (10,000 meter cubic)	Money invested for environment protection (10,000 Yuan)
2007	1001	124	4700	N.A
2008	779	176	5336	876
2009	701	171	3188	569
2010	698	173	2865	5588
2011	642	113	1744	75
2012	604	121	1,926	965
2013	577	108	2,007	1,377

Source: Sustainability Reports of PetroChina 2010-13

Based on the tables it is seen that PetroChina has been steadily reducing its pollution making effluents and is contributing towards conservation of both quantity and quality of water in China. However, it is a strange observation that while its investment in the environment increased during the period of recession (2008-2010), it reduced drastically in 2011 and so reduced the amount of energy and water conservation.

CNOOC, on the other hand, has been concentrating on investment in research and development (R&D) and science and technology (S&T) to earn brownie points both for the environment and the economy through technological breakthroughs (See Table 4.4).

Table 4.4 Environment Parameters of CNOOC

Year	Investment in R&D (100 million Yuan)	Investment in S&T (100 million Yuan)	Energy conservation (10,000 tonnes of coal equivalent)	Energy Conservation and Emission Reduction Investments (100 million Yuan)
2009	19.7	44.3	41.6	N.A
2010	20.9	56.1	47.2	N.A
2011	17.4	54.0	48.9	4
2012	26	N.A	53.8	3.5
2013	28.2	N.A	29.9	2.8

Source: Sustainability Reports of CNOOC (2011-2013)

In comparing the data of energy conservation of both PetroChina and CNOOC we can see that despite less investment PetroChina has conserved more energy than CNOOC. Yet, we should not forget that CNOOC operates on a smaller scale than PetroChina and hence has lesser scope to maintain growth rates along with ecological balance (Sustainability Reports of CNOOC 2010-2013).

Sinopec, under the slogan of 'care for energy, care for you' has also been a steady participant in the race to save the environment. In a trend analysis from 2005 to 2011, the following observations have been put forth (Sinopec Sustainable Development Report, 2011):

Number of clean production plans – 4684
Investment deployed- 1434.64 million yuan
Waste water reduced by -39,880 ktpa
Cod in waste water reduced by-4.341ktpa
Waste gas reduced by- 871.3 million cubic meter
Sulphur-dioxide in waste gas reduced by- 23.229ktpa
Industrial residue reduced by- 18.341ktpa

China's oil and gas companies though significant are not the substantial part of the Chinese lobbies since they rely on a fuel on which China cannot stand by its principle of 'self- reliance'. Coal and power is what makes China and the companies dealing with them are what the China of the past the present and (perhaps) the future can rely on. The next section shall discuss the coal and power companies into 'making and being' the energy of China.

China Guodian Corporation

Under the vision of 'home, stage and dream' China Guodian seeks to build up new energy technology and innovative enterprise. It relies on five focus and five enhancement as its core strategy area (The below section is based on Annual Report of China Guodian Corporation, 2011).

Five Focus (Ibid, 10-11)

- Promotion of clean coal power technology to build up environment friendly coal power plants.
- Focus on improving the scale and quality of hydropower development to increase the proportion of renewable energy.
- Focus on building all clean renewable forms of energy like solar, wind nuclear to reach commanding heights of new energy development.
- Focus on promoting comprehensive development and utilization of coal and construction of large low carbon energy bases.
- Focus on building high tech new energy to form a leading cluster of new industry.

Five Enhancements (Ibid, 16-17)

- Enhancing the operation and management innovation
- Enhancing the system mechanism innovation
- Enhancing the science and technology innovation
- Enhancing the talent development innovation
- Enhancing the corporate culture work

As a corporation structured into 45 companies, 2 research institutes and 200 primary power generation companies Guodian claims all commitment to emission reduction and environment protection. It has shut down low efficient small thermal power plants as targeted under the '11th Five Year Plan' and has maintained targets of sulphur dioxide emissions even lower than those allowed by State Environment Protection Administration (SEPA) (Report from *International Rivers,* n.a).

Table 4.5 Environment Parameters of China Guodian Corporation

Year	Coal consumption per kilowatt hour generation (g/kwh)	Sulphur-dioxide emissions per kilowatt hour (g/kwh)
2002	375	n.a
2003	371.3	9.75
2004	365.7	9.88
2005	361	7.54
2006	355.5	6.65
2007	349	4.47
2008	340	3.30
2009	331.8	2.58

Source: Annual Report of China Guodian Corporation, 2010

By June 2010, 10 percent of its power capacity came from hydropower generation. However its entire tall claims to responsibility towards environment and ambient corporate culture draws flak when its environment record undergoes a third party claim. Reports have claimed that Guodian had to even postpone its IPO after a crackdown by SEPA over unauthorised construction of Shizuishan plant in Ningxia and also demanded the construction of desulphurization units in two of its coal plants if it wants to continue their functioning (Ibid). Again in 2007 SEPA had suspended 1.98 RMB billion worth of projects of Guodian for failing to pass the environment norms (Ibid). Also it was facing various bottlenecks over it cannot be doubted that strict and swift action by SEPA prompted it to work conscientiously towards environment and not pass it as mere philanthropy (Report in *International Rivers,* n.a).

However, a company earns its reputation not just by the profit it earns but the amount of work it can show for the public welfare and remain in sync with its claim of being 'for the people. No governments (no matter how much corrupt or authoritarian) can encourage a corporation which blatantly believes in filling its coffers only. Hence the environment quotient is a reserve options in the form of corporate social responsibility to retain its claim to being the 'future of China'. Huadian Corporation has diversified its installed capacity into not just thermal generation but also into non-fossil fuels like hydro, nuclear and wind (Website of China Huadian Corporation). Similarly Huaneng Corporation prefers to call itself a 'green corporation' even while engaging in coal to produce power (Website of Huaneng Corporation).

China Power Investment Corporation

CPI releases its indicators of discharging of main pollutants like dust, sulphur-dioxide and waste water annually in contrast to its net coal consumption for thermal units

Table 4.6 CPI environment indicators

Year	Dust (g/Kwh)	Sulphur dioxide (g/Kwh)	Waste water (kg/kwh)	Net coal consumption for thermal units (g/kwh)
2007	1.09	5.27	0.54	357.57
2008	0.68	4.45	0.37	350.24
2009	0.41	3.7	0.26	343.22
2010	0.34	2.88	0.23	331.75
2011	0.3	2.36	0.2	321.77
2012	0.26	2.15	0.17	317.07

Source: Website of China Power Investment Corporation

With reducing pollutants released each year and decreasing coal consumption, China's 'go green campaign' seems to have its traces being felt even in routine working of power companies. China has come a long way from self sufficiency of energy supplies (self-reliance as the first stage) to self- sufficiency of energy at reasonable price (go abroad policy as the second stage) and energy conservation and low carbon economy (a shift from decreasing energy intensity and reducing carbon intensity at the third stage) (Li Xinlei, 2012:1).

Suntech Power Holdings Company Limited

Founded in 2001 as a solar pv manufacturing unit. This private enterprise in a socialist country has seen a meteoric rise by getting listed in New York stock exchanges within four years of its operation (Lee, 2012:61). By 2012 it has become the largest producer of solar panels and is lauded for its ingenious ideas of using silicon wafers to promote energy efficiency (Ibid). However its 'early rise has led to its early demise', as it's Chinese subsidiary declared bankruptcy in March 2013 (Bradsher, 2013). Having once reached to the zenith of market capital of 16 billion US dollars the company had a sad demise with the closing of 59 cents a share (Ibid). However, the surprising factor was that the Chinese government which often comes to the rescue of its 'sick units' (and more so in the overseas market), chose to let its 'green business' die an early death rather than trying to revive it (Ibid). This happened despite the stalemate in the hydropower sector because of which China is vying the solar industry with renewed aspirations to fulfill its energy needs by supplanting the pollution generating fossil fuels. This company clearly held the potential to become one of the major and perhaps the first monopolistic private company of China. Suntech was not an exception but a rule as the solar industry in China seemed to be reaching the pinnacle of its boom. Another company in this 'sunrise industry' is the Himin group, whose leader Huang Ming played a major role in the formation of provisions of laws in favour of renewable energy especially the solar industry (Lee, 2012:85). Himin is also credited for educating the Chinese masses about the various problems related with the fossil fuels and various nuances of the solar energy (Lee, 2012:84).

Efficient policy for implementing energy efficiency

The period of the 1980's was a 'digital divide' for China's energy conservation projects projects (Zhao, 2001:20). A period, in which China's government in earnest had concentrated on undoing the wrongs of the Mao era. Fortunately this focus was not just on economic salvage although this was the most hyped part both by domestic and international media. Despite fluctuations in the level of investment during the various five year plans the government had shown strict commitment from the Sixth Plan onwards towards conservation of energy. Administrative changes, institutional establishments and sector investments were the order of the day reducing the energy intensity by one third (Zhao, 2001:21). Given below is the change in energy consumption of major sectors during the period of the 1980's.

Table 4.7 Changes in Energy Consumption of Major Sectors during the Period of the 1980's.

Product	Unit	1980	1990	Percentage change (1980-1990)
Fossil fuel electricity (more than 6000 kwh)	Mj/kwh	13.1	12.5	-4.7
Steel (total energy)	Gj/tone	59.8	47.2	-21
Aluminium (large plants)	Gj/tone	596	475.3	-20.2
Ammonia (large plants)	Gj/tone	41.9	39.3	-6.1
Ammonia (medium plants)	Gj/tone	71.5	63.8	-1.1
Ammonia (small plants)	Gj/tone	88.5	66	-25.3
Cement (large plants)	Gj/tone	6.1	5.9	-3.4
Caustic soda	Gj/tone	54.8	48.6	-11.2
Calcium carbide (large plants)	Gj/tone	75.3	64.8	-13.9
Plate glass	Mj/50kg	951.7	923.8	-2.9

Source: Zhao Jimin (November 2001:21)

In all the above cases China has been instrumental in reducing its energy consumption fluctuating only in the amount. The centralisation of the environment cases had brought a positive note at least on the industrial front. However by the turn of the decade all this good work began to be undone by those who had not so long ago so vociferously advocated for it. By now economic reform had completely absorbed the government and it was in no mood to waste time on petty issues like environment protection and energy conservation. While in the 1980's it was developing a solid basis for technology absorption both through indigenous built up and outside support, it dismantled all of it by taking a reverse gear in the 1990's (Zhao, 2001:25). The economic paranoia was so mind boggling that it went back to its pre reform tactics of administrative regulation and over centralisation in the energy conservation programme (Zhao, 2001:8). The biggest blunder committed by the government at that time was to remove all financial incentives and economic sops associated with energy efficiency both in product and process (Zhao, 2001:25). Simplified and uniform tax laws meant that preferential treatment given to energy efficiency and environment conservation projects were disbanded (Ibid). The after effects of this move meant that banks too became indifferent as now economic gains again at the upper hand over social benefits (Ibid). In fact many conservation centres which had sprung up in the 1980's to provide advice, directions and services for boosting energy efficiency also closed down (Ibid). In fact the decade of the 1990's was a transition phase for the energy sector wherein the old administrative structure was in shambles and the new market rule had not begun to produce its positive fruits to channelize and streamline the energy sector (Ibid). Nevertheless this was the same decade which led to diversification of energy resources in favour of renewable and had witnessed series of laws and regulations which were instrumental in laying the groundwork for the future conservation programmes. Given below is the list of such environment policies issued in the 1990's (Zhao, 2001: 22).

Table 4.8 Various Environment Policies of China

Year of formulation	Policy	Targeted rationale
1992	China Agenda 21	Energy efficiency, renewable energy, clean coal technology, combined cycle power plants, nuclear power
March 1994	Sustainable energy Programmes under Agenda 21	Renewable energy and energy efficiency

1996-2000	Brightness Programme, Integrated and Comprehensive Rural Electrification, energy efficient lightning, riding wind programme	Environment protection
January 1998	Law of Highway	Fuel based taxation system intended to save energy, reduce pollution and promote automobile technology development
1995	Electric Power Law	Government support of all small hydropower systems, solar energy, wind, geothermal, biomass and other renewable resources for rural electrification
1996	Parallel operation regulations for wind power generations	Power grids allowing interconnection and parallel operations of wind farms, power grids must buy all electricity generated by wind farms at a price that covers the production costs
1998	Energy Conservation Law	Using renewable energy to reduce emissions and to protect the environment through project management and bank loans
April 29 2000	Air pollution Control Law	Enterprises should use energy efficient low polluting clean production technologies, SDPC and SETC to promulgate lists of retired equipments (Article 19), sorting and washing of high sulphur and high ash coal for efficiency in end use equipment, household heat through district heating systems (Article 24), establishing desulphurization equipment on some new and re powered power plants (Article 30),

Source: Zhao (2001:28)

Chinese government have often been very idealistic about their goals of achievement by setting high bench marks and constricted time for maximizing their potential. Perhaps it is this over enthusiasm which often makes them fall short of their own targets. Also lack of simplification in both implementation and application has exacerbated the problems despite granting maximum autonomy to the implementing authority. Li Xinlei (2012) in her paper presented at the Berlin conference etches out various perspectives regarding the 'Climate Change Policy of China' and the genuineness of China's commitment to mitigate energy emissions. China is often viewed as the growth obsessed country whose delusional fear of energy security has forced it to carry energy efficiency as a 'beast of burden' along with its energy policy rather than genuine concerned attempts of alteration of China's energy structure. However this logic treats the national interest and cognition preference of China as the static one and ignores the evolution itself of energy security concept in China. (Ibid:2)

She vouches for the rapid development of the renewable sector as the 'green miracle' in China and rubs of the 'cynical' intelligentsia by quoting the constructionist perspective which does not make a distinction between energy security and climate change as separate concepts of different interest (Ibid:3). Energy security has been dubbed as a 'conceptual revolution' whose effect has brought a cognitive transformation in national socio-economic policies and structural shift in resource allocation (Ibid). It is widely believed that the environment and other social factors constitute the fourth dimension of the definition of energy security which is acceptability (apart from availability, affordability, accessibility as the other three dimensions) as it is the new energy sources which can be an effective medication for both poverty and pollution (Ibid). The Club of Rome in its proposed theory of 'growth limitation' believes that it is not just the 'quantity' but also 'quality' of energy supply which matters in determining energy security (Ibid:4).

Figure 4.8: Conceptualisation of China's National Energy Security

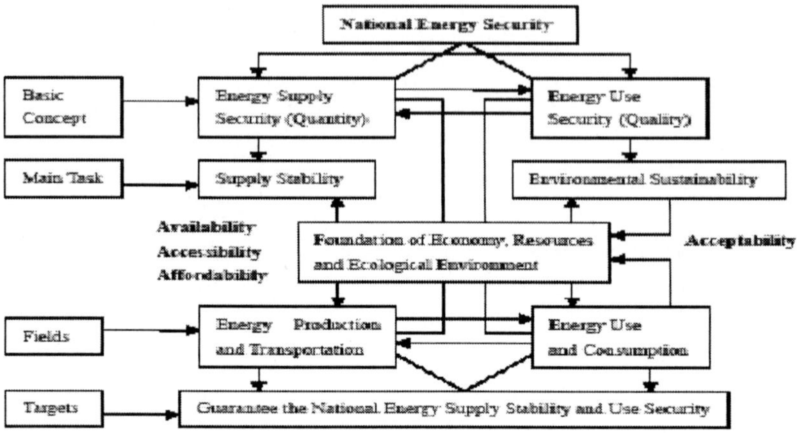

Source: Li Xinlei (2012:4)

In synchronising environmental, economic and strategic objectives it has been seen that to gain advantage in the international green market, technological innovation is not just a platitude but an imperative. Similarly, in order to achieve the twin environmental objectives of reduction in GHG emissions and sustainable development one has to gain advantage in carbon trading market and enhance efforts towards achieving low carbon economy (See Figure 4.9).

Figure 4.9: An Analysis of China's Economic, Environmental and Strategic Objectives

Source: Li Xinlei (2012:6)

China's high energy consumption rates (exceeding GDP rates almost by 5 percentage points), lower energy efficiency, static oil production from 2001 to 2003, while at the same time rise in automobile consumption put further strain on energy demand writes (Li, 2012:7). It were these pressing issues that China in its Tenth Five Year Plan (2001-2005) for the first time officially recognised the issue of 'energy security' and soon after in 2003 allocated 100 billion US dollars for 'futuristic strategy oil security system' in a policy document titled 'Twenty-First Century Oil Strategy' (Ibid:8). The 'scientific development' concept introduced in the Hu-Wen led Sixteenth Party Congress (Third Plenary Session, October 2003) spoke explicitly of a socio-economic society whose development is people-oriented, extensive, coordinated and catering to sustainable development (Li Xinlei, 2012:8). Again it was in 2004 that the executive meeting of the State Council passed the 'China's energy and long term development plan (2004-2020) aiming to conserve energy every year by at least 3 percent (Li, 2012:8). NDRC's initiative of ten major conservation projects in 2005 under the project 'medium and long term energy conservation for China', the '11th Five Year Plan target for reducing energy intensity by 20 percent and pollution intensity by 10 percent from 2005 level, former President Jiang Zemin's 2008 paper declaring 'China's new energy development road with Chinese characteristics' in his paper 'reflections on energy issues in China' and former premier Wen Jiabao's notion of a 'recycled economy' where management of mineral resources and conservation in production and consumption modes are highlighted reflect the seriousness of the Chinese government to 'build a reliable energy production, circulation and consumption system'(Ibid). The proposal of introducing per unit GDP carbon dioxide emissions as a compulsory indicator in the 12th Five Year Plan was initiated by NDRC in the thirteenth meeting of the 11th NPC Standing Committee as early as February 2010 (Ibid:9). The 12th Five Year Plan has already resolved to establish a competitive renewable energy system and in December 2011 introduced differential reduction targets for different provinces (Ibid:9). NDRC too has introduced different city campaigns and climate initiatives for different provinces suited to local conditions and requirements. For example, in August 2010 the 'low carbon pilot cities and provinces projects' was introduced in five provinces and eight cities to promote low-carbon economy structure and integrate carbon intensity reduction with energy security concept (Ibid:9). Yet many scholars opine that introducing a carbon tax and skepticism to reduce GHG emissions is just a smokescreen of the Chinese government to gain an early bird advantage of the renewable energy market while at the same time acquiring a new opportunity to tax its private corporations (Ibid). China has been vehemently trying to cover up the ideological vacuum left after the 'Deng Xiaoping theory' and Jiang Zemin's 'Three Represents' by voicing eloquently about the climate world. Tall claims to 'green GDP' (introduced in the Seventeenth Party Congress), 'scientific development', 'recycled economy' etc. might sound sheer political jargons but are some rudimentary steps into directing the thought process of the whole nation into the sensitivities of the environment (Ibid:13). It seems every party congress comes up with a new terminology to reiterate its adherence and to restore the confidence of its masses and environmentalists across the globe towards its contribution to the Chinese characteristics of sustainable development. The 'harmonious society' dream of Mr. Hu Jintao too carries some remnants of emotional proximity between man (read economy) and nature (read environment) (*ren yu ziran hexie xiangchu* 人与自然和谐相处) (Ibid:14). China has long graduated from the concept of 'conservation society' (reducing wastage and increasing efficiency) to 'circular economy' (transition from linear growth economy to eco-development) (Ibid: 15). Ma Kai the then president of NDRC (Ibid) detailed the concept of conservation society in the Tenth Five Year Plan and vociferously spoke about technological innovation. The Fourth Session of the Eleventh National People Congress Standing Committee took a historic decision by passing the Circular Economy Promotion Law on August 29, 2008 granting its legal acceptance to circular economic pattern (Ibid:15). The coming of this law into effect on January 1, 2009 meant that energy conservation was no more a pipeline dream meant only for grandiose speeches and political manifestoes of the party congresses but along term goal with short term targets and strategies meant to make it achievable at the stipulated time (Ibid:15). Also debates and planning on 'low carbon economy' are no longer reserved for ceremonious opening or closing sessions of the party congresses and annual work reports but have also entered into routine board room discussions of national party congresses and Chinese People Political Consultative Conferences (CPPCC) (Ibid: 16). Given below are some of the few laws passed in the recent past to balm the writhing sprain of the climate question at least to a certain extent (Chen Nicholas, 2008)

- Renewable Energy Law- enacted in 2006, it aims to enhance the installed capacity of renewable energy resources by 15 percent till 2020. To achieve this target it had invested 180 billion dollars between the period of 2006-10 and grants sops like financial subsidies and tax incentives to bulk consumers of renewable energy resources (Ibid).
- Circular Economy Law- passed in 2008 and gaining effect sin ce the dawn of 2009 the law exclusively targeted the corporate for their

misdemeanor towards environmental standards prescribed by the government. It also included in its ambit raw energy suppliers and consumer industries and raised a finger on mishandling of both the producers and the consumers of energy resources (Ibid).

- Energy Law- it was a proposed law due to be enacted in late 2009 but met a sad demise after vehement opposition from NDRC. This law if passed would have superseded all other laws by setting up an energy ministry and ensuring central coordination of all energy policies. Its contents were viewed as an attempted coup by NDRC to supersede over its powers and hence never saw the light beyond closed quarters (Ibid).
- New Building Code - from 2006 onwards China requires all up- and-coming buildings to be energy efficient by at least 50 percent and metropolis like Beijing and Shanghai by at least 65 percent (Ibid).
- Green reporting standards- with the passage of circular economy law, all corporate enterprises and stock markets (in Shanghai and Shenzhen) shall implement 'green reporting' standards and also publicly blacklist those companies who fail to implement these standards (exclusive purview of CSRC). Xinhua and China Daily serve occasional dosage of environment defaulters under the jurisdiction of NDRC and its provincial branches (Ibid).

Economy versus the Environment: Whose side should Energy take?

Traditional energy practices in China have led to a belief that energy consumption and environment protection are incompatible and contradictory in nature. However the real challenge is to convert the outlook into a scientific format of development which optimises the utilisation and conservation of energy resources (both renewable and non-renewable) simultaneously.

However a few other researchers believe that encouraging energy efficient products is like digging one's own coffin as such products do not resist but encourage the wastage of energy resources (Churchill, 1993). They begin with an assumption that efficiency and price of a product or a service share an inverse relationship, and the more efficient a product or a service is the lower the price becomes for that consumer (Ibid). For example an energy efficient light bulb will be consumed and a car with a better mileage will lower the cost of that service (in case of the bulb) and the number of vehicle kilometers (in case of the car). However, the consumer buys the service and not the fuel needed to run it and fuel efficient products lowering the price of the service or commodity shall increase the consumption of that commodity/service even to the extent of wastage (Ibid). Such researches ridicule those environmentalists who they believe are living in a delusional world where energy services are assumed to be price inelastic (i.e. consumption does not change with change in price). In any case, a perfectly inelastic demand curve is considered hypothetical even in economics and deeper market analyses would reveal that energy services and products do bear positive price elasticity –i.e. reducing price leading to increasing consumption (Ibid). However whether increased consumption would lead to increased fuel usage varies for individual products in the ratio of fuel costs and utility to total services cost (Ibid). Also, energy efficiency does not only enhance the consumption desire of the existing consumers but also leads to creation of newer markets and enhancing of existing markets as in the case of electricity where enhancement of heat efficiency from less than four percent to more than fifty percent in combined cycle plants has made the real price of electricity fall causing extravagant electricity consuming products like air-conditioners, refrigerators, laptops and others to expand their sales in the market (Churchill Anthony, 1993). The developing world (like China) faces the situation of 'double whammy' as inefficiencies exist not just in production and consumption but also in distribution due to which large chunk of masses lie outside the grid connection of electricity (Ibid). Hence these inefficiencies are covered up by subsidies which are neither enough to produce more electricity nor sufficient to overcome the losses. In fact subsidies and inefficiency create a 'Catch 22' where each seems to be fuelling each other's presence (Ibid). This has led to emergence of a parallel industry of invertors and generators who consume double the electricity on recharging (Ibid). On the other hand those who lie outside the ambit of grid also pay multiple per unit price for the expensive alternatives they resort to like kerosene lamps or hand pumps (Ibid). Another study was done for the analysis of influence of tax policy on energy buying behavior of the consumers. The study had aimed to identify the future of sustainable energy on China's transportation sector. It had considered the influence of factors like energy price, interest rate, energy tax rate and energy saving marginal cost (Tao and Xue, 2008:17). As a macroscopic adjustment measure energy policy has always meant to promote rational development of energy resources and economise on the use of policy instruments with other economic measures. This role of the taxation policy is unique as it cannot be replaced by any other economic measure (Ibid). The energy tax system is implemented by the state and is a fee levied to channelise the production, development and consumption behavior of energy resources (Ibid). The energy tax has a wider scope than the environment tax because it also entails the provisions of the environment law as well as of the energy conservation laws (Ibid). The energy tax has been particularly instrumental in reducing the end use consumption of energy resources- a move which has been suggested by various economists throughout the energy history of China (Ibid). Currently many developed countries already have an elaborate energy tax structure which is one of the major revenue generating resource of their country. However in China the biggest bottleneck is the mismatch and sometimes even conflicting provisions in the energy policy and the financial tax policy of the Chinese economy (Ibid). This has distanced the Chinese government from its goal of applying speedier and concrete energy conservation measures (Ibid). The present tax on crude and petroleum products in the domestic market of China covers merely 28 percent of its costs which is far lower than the world average (Ibid). This is not only because of a liberal tax structure but also because of the prices of gasoline and diesel fuel being far lower than the world average. Obviously this 'low tax low price' policy (*di shui di jia*) (Tao and Xue, 2008:18) has done more good than harm for the judicious use of crude and other fuels. The current economy of China is undergoing an expansionist phase in the infrastructure industry of China. While the dictum of 'more roads, shorter distances' is undoubtedly a good move to reduce the transportation costs, it is also a big boost for freight carriers and general passengers to ply more number of times on the road (Ibid). Rising incomes and rising urbanisation in China has led to rising specialisation of services (especially in agriculture) which are also becoming increasingly energy intensive (Ibid). Moreover transportation costs have also expanded as an added appendage. Rising income elasticity and consumption elasticity (due to better efficiency) have all caused the fall in real prices and lead back to square one of 'energy dilemma'(Ibid). However the answer lies in one simple solution. Pragmatic policies by a visionary government without resorting to anything populist or coercive are the need of the time. Aping the developed world that has already reached the stagnation point of per capita energy consumption is no cleverness. For a country claiming to be developing with the 'Chinese characteristic model', it should suck up the efficiency gains and consumer surpluses through tax and stock options for individual consumers.

For a large number of years China's energy policies have relied on making the energy dance to tunes of the economy. The economic requirements and needs have always been the prime concern for both the government and the average consumer. The drive for modernisation and industrialisation has shifted the energy mix of China's consumption basket from being coal based to being oil and gas based (Liu, 2003:17). While the influence of continuous economic adjustments have been beneficial to the energy mix of the consumption basket it has neither been able to change the basic structure of the energy mix nor has it been able to assuage the basic fears of energy scarcity or fulfill even partially the long cherished dream of self sufficiency of the Chinese government. Coal is still the major supplier of electricity with oil and gas just pitching in for one fourth of the total electricity of China (Liu, 2003:18). No wonder the coal rich China is unable to identify how to contain the rising dominance of crude and gas both in its transport and its import bills. For the average consumer this is the call between the devil and the death as coal consumption robs him of his air quality and crude consumption from his financial stability.

Many sociologists have believed that the prime purpose of energy generation was to expand the production of human civilisation, provide various capacities to the human life and ensure economic growth not for the sake of GDP but for the sake of providing material benefits to the general population (Cui and Wang, 2010: 107). Hence energy scarcity is not an economic issue but a social issue. Energy problem gives headache not only to the realisation of economic goals but also to the realisation of the modernisation goal, the goal of the establishment of a well off society and the goal of establishing socialism in the Chinese society (Ibid). The tenets of the commodity economy state that energy like any other economic commodity has to pass through various hands of trade to transfer from the production stage to the consumption stage (Ibid). However what transpires between a supplier and the buyer in the energy market is not just the fulfillment of a need or a want but factors like consumers income standards, the price of the comparative fuel (in China's case it has been coal) and the speculation of the consumer towards the probable price of the energy resource in the market (Ibid). In China after the supply susceptibility of the external market outside and various populist measures taken inside; the energy market is heavily influenced by various factors like energy prices, economic growth, population, production structure, energy consumption structure and living standards and income capacity of the consumer (The below section is based Cui and Wang, 2010:107-8).

- Energy prices – in economic aspects price has played an extremely crucial role in the trade of any commodity. This is especially true in the case of China which has seen a rapid transformation from state administered prices to market prices ruling the market. However the condition of vital commodities like energy is different as the prices are caught in the conflict of different pulls of the state and the market. The energy law specifies that although the energy price structure is governed by the market conditions yet it should be a perfect combination reflecting adjustments both in the state and the market. In the case of energy as a commodity two views have emerged. One where it is postulated that rising prices would be followed by slowing demand and greater efficiency versus the debate of demand falling to a certain extent and then rising with rising prices contributing to inflation. Such debates are a common discussion at an almost daily basis in the board rooms of government agencies and energy lobbies as well as the drawing rooms of the average consumer.

- Economic growth- economic growth is defined as the growth which raises the real per capita production output and real production capacity of a particular area or country in a given period of time. When we say that energy promotes social development we are obviously talking about economic growth and production. Energy and economy share a mutually existing and dependent relation where the former fuels the latter's growth and the latter provides investment for development of the former. The patterns of energy production and consumption structure are a big indicator of the economic growth and the general living standards of the people of that area. The unit of energy consumption elasticity reflects the relation between the rising GDP and energy consumption numbers. When the economy is on the rise the elasticity becomes near or equal to one and is very less in low growth period.
- Population- population is an extremely important factor in the dynamics of the energy patterns of a nation as it has a direct bearing on a number of issues like determining the per capita production, individual lifestyles which in turn determine the per capita energy requirements. Population affects not just by the sheer value of its quantity but also by the increase in value of its quality (like income and education) and expansion of the populated space (dividing into rural and urban space). Any change in the above indicators brings changes in the quality and quantity of population thereby bringing changes in the energy consumption pattern.
- Production structure- differences in the characteristics of different production structures also brings changes in the energy consumption structure which is also influenced by production structures established in different periods of time. Hence while calculating the issue of changes in energy consumption, the issue of changes in the primary, secondary and tertiary sector should also be incorporated. Since a long time the industrial sector has dominated the Chinese economy and production set up and has also been a major determinant of the energy consumption practices. The domination of the industrial sector over the tertiary sector is also the reason responsible for high energy consumption of China.
- Consumption structure- for a long time China's energy structure has been a coal dominated one but is almost on the verge of replacement by other fuels namely oil and gas and perhaps in the distant future renewable resources. A country's energy consumption structure determines the progress of the civilisation as well as the level of development of

social production of its citizens. Changes in the energy structure are the resultant of changes in the energy consumption standards as well the elasticity of energy consumption.

- Income levels of the consumers- price and income are two main determinants of the trade of a commodity. The higher the disposable income of a consumer, higher is the desire for a better quality of life. While a while ago better quality of life involved equipment which produced more combustion of fossil fuels, the trend is fast changing with the upcoming generation going in for energy saving products due to extensive promotion in the media and government incentives.

Based on the above factors a tabloid was constructing analysing these factors from the period of 1990 to 2013

Table 4.9 A Period Analysis of Energy Consumption and Economic Parameters

Year	Total energy consumption (10,000 tonnes of standard coal)	Energy price	GDP (100 million Yuan)	Total population per year (10,000 people)	Proportion of secondary sector to the tertiary sector (percentage)	Proportion of coal consumption in total energy consumption (percentage)	Per capita disposable income (Yuan)
1990	98,703	104.2	18,667.8	114,333	41.3	76.2	903.9
1991	103,783	112	21,781.5	115,823	41.8	76.1	975.8
1992	109,170	113.4	26,923.5	117,171	43.4	75.7	1,125.2
1993	115,993	142.6	35,333.9	118,517	46.6	74.7	1,385.1
1994	122,737	125.5	48,197.9	119,850	46.6	75.0	1,869.7
1995	131,176	110.9	60,793.7	121,121	47.2	74.6	2,363.3
1996	138,948	110	71,176	122,389	47.5	74.7	2,813.9
1997	137,798	106.4	78,973	123,626	47.5	71.7	3,069.8
1998	132,214	94.3	844,02.3	124,761	46.2	69.6	3,250.2
1999	133,831	96.5	896,77.1	125,786	45.8	69.1	3,477.6
2000	138,553	106.8	992,14.6	126,743	45.9	67.8	3,711.8
2001	143,199	101.8	109,655.2	127,627	45.1	66.7	4,058.5
2002	151,797	104.1	120,332.7	128,453	44.8	66.3	4,518.9
2003	174,990	105.7	135,822.8	129,227	46.0	68.4	4,993.2
2004	203,227	111.6	159,878.3	129,988	46.2	68.0	5,644.6
2005	224,682	114.8	183,867.9	130,756	47.5	69.1	6,366.6

2006	246,270	105.4	210,871	131,448	48.9	69.4	7,174.7
*2007	280,508	n.a	265,810.3	132,129	n.a	71.1	n.a
*2008	291,448	n.a	314,045.4	132,802	n.a	70.3	n.a
*2009	306,647	n.a	340,903	133,450	n.a	70.4	n.a
*2010	324,939	n.a	401,513	134,091	n.a	68	n.a
*2011	348,002	n.a	473,104	134,735	n.a	68.4	n.a
*2012	361,732	n.a	519,470	135,404	n.a	66.6	n.a
*2013	375,000	n.a	568,845	136,072	n.a	66	n.a

Source: Cui and Wang (April 2010) *China Statistical Yearbook 2014

The above table has revealed some startling features about the impact of these factors on the energy consumption. It has been seen that the impact of the production structure has the maximum affect while population, energy price, economic growth, consumption structure, consumers income standards affect in decreasing order of magnitude. Yet this is not to say that the other factors have miniscule effect on the energy consumption pattern of China (See Table 4.9).

Energy security is the third stage in achieving the aim of well off society (Cui and Wang 2010:110). It is also considered as the base for rational development of socio economic sustainable development in the twenty first century. Perhaps the biggest challenge for China is to maintain the sustainable development of the three big E's namely, energy, economy and environment.

Advanced technology

Up till now the buzzwords of discussion in energy dynamics has been 'investment', 'plans and projects', 'Chinese companies', 'installed capacities' and 'low carbon economy' but conference room discussions and internet based researches are nothing but mere debates if ground realities do not corroborate with the affirmed statements. However, like many other whimsical ideologies and plans, projects and targets too take a long term to realise, materalise and reap effects substantial enough to be seen, felt and talked about. In 2012 China for the first time launched the National Energy Technology Twelfth Five Year Plan focusing on technical study, technical equipment, demonstration projects and technical innovation platforms (Li Xinlei 2012: 11). The white paper on energy released in October 2012 also explicitly points out working on the dictum of 'high content of science and technology, low energy consumption, less ecological pollution, good economic results' (*White Paper on China's Energy Policy*, 2012). A leading Chinese energy analyst Ceng Xinqiu believes that the white paper has divided China's energy priorities into the time frame of past and the future (Xia, 2012). The past which relied on priority to energy conservation, based on domestic conditions and building energy structure on coal to the future of not only maintaining priority to energy conservation based on domestic conditions but also incorporating pluralistic development, protect the environment, innovation in science and technology, intensify reforms, promote international cooperation, improve people's livelihood (Xia, 2012). The last point mentioned in the white paper has a special significance as it corroborates with the spirit of the Eighteenth Party Congress. Ironically this point is also the initiating point as well as the 'Achilles heel' of energy development (Xia, 2012). Improving the livelihood of people through energy essentially means reducing the energy divide between the rural and the urban and the rich and the poor. It also involves solving the '*san nong*' (three main problems of the agricultural area) as well as the energy deficiencies of the border areas (Ceng Xinqiu interviewed by Xia Lihong, 2012:1).

The Energy Conservation Law was promulgated in the period of November 1997 to 1998 (Zhao, 2001: 26). It apart from its other provisions of promoting energy efficiency and energy conservation had been explicit about the issue of development of advanced technology. 'To stimulate and support technology R&D and scientific research in energy conservation as well as application and dissemination' (Zhao, 2001:26). However the biggest lacuna in the law was that it did not give any guidance on how to implement its programs for realisation of its lofty principles (Ibid, 27). Yu (2010) points out to lack of effective laws which can regulate the oil, gas and nuclear sectors of the energy field. The nuclear sector has the Law on Protection of Radioactive Pollution which is the only security measure related to nuclear disasters, as the rest of the laws deal only with administrative provisions (Ibid: 2163). Also the issue of laws for public energy services is not addressed (Ibid: 2163). Public energy services means that those services and products which are provided by the government to the people for their energy needs like electricity, oil, LPG etc (Ibid: 2163). All consumer based laws regarding energy issues focus more on rights of the consumer rather than his duties in contribution to energy conservation. Yu Xiaojiang (2010:2162) also points out to the expiry date of various energy laws as they were formulated during the period of planned economy and have lost relevance during and after the economic reforms. Also lack of a unified energy ministry has resulted in marginalization of national interests over sector specific or institution specific interests in the formation of energy laws (Ibid, 2161). The author cites the example of Law on Coal Industry (1996) whose outdated provisions are unable to contain any of the menaces of the coal industry be it wastage of resources, mining hazards etc (Ibid, 2163). Also 'auxiliary legal documents' which accentuate the importance as well as the implementation factor have not been issued due to political delays and internal infighting. 'Without them many laws may fail to constitute a whole, hence they will be impossible to implement and enforce.' (Ibid) The author has cited the case of Article 11 of the energy conservation law where the governments are directed by a 'shall' speech rather than a 'have' command to implement the provisions (Yu, 2010:2164). Also the government agencies have over stretched themselves by not only involving themselves into policy making but also into supervision, management and complaint reprisal mechanism which leaves them with no scope to effectively handle even one aspect of the energy issue (Ibid).

Expectations from the 2012 White Paper are high yet too idealistic targets give little leeway for workable solutions and white paper is no exception. Moreover issues like promoting international cooperation while following those energy policies which are based on domestic conditions are conflicting propositions in the white paper. In 2011 China had shared the dubious distinction of producing 31.800 million tonnes of total energy production as well as becoming the largest consumer of energy in the world (Ceng Xinqiu interviewed by Xia Lihong, 2012:3). Having become the world number one in hydropower and number five in wind power capacity, China is also increasingly making its presence felt in important low carbon technologies like solar PV, wind turbines, solar water heaters, electric vehicles, rechargeable batteries and energy efficient home appliances (Chen Nicholas, 2008) as the world's third largest ethanol producer China is witnessing its own 'green revolution' by a spiral increase in sales of electric bicycles and compact cars (Ibid). Sporadic reports of resorting to coal cleaning technologies to reduce pollution emissions and increase efficiency or adopting of 'combined cycle' technology (an electricity technology where electricity is produced from waste heat of gas turbines which is more energy efficient and less pollution making than traditional technologies) (Austin Angie, 2005:6) do motivate the researcher to give more than a passing glance to China's 'innovation' spirit. Especially so when this is backed by a strongly wired regulatory framework on establishing codes of appliance efficiency standards and efficiency designs, imposing carbon tax or pollution tax (20 percent surcharge on SUV) and promulgation of various laws like Renewable Energy Law, Circular Economy Law, compulsory 'green reporting' for listed companies etc (Chen, 2008). However it is seen that much of the advanced technology thrives on foreign participation and investment where China is a mere second fiddle even in its own domestic boundaries (Ibid). This is in sharp contrast to the traditional energy production where China has completely banned foreign participation in its domestic sphere despite constantly advocating international cooperation in its white papers and being an aggressive player in upstream and downstream activities of other countries (ibid). The 'guidance catalogue for foreign investment' exclusively weeds out the non-Chinese corporate from high consumption energy industries, supply of conventions like gas and electricity and mining of scarce resources and rare earth metals in China (Ibid). However all industries catering to recycling, solar cell manufacturing, anti-pollution equipment, processing of urban waste, garbage collection and handling, environment protection techniques, renewable energy production are encouraged to engage in exchanges and cooperation with foreign players (Ibid). Example: while mining is not allowed by foreigners, mine gas utilisation is increasingly encouraged. Similarly while crude production in China dominated by state owned enterprises foreign participation is allowed in production of oil shale, oil sand, heavy oil and extra heavy oil. However, no foreign enterprise can venture into the Chinese market independently but must by law engage into a joint venture with a Chinese company (Ibid). The reasons for such difference are obviously well known. Lack of experience and a history or perhaps politics of technical disjunction has led to the government seeking foreign intervention and guidance to seek initial support and promotion for its industry (ibid). On the other hand, the well established traditional sectors already bordering on xenophobic tendencies and delusional fears for commodities as scarce as energy do not require and cannot afford any foreign participation which is viewed more of an interference than intervention (Ibid).

It has often been seen that, since many of the renewable energy firms are private enterprises and so they are often not provided the 'safety valve' of financial security like their state owned brethren. Suntech bankruptcy is a point in this case. Obviously in such cases resorting to advancement of technology through stronger policies and reduced costs in expanding solar technology are an imperative. A white paper on China's energy conditions and policies released in December 2007 by the Information Office of the State Council has stringently focused on 'accelerating the programme of energy technologies' and has highlighted a number of new and innovative technologies which have been adopted by China in the recent past (*White Paper on China's Energy Conditions and Policies 2007*). Some of them are: coal gasification based poly-generation technology, third generation pressurised water reactors (pwr), nuclear power generations, heightened gas cooled reactors (htgr), research and development of coal liquefaction and gasification, coal to olefin conversion, wind driven generators, conversion from fossil fuels, biomass and renewable energy resources to hydrogen, circulating fluidised bed (cfb), high efficiency hydrogen storage, fuel cell power generation, automotive fuel cell power system, building of gas cooled fast reactors, magnetic confinement fusion and natural gas hydrate technology (Ibid). However these technologies are yet to have a direct impact on the end consumer as most of them cater to redirecting production techniques towards higher efficiency standards.

China realizes that no other form of energy can replace coal and hence in its 'Action Plan for Energy Development Strategy 2014-2020' has offered to limiting coal consumption (till 62 percent) and re direction of finances towards clean coal technologies (*China Energy Focus*, 2014). In fact the significance of clean coal technology can be analysed from the fact that the President Xi Jinping chose to refer to it as 'one of the five core pillars for comprehensive reforms' at a meeting in June 2014 (Ibid). However the caveat lies in the cost of these clean coal technologies which shoot up the costs of electricity at an all time high. For example, average cost of electricity generation of an IGCC unit is five times higher than the cost from a conventional coal plant (Ibid). Also the current gasification structures lack the technological maturity to accommodate production from these clean coal technologies. MOST has launched the blueprint for developing clean coal technology under '12th Five Year Plan for Clean Coal Technology Development' (Ibid). Perhaps the best way to harness advanced technology both domestic and foreign is to lay the 'bait for economic incentive'. China has vehemently sliced down its import duty rate for renewable energy technologies.

> The average import duty now stands at 23 percent, but renewable energy technologies enjoy special low rates, 3 percent for components of wind power plants, 6 percent for wind turbines and 12 percent for photovoltaic (PV) systems (Zhao,2001:29).

Another economic incentive for renewable energy technologies is tax rebates on income tax and value added tax (VAT). VAT has been reduced by the central government for technologies of biogas (3 percent) and small hydropower projects (6 percent) (Zhao, 2001:30). This is in sharp contrast to standard vat rate which is 17 percent (Ibid). Regional income tax laws have also been initiated by local governments to encourage renewable energy enterprises and insulate them against standard corporate tax of 33 percent especially in areas which can bank upon the abundant supply of wind and solar like in Xinjiang and Inner Mongolia. China has also been giving loans at minimal rate of interest to encourage renewable energy and electricity built up especially in rural areas (Ibid). China not only subsidises the producers of renew able energy but also its consumers. While the central government facilitates any unit undertaking R&D in renewable sector, the local governments provide commercial raw materials at low costs to reduce the overall cost of production of renewable energy by pitching in for construction or equipment costs. The subsidies are also a stimulator of building up market and investment of the renewable sector (Ibid). Under the Torch Programme and the Spark Programme the central government has been in instrumental in encouraging the R&D prospects of the renewable energy sector (Zhao, 2001:31).

Another recently released white paper on climate change has also declared that China's non fossil fuel consumption is up by 8.1 percent and installed power generating capacity from non fossil fuels by 27.7 percent till 2011. Also China was the forerunner in developing on-grid wind power capacity by 2011 (White Paper on China's Policies and Actions for Climate Change, 2012). Notwithstanding transmission and grid integration problems it is true that regular emphasis by successive governments and ministries on non fossil fuels (like the 15 percent non-fossil fuel energy target by 2020 declared by NDRC) has retained the investor confidence into the renewable energy market (Business Vibes, 2012) and granted hope to the corporate and local officials into enhancing both their profits and morality.

It cannot be denied that no matter how much of energy conservation China implements, no matter how much of adjustments it makes in its energy structure or no matter how much of investment it incurs in its renewable energy sector, China will not be able to shift its reliance from the volatile imports of oil and gas. Also many in China have begun to believe that in this technology dominated world it is not feasible for China to strive for achieving self sufficiency in those energy resources in which it already is in a disadvantaged position like oil and gas. Hence it cannot harp on its early plank of developing its energy resources in isolation (Ceng Xinqiu interviewed by Xia Lihong, 2012:4-5).

Conclusion

The factors as a role of being the domestic determinants of energy policies gained recognition only after the introduction of post Mao reforms. The era preceding that (as discussed earlier) had undermined the importance of technology, (though Soviet assistance was received with much gratefulness), the market (as economy was just beginning to frame itself) or the environment (economy building and resource exploitation gave much less scope for further thought about it.) However as time fast forwarded the clamour for economy began to gain grounds and led to the rise of two major determinants- the energy companies and the market. It increasingly began to be felt that politics had enough of its share in administering the energy sector and it was now the turn of the market mechanisms to rule the roost. In this case energy companies came in handy with their administrative experience as they were none other than the former discarded energy departments in the ministries. And yes, environment which had long been taken for granted for ages immemorial was now in no mood to take a back seat. The pollution levels were rising and the results were fast appearing in the soot rimmed horizon of the Chinese sky. A new tussle began between energy and environment and the rest of the determinants were granted with the new task of synchronising the development of the two without annihilating the economy, thus giving birth to the idea of sustainable development. This is proved by Beijing's recent release of 'Clean Air Action Plan (2013-17)' holds stringent moves and concrete measures to contain the menace of 'grey skies and dusty air' for which it has already earned enough disgrace from the international community. Its provisions include monthly limit on car registrations, market policies to increase the cost of car use, impose congestion fee, create low emission zone, development of public transportation, promote reforms of public cars and check on vehicle exhaust fumes and industrial emissions (*White Paper on Beijing Clean Air Action 2013-2017, 2013*).

Having discussed all the domestic determinants it seems an acceptable argument that China's domestic determinants are at variance with each other. In fact, having discussed them individually we can safely conclude that they are not only at variance with each other but are also conflicting with each in their execution despite sharing the same interests of self-sufficiency. CCP and energy companies despite intricately entwined into each other's administrative capacities seem to be playing a tug-of war in superseding each other rather than joining hands too act as co-actors in China's energy field. Similarly while on surface it seems that the market and environment are mutually exclusive from each other they seem to share a greater bonhomie with each getting a piece in the other's pie. As far as technology and the poor consumer is concerned it seems that they are mere instruments in the hands of the above mentioned major players and have no role or say worth being recognised by the others. However, this is not to discount their importance who can (and have) changed the course of a government's thinking capacity, a company's installed capacity, a market's productive capacity and an environment's changing capacity in the long run. The idea of China's energy policies having always aimed for self sufficiency through optimum utilisation which can be based true albeit with a condition that the optimum utilisation of one or two determinants be it political control, business expansion of energy companies, market mechanisms or environmental which in turn will severely stunt the growth of the other determinants. It seems that either the market will trounce upon political dictatorship or economic development will turn in to a graveyard for ecological sustainability. This gives an impression that not only are the domestic determinants at variance with each other but also create problems for formations and implementation of energy policies by their mere co-existence. However findings have suggested that despite variations, it cannot be assumed that mutual coexistence of the domestic determinants is a threat to the development of the energy policies or energy structure. In fact it is these determinants which not only give a variety to the contents of the energy policies but also aid in incorporating the interest of various different groups while at the same time producing a holistic framework for the development of the energy structure.

5. Interplay of Domestic Determinants: The Duel of the Stalwarts

This chapter shall outline the complex relationship between the domestic determinants of the energy policies. In the previous chapter we had identified six main determinants affecting and affected by the energy policies of China, namely: bureaucratic control, energy companies, environment, advanced technology, market mechanism and consumers. Having identified the domestic determinants and the historical trajectory of China's energy policies, we seem to have identified a patchwork of chequered movements with no shape or design to examine. How should, then, such polka dots be adjudged to exhibit a virtuous (or perhaps a vicious) pattern. Can these domestic determinants behave independently of one another? Are they in conflict? And if yes, then who rules? If not, then why not? Is isolation of any one of these determinants a thumb rule for achieving suzerainty over the other? Are natural factors superior to human actors in determining the energy policies? Or is it vice versa? Is this a tussle between actors and factors, or more aptly called man and nature? Does energy lie between the two groups? Is energy a natural commodity with a humane vitality? In an attempt to answer these questions, a few models identifying the complex relationship between various determinants have been discussed. Also how the legal framework corresponds to the energy structure and in turn determines the energy policies is also addressed. Each energy source has witnessed its pinnacles of glory and nadirs of anonymity and it would be unfair to club all energy resources into one category and analyse them holistically. Hence a balance sheet is prepared where the influence of each domestic determinant on each energy resource is analysed. Also the impact of these domestic determinants on various regions of China is considered.

"Energy security should pay attention to domestic factors which shall strengthen and guarantee the policy structure of China" (Li Chun Mei, 2003: 4), says China's energy analyst Chen Xinhua. He had written a book titled *Kaifa Zhongguo de Tianranqi Shichang: Nengyuan Zhengce De Tiaozhan* (Exploring China's Gas Market: The Biggest Challenge of Energy Policy)

(Ibid). In May 2003 *Zhongguo Nengyuan* (China Energy) had published paper highlighting the importance of domestic determinants in charting the course of energy policy (Ibid). China today calls itself the "socialist market economy" (*shehui zhuyi shichang jingji* 社会主义市场经济) and hopes to work in future under the same model. In such a set-up, energy issues also cannot be dealt with purely on ideological or business grounds. From an economic perspective, it has been increasingly felt that definition of "energy costs," which is limited to calculating only exploration, production, transportation and distribution costs, is too narrow in scope and should be widened to include environmental implications too (Lester and Steinfeld, 2007:35). At a time when "sustainable development" is a morally persuasive topic, the government is keen on encouraging consumers to adopt energy saving habits through various sops like tax avoidance, credit facilities, etc. However, China is so terribly mired in the conflict between its political and economic measures that the efficacy of all its measures is lost. Many say that problem of "price and scarcity" is considered only at the central level while the local governments who have just begun to eat the fruits of economic growth are in no mood to control the "growth spurt" on mere grounds of energy scarcity (Ibid). Moreover, many state-owned enterprises are either unable or uninterested in responding to energy price signals because there is neither any incentive from the top brass nor are they interested in tightening the strings of their already tight purses (Rosen and Houser, 2007b:34). Strangely, despite being a one-party rule, such conflicts between local and central governments exist between almost all levels whether administrative or legislative. China's energy analyst Chen Xinhua believes that China's energy policies are getting increasingly influenced by international dimensions and situations (Li, 2003:4).

The current Chinese situation does not build an optimistic future for itself. The economy is overheating, energy consumption is skyrocketing, prices are escalating, pollution is expanding and political and administrative capacities are stretching beyond the requisite limit. Many energy analysts have attempted to understand the complex relationship between various domestic determinants through the CGE and the PREEST model. These models try to establish the close nexus between energy, economy and environment and their impact on the government psyche and vice versa.

Models of Identifying the Connection between Various Domestic Determinants

Wei Weixian based on Computable General Equilibrium Model (CGE) has drawn a relationship between energy, economy and environment and their mutual utilisation effects on each other. In a graphic representation the model illustrates various points. The first and foremost point is that energy resources are the motivational factor which give assurance to economic development. Speedy and sustained economic development requires a guaranteed, long-term, stable energy supply. Secondly, in the process of economic development requirements of expanding production scales and rising living standards increase pressure on land, mineral resources, hydropower, environment and energy. When this happens, the drive to satisfy these resources would mean intensified exploration of energy resources and in turn excessive production and consumption which would mean rising levels of pollutants in the environment. Once the quantity of these pollutants exceeds the enduring capacity of the biosphere, the ecological balance is seriously disturbed, producing unhealthy repercussions. Once the ecological quality goes down it inevitably affects the quality of energy resources, physical power and other basic constituents of production, ultimately undermining the level of total economic development. This model was then placed in the Chinese context to study the mutually progressive and regressive effects of energy, economy and the environment (this section is based onWei Weixian, 2009: 3-5).

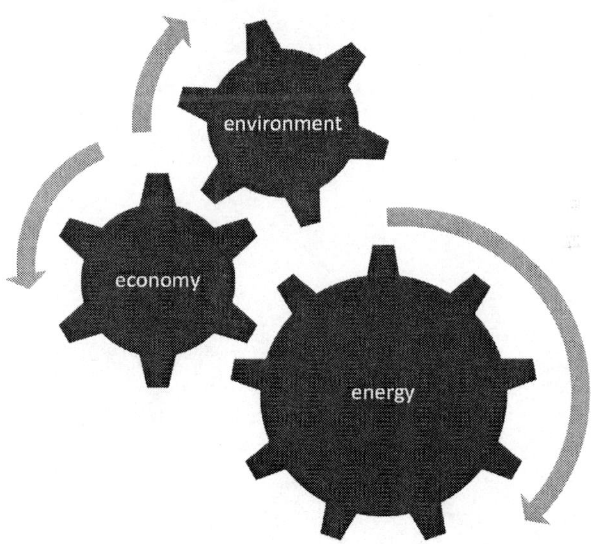

Another model which has been the most highlighted in the recent past is the sustainable development model. It is also called the PREEST model in some circles (Cai Weiying, 2007: 9-13). We shall analyse this model against the backdrop of our identified domestic determinants. It involves five basic components which are: population, resources, economy, environment and science and technology. The relationship between these five constituents is not the same, ranging from being strong to weak, long-lasting to being temporary, and hence continues to be intermittent. In analysing the interplay of these constituents we shall dwell on the question of energy issue in understanding the interplay of our domestic determinants. In this case, population has been identified as consumers and resources as energy.

- Consumers and energy: When the issue of social development is discussed, population is considered as the highest priority and energy exploration and production as a mere economic activity to satisfy the wants and desires of its consumers. Hence we can say that expansion of human capital is not only the cause but also the effect of energy production and consumption. However consumers and energy are inversely related in the sense that quantitative expansion of consumers causes a qualitative and eventually a quantitative decline in energy resources. Hence the concept of sustainability development seeks to bridge the gap between this inverse tendency by encouraging energy efficiency and qualitative as well quantitative inculcation of energy saving habits among the consumers (Cai 2007:9-13).

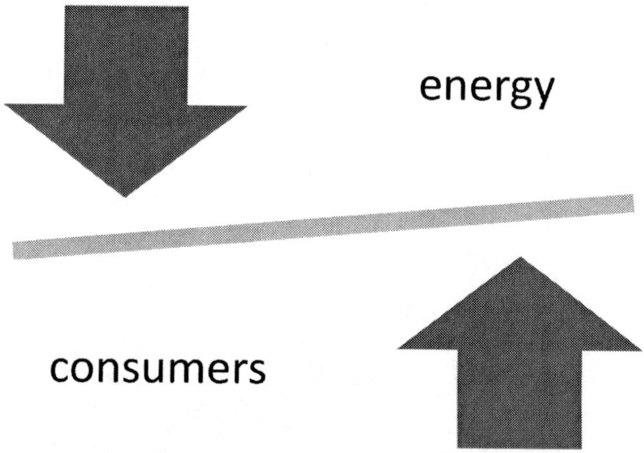

- Environment and energy: Both are the constituents of "nature" and form important parts of the natural habitat. Yet recent trends have led them to become "sworn enemies" where the development of one is debilitating to the very existence of the "other." While many in the world understand the harmful effects of "energy activity" on environment, few people are aware of declining recycling capacity of fossil fuels due to deteriorating environment quality. Since fossil fuels are derived from the humus, the quality of humus essentially affects the quality of fossil fuels like coal, oil and gas. Sustainable development brought reconciliation among the two by emphasising exploration of renewable resources as an alternative to fossil fuels (Cai, 2007:9-13).

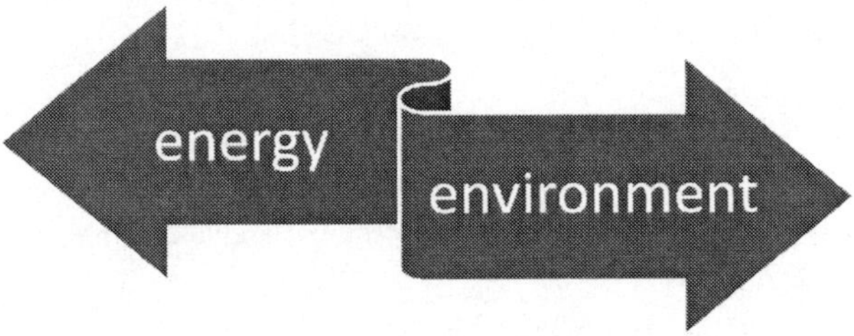

- Technology and energy: Advanced technology is an essential "reconciliation tool" of "sustainable development" and it would be no exaggeration to say that all grandiose talk would be defunct if adequate and affordable technology is not there to support it. Until now technology has assisted in expanding and intensifying the exploration activity of fossil fuels, causing the "energy scare." Hence sustainable development desires to tame this "wild horse" by utilising it to promote energy efficiency as well as the exploitation of renewable resources to supplement and then eventually displace the existing energy structure (Cai, 2007:9-13).

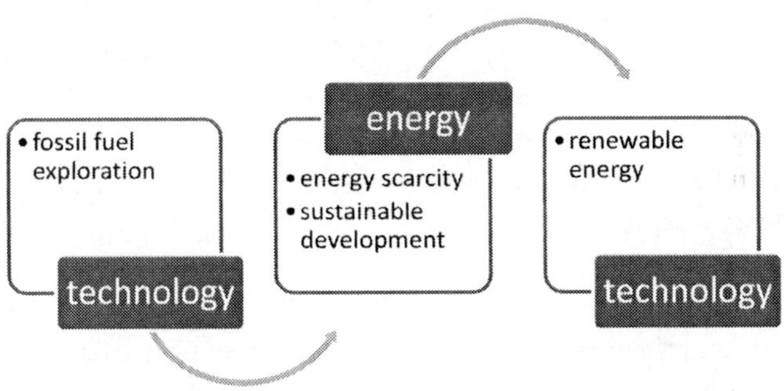

- Energy and economy: Energy is the basis of economy. Through renewable energy this link also adds a third dimension called the environment. The quality of energy resources affects the level of economic development. It has been seen that despite possessing a sufficient quantity of oil China was unable to utilise the crude in its possession as the quality was unsuitable for its refineries. Similarly domestically produced coal had a lot of sulphur content resulting in excessive pollution. The value of energy consumption is measured by calculating the ratio of energy consumption to economic increase (which constitutes increases in GDP, GNP and

National Income) (Cai Weiying, 2007: 9-13).

> China has multiple players with multiplicity of interests and multiplicity of roles to play. No player is typecast in a particular role ranging from commercial "hat" to societal "hat" and for some a government regulatory "hat" (Lester and Steinfeld, 2007: 35).

A general level of lack of coordination exists between the central agencies and the subordinate actors (Lester and Steinfeld, 2007: 35). Coordination lacks not at the point of what to do but how to do (Ibid). Physical infrastructure which could be decisive in incrementing and channelising the energy needs of China are made on an interim basis by grassroots agencies (Lester and Steinfeld, 2007: 35). China's central government is its political fulcrum declaring its major decisions into laws and policies yet it cannot be denied that China's infrastructure build up is dependent on decisions taken by local governments relying on the interests of local industries and local fuels, missing out on comprehensive national strategy or the "big picture" (Lester and Steinfeld, 2007: 35).

Just like the domestic determinants that vacillate in their relationship with energy resources through cooperation and conflict, a similar condition exists between their related laws and energy laws. Whether these laws persist or resist the realisation of the provisions of energy security is discussed below.

Analysis of Energy Policies versus the Energy Structure of China

An energy structure of a country is a reflection of the mutual impact of energy policies and the other policies on each other and on the country's general political and socio-economic strength (Xiao Guoxing, 2010: 78-84). This mutual impact determines the efficacy and the tenacity of the energy policy and the cost required to build a stable energy structure. As discussed above, the cost of an energy structure is not just economic but dwells on all contours of the complex reality that exists in countries today and more so in emerging economies. While the energy polices lay the foundations of an energy structure it cannot be denied that the strength and the durability of that structure is derived from the impact of other policies (Xiao Guoxing,

2010: 78-84). It is not that the policies are engaged in a battle for "survival of the fittest" but it is the survival of all the policies (whether related to energy or not) that the fitness of an energy structure is determined. In the document of China's legislative laws the seventh clause, second section writes that "National People's Congress can determine and alter Criminal Law, Civil Laws, laws related to the country's structure and other basic laws." (Xiao Guoxing, 2010: 78-84) This means that in China's legal structure, apart from the traditional "six laws," there is also a provision of "other basic laws." (Xiao Guoxing, 2010: 78-84) China's energy law belongs to this sphere of "other basic laws" as it fulfils the conditions of the adjustments, and changes in the energy laws are based on the concomitant relationship shared between energy and society, which is the basic social relationship determined both by the consumers and the producers (Xiao Guoxing, 2010: 78-84). Xiao (2010) writes that energy is the source as well as the driving force behind the road to sustainable development, as well as a bottleneck in the socio-economic development of a country which is usually manifested in the rising living standards of the people in particular, and massive infrastructure build up of the country in general. The direct engagement of energy with society had begun with the exploration and utilisation of its resources way back during the liberation period and since then has been the basic elixir of intertwining society towards the development of the sustainable structure. In fact, lately the working draft of the Energy Law of China has received emphasis by the country's leadership, various departments of the government and the different intellectuals of society, particularly for this point (Ibid). The energy laws govern not just the consumption pattern of energy but also the laws related to the scale of energy production, the system of energy administration and supervision, taxes and prices for the usage of energy and its technical equipment, investments and market capacities of the energy structure, etc (Ibid). Currently China's energy law is composed of five parts, namely, Electricity Law, Coal Law, Energy Conservation Law, Renewable Energy Law and Law related to Protection of Pipelines of Oil and Natural Gas(Ibid). It is also predicted that the future would see the promulgation of laws going beyond coal and pipelines like the Oil and Natural Gas Law, Nuclear Energy Law, which would be included in the ambit of energy laws (Ibid). The guiding beacon for the energy law administration is the economic system and the political administration of China. In the field of energy law the equipment of market system exhibits a control of property rights—this happened when energy began to be searched and exploited and it became a state property (Ibid). It has also been argued that introduction of the energy market which has withstood the transient economic system has been the major source of creating innovation (Ibid). The political influence in the energy law is visible in the formulation of energy strategies, energy administrative system, scale of energy production, limitations of energy market expansion, supervision of energy market, etc. It also determines the targets, direction and process of production (Ibid). However, does the energy law coexist with the other laws of China? Are they in conflict or coordination? Each law shall be analysed individually in tandem with the Energy Law of China (The section below is translated from Xiao Guoxing, 2010: 78-84).

- Energy policy and the PRC constitution: Energy law is part of the constitution and hence naturally abides by its principles and values. It defends the political economic structure of the country and abides by the spirit of socialism pervading the market society. Obviously as China increasingly takes to adopting the political slogan of a "sustainable development" and "green GDP," these changes are bound to get reflected in the future laws and policies related to energy (Ibid).
- Energy policy and the Company Law and Competition Law: Both the Company Law and the Competition Law correspond to the power capacity of the market structure as well as the system by which the energy investors operate. The environment of these aspects of the market lay the conditions for the formulation of energy strategies and are many a time the preface of the document of energy policies. The scarcity of energy resources and the competition involved in exploration and exploitation require the creation of a separate energy policy which reflects the role played by the market in providing basic aid to the sphere of allocation of energy resources both within and outside the country. Energy policies deal with the multi-pluralistic power of the energy investors, price administration, ownership of energy resources, entry and exit of the market, equality of competition versus the monopolisation of the market, protection of the consumer and conservation of the market socialism, etc. (Ibid)
- Energy policy and the Price Law and the Wealth Tax Law: The price of the energy resources are not the general market price influenced by demand and supply patterns but a calculated administered price. For this "shadow price" to work effectively, the energy policy works in tandem with price laws and the energy market. The energy policy marks different prices for renewable energy resources and new energy industries versus the industries which encourage high consumption, increased pollution and rapid utilisation of already depleting thermal resources. However, the current law on wealth tax does not favour equal distribution of profits among the energy industries. Moreover it seems that its provisions are completely antagonistic to encouraging investors

in the energy market. However, the current tax structure determines that the custom duties in the energy sphere shall be laid down by the provisions of the administrative laws. In fact in the current law structure the ambit of the wealth tax does not interfere in any of the provisions of the energy policy apart from the conservation law and the renewable energy law. For example, the Eighth Provision of the Legislative Law, the legal clause of tax revenue and the tax provisions of the energy law are in complete sync with each other. (Ibid)

- Energy policy and the Law for the Progress of Science and Technology: The most dynamic aspect of the energy industry is the innovation in its S&T department. Innovation in the energy industry has donned many a form since its inception. Whether it was the Soviet assistance used for exploration and exploitation of fossil fuels, or the process of energy conservation, the advent of renewable technology or the utilisation of new energy resources all were started with the concept of innovation at its foundation. The energy policy and the law for advancement of science and technology were committed to expanding both the quantity and quality of innovation in S&T. Moreover the policy for science and technology has also been instrumental in promoting energy education and the nurturing of energy personnel, etc. (Ibid).
- Energy policy and the Safety Production Law: Energy production is risky and accident prone. The safety production law deals with the practical feasibility of production without incurring the costs of damage to society. The energy policy under this law deals with the rules and regulations regarding energy exploration, safety conditions for the transformation of processing industry, etc. (Ibid)
- Energy policy and the Environment Law: Energy resources possess all the common characteristics of being a resource for the country and hence the energy policy is made in consonance with the provisions of Mineral Resource Law of China. However energy resources also possess the specialty of being "energy" for China. This special characteristic provides space and the requirement for energy policy to build up additional legal clauses which prevent the misuse of energy or the misuse of any other resource through the usage of energy. For example, the excessive exploitation of minerals has laid a great strain on the ecological habitat of the local surroundings and has questioned the government's sensibilities in allowing it to continue unabated. While it is a general tendency to assume that both the energy law and the environment law are antagonistic to each other, it is often forgotten that both are laws meant for the preservation of natural endowments

of the country and hence operate under the same blanket of principles, values and ethics. As far as legal provisions are concerned the two policies are not "sworn enemies" but the "best of friends." The twenty-first clause of the Water Law clarifies that water is public property and the right of first use is possessed by the residents of the surrounding areas. The left-over water then shall be distributed for purposes related to agriculture, industry, ecological habitat and transport in decreasing order of importance. However, it can also not be denied that many of the environment problems have stemmed from the excessive exploration and exploitation of energy resources questioning the validity and relevance of the energy law. The energy law holds a clause where an evaluation of the interference of energy policies or strategies in the sphere of ecological influence is done. While on paper the policy restricts the exploitation of energy resources which disturbs the ecological balance, in reality, the measurement of this disturbance is laid at the discretion of the local officials affecting the resilience of this clause. (Ibid)

- Energy policy and the Circular Economy Law: No matter whether this law falls under the protection of environment law or economic law, it is no doubt that its main motive is to promote the synchronisation of the three Es: energy, economy and environment. Moreover this law also intends to promote the consonance of energy law with the three Rs—reduce, recycle and reuse. Xiao Guoxing believes that both the 3E and the 3R need a mature market economy and it is the correct time for this amalgamation to be advocated in China. (Ibid)
- Energy policy and the Foreign Trade Law: The foreign trade law ratifies the utilisation of energy markets of both the sides. The main target of the energy policy in this matter is to promote the utilisation of energy resources without over-exploitation as well as the protection of a guaranteed energy supply for China. In fact the foreign trade department and the NDRC work in close proximity with each other to encourage China's trade in petroleum products, technology and services with other countries. (Ibid)
- Energy policy and the Statistics Law or the Standardisation Law: The NDRC works in tandem with the statistics department to publish authentic energy data as well as the concerned news about it. At the same time in order to guarantee the quality of energy products, the energy law provides legal efficacy in strengthening the main energy products and maintaining the national standards of quality of both the energy products and its equipment (Ibid).
- Energy policy and the Energy Law: Energy law is the legal aspect of the energy policy providing it a status and significance in the country's legal

domain. It can also be said that energy law is the practical application of the energy policy and hence is a testimonial to the viability and sustainability of the energy policy. Energy law of a country in totality is the summation of the energy culture of that country. In fact, in the case of China the enunciation of the energy law is not just a revolution for law but a revolution created by law (Ibid).

The energy law of China is a salient feature of not only the energy culture of China but also the entire legal system of China. However the logic of the existence of an energy law is determined by the following components which sometimes duplicate (or perhaps strengthen) the terms of the energy law:

- Energy Law versus the Energy Conservation Law: Energy conservation is the rate of efficiency of energy utilisation in a given situation, however the two conditions which necessarily precede the efficiency of the utilisation rate is the efficacy of the energy structure and its industries. Yet the foremost of all the efficiencies is the tenacity of the market and the prevailing competition as well as the guarantee of a stringent administration system by the government. This brings into play the importance of an energy law which, while working under a market augmented government structure, pervades the general energy system, deals with the pluralism of energy investment, determines the trade of energy products, expands the competitiveness of the domestic energy process and yet retains the issue of energy conservation as its major priority (Ibid).
- Energy Law versus the Renewable Energy Law: As the cost of investment in the renewable energy sector is high, the latent capacity provided by the industrialisation and commercialisation of this sector has not been visible as it still relies on government support and encouragement. The Energy Law too gives special emphasis to the development process of the renewable energy sector. After understanding the guidance for development laid down by four decades of continuous industrialisation and commercialisation, it is only recently that the renewable energy sector has begun to foray into the ambit of market. The nuances of trade and investment regarding the technology, capital and products of renewable energy are still discussed extensively in the energy law rather than the separately enunciated renewable energy law (Ibid).
- Energy Law and the Coal Law: It is a known fact that for a resource which is the pride of China and caters to all its aesthetic sensibilities of self-sufficiency and energy security, issues related to its exploration

and production, such as environment depreciation and poor quality, can at best alter its production technique rather than replacing it completely with some other fuel. With the scourge of industrialisation being copiously visible and the era of a low-carbon economy gaining ground, the Energy Law is the bridging factor between excessive coal production and the fast deteriorating environment (Ibid).

- Energy Law and the Electricity Law: From the electricity revolution to the energy revolution, from the clean energy slogan to energy efficiency revolt, electricity production and development has always been a product of change and revolution. From coal electricity to electricity from oil and then the era of hydropower, wind power and solar power. It has been seen that all the energy resources are competing to be the best resource for producing the cleanest, safest and guaranteed supply of energy. This competition has always disrupted the existence of a continuous structure of electricity in China. At such juncture the Electricity Law has also been a series of fragmented clauses which have not done much to alleviate the power woes of China. Thus it is the onus of Energy Law to cater to establishment of rules and regulations, development, market competition of electricity production and distribution in China (Ibid).
- Energy Law and other related laws: In the wake of rise in oil and gas prices and the disruptions in guaranteed supply of fossil fuels, a series of laws have come into force in the form of Nuclear Energy Law, Atomic Energy Law, Administration of Oil and Gas Law and the Energy Law needs to fortify itself with more stringent laws and regulations to face future challenges in the energy sphere (Ibid).

The Balance Sheet

China sacrificed its energy to build up its economy and is now using the economy to buy back its energy. This is the general perception of most energy analysts both inside and outside China. A balance sheet is formulated to determine to what extent each energy industry has been an asset or liability in the economic balance sheet of China. Note that assets here are measured not just in terms of how much economic gain has been made or lost but also how much of energy capacity and environmental capability was made or eroded during the process of energy development (The section below is based on the translation and analysis of Andrews-Speed Philip's book *Energy Policy and Regulation in the People's Republic of China (2004)* by Wang Yanyan in 2005:33-34) .

- Coal industry: China's energy capital, coal has historically blessed China with its copious availability and ubiquitous consumption in almost every industrial use. The basic ingredient in China's energy recipe, coal still constitutes nearly seventy per cent of the consumption basket, showing only a slight dip in the past sixty years. It has achieved this feat when throughout the past, present and definitely the future, both the domestic and global limelight has been hogged by other energy resources ranging from other fossil fuels like oil and gas to renewables like hydro, nuclear, wind, solar, etc. So far so good as coal has been the omnipresent and omnipotent asset of China's energy balance sheet. The aura of low exploration costs and low prices blinded the administrators from the liabilities from low quality, inequitable distribution and environmental destruction. Even when the government took up the cause of energy conservation, the clean coal technologies used were extremely sub-standard (Wang Yanyan, 2005: 33-34). Unfortunately the economic costs of such nuances did not stay within the coal industry but also spread to related industries inhibiting the economic efficiency of the overall system. Coal as a liability is not only short term but is a burden for a long time. This is because coal distribution requires a well-developed transport system as production areas are far away from consumption areas adding to the fuel costs and robbing the benefit factor of being an asset (Ibid). This investment in infrastructure has many a time been at the cost of various social projects which have extinguished due to dearth of funds. In fact it is believed that coal can act as an asset neutralisng all its "liability" aspects simply by utilising its latent capacity of energy conservation within the industry. For example, a lot of energy can be saved simply by converting solid coal into liquid and gaseous forms before consumption (Ibid).

- Power industry: Apart from coal and oil industry, power industry was the third part of the trident which witnessed exponential growth rates. In the period of two decades from 1980 to 2001, when China underwent the "double digit" phase, the power industry enhanced its capacity by five times, although the northeast part of China also witnessed some massive power cuts during the same period (Ibid). Although the power cuts did not happen because of production lapses but because of lower capacity of transmission and allocation of electricity, it is also true that that the lower efficiency of the power industry means that the power factories and equipments are facing massive losses due to poor transmission (Ibid). How can the power industry become an asset? Perhaps the simplest way is to contribute massively in energy conservation which it can do simply by enhancing its energy efficiency. Statistics have revealed that coal consumption to produce every single unit of energy is very high, especially when it is produced by small-scale factories using outdated technology (Ibid). Distributed energy generated through co-generation, small-scale hydropower units, utilising wind and solar energy for regional generation can be a better alternative. China had begun the practice of establishing co-generation plants way back in the 1980s which by the end of the twentieth century were producing 15 per cent of China's total generation capacity (Ibid). However the abolishment of the encouragement given by tax revenues, as well as the ambiguous policies of the power industry and the administration system, stopped the production from co-generation plants, resulting in a reversal of the power industry from being an asset to becoming a liability (Wang Yanyan, 2005: 33-34).

- Energy consumption by other industries: Despite continuous changes in the economic structure of China, the contribution of the secondary sector has always been pegged at a flat 40 per cent, long before it became the "factory of the world." This happened because the rest of the contribution was a mere replacement by the service industry which was earlier contributed by the agricultural sector. It is already known that heavy industries were not only the biggest contributors to GDP but also the biggest consumers of energy. What is perhaps less known is that employment generating village and town enterprises have wasted such colossal amounts of energy resources that they managed to create a dent in the rising GDP of the last two decades of the twentieth century (Wang Yanyan, 2005: 33-34). Currently, inadequate consumption, lack of supervision and wastage of generated energy are some of the biggest problems faced by the energy industry (Ibid).
- Construction: Like all other industries it gets blacklisted for the wrong-doings of the offices and for using equipments which waste resources. The problem gets aggravated when low-efficiency central heating systems are used (Ibid).
- Transport: China had quite an early realisation of the shortage of oil resources yet was unable to contain its consumption or look for quicker options to supplement the fuel supply. The result in the period 1980s to 2000 was that China increased its oil consumption by three times, turning China from an exporter to importer (Wang Yanyan, 2005: 33-34). Obviously more trade means more usage of transport and the best and perhaps the only option is to focus on fuel efficiency of the plying automobiles (Ibid).

Energy as a Resource

Earlier in 2010 the International Energy Agency reports of China having surpassed the US in 2009 to become the world's largest consumer of energy was challenged by many Chinese (and especially the government) as a ploy to make China take the blame of all the pollution and weaken its "Third World position" into accepting various environment protocols and bindings (Swartz and Oster, 2010). However IEA reported that although the US was the biggest culprit since records for energy consumers began to be measured, after the past decade China went slightly ahead of the USA in consuming energy worth 2.26 billion tonnes of oil while the US maintained a figure of 2.17 billion tonnes of oil. (Note that this measure is not for consumption of oil only but a measure of consumption of all forms of energy including non-fossil fuels measured in terms of oil) (Ibid). However IEA defends the figure by alluding to the only exuberant economy (the Chinese economy grew at 8.7 per cent in 2009) after the 2008 financial crisis and hence a natural corollary of emission rise (9 per cent for China, the highest for that year by any individual country)(Ibid).

Oil sector: While debates are raging about who is the biggest culprit it cannot be denied that China's living standards are rising as its lifestyle is changing very fast, getting more urbane and consumption oriented. While hundreds of tiny hamlets still silhouette the glitzy landscape (or rather the cityscape), it cannot be denied that more and more Chinese are venturing for energy intensive products to match the lifestyles of Europeans and Americans. Despite being referred to as the "bicycle country" by the international media, China is the largest seller of new cars in the world while its average citizen continues to thrive on energy consumption one-fourth of that of an average American or European. Zhao Fang (2008:66-70) in his dissertation identifies the environmental consequences of utilisation of different types of energy resources in the country. In the case of oil, it is not just lifestyle factors like ordinary consumption increase which matter but also various other potent market indicators like supply and demand, development and business of the oil companies, international fluctuations and most importantly the domestic oil prices which matter more and have varied ramifications.

- In 2005 a new tax on gasoline was passed replacing all the road tolls, which significantly boosted the price of gasoline in the domestic market. After the lull of 2008 the prices declined in 2009 only to rise again in 2011 and since then there has been no stopping its meteoric rise (China Energy Report, 2012).
- In May 2009, NDRC issued a "petroleum price management trial method." Here, if within any 22 business days, the international oil price varied by 4 per cent, domestic oil prices would be revised. This was done to limit the upper ceiling of the price of the domestic oil products and to insulate the common man and the companies from large fluctuations in the international oil price (Xie, 2010).

"Excessive supply does not guarantee lower prices" believes Xie Xina (2010) in her article "Chinese Oil Companies Taking Advantage of Energy Consumers" and holds the national oil companies (NOCs) guilty of purposely exporting crude products at lower prices to create artificial scarcity in the domestic market and forcing the government for an upward revision of the prices of petroleum products domestically. The author also denies that the government price mechanism is a guarantee of low market prices in almost all situations. She quotes the prices of April 14, 2010 when the NDRC announced the gasoline and diesel price increase of $47 per tonne (i.e., $ 0.13 per gallon for gasoline, and $ 0.15 per gallon for diesel) when by the end of March there was an excess of oil products worth 18.54 million tonnes. She also cited the case of 2009 where China exported 14.96 million tonnes of oil products at the rate of $ 1.337 per gallon while at the same time domestic prices in Beijing were pegged at $ 3.70 per gallon. Obviously when it is time for the blame game both the NOCs and the government wash "their dirty linen in public" by transferring the guilt to the other side. Perhaps the only person from the side of the oil companies who agrees with the existence of such a precarious situation is the CEO of PetroChina Jiang Jiemin who publicly expresses his frustration with the pricing mechanism albeit on a softer note. "Although generally the NDRC pricing mechanism runs smoothly and fits Chinese characteristics, it has ill effects on oil products, processing and marketing." (Ibid) He too is an advocate of allowance by the government to reflect the international volatility in the domestic government as the only solution for a stable supply of oil to China (Xie, 2010). However Xina supposes that philanthropy of the state-owned companies in its claim to operate according to a socialist set-up is a mere smokescreen and they could go to any lengths either by increasing the wholesale prices of the gasoline products or disrupting the supply to force the government to increase the prices, in order to retain both their business and profits in the refining sector. If this happens, the government would be in a complete quandary by facing steep pressure from all sides: the companies, the market, the public and the international community for not abiding by the diktat of "socialism with Chinese characteristics." (The above section is based on Xie Xina, 2010)

Guy C. K. Leung (2011) in his article "China's Energy Security: Perception and Reality" has attempted to explode some myths related to oil in the issue of energy security. He articulates that the concept of "energy security" emerged because of the insecurities created by oil. Also, neither laying down extensive pipelines nor acquiring foreign reserves could assuage the convulsions of energy security no matter how much of a "feel-good factor" is projected by the companies or the government. Despite popular opinion otherwise, he holds the transport sector and not the industry in the "world's factory" culpable of driving up the national oil demand. He sums up with a belief that the Chinese government should change their perceptions from making energy security as a goal to be achieved into turning it as a means to achieve the more idealist goal of self-sufficiency (Leung Guy, 2011: 1330-1337).

Renewable energy: The government plans to spend a whopping US$ 1.54 trillion in the clean energy sector sourced from various channels like financial institutions, tax policies and government investment vehicles like the China Investment Corporation and China Energy Conservation Investment Corporation (China Briefing, 2011). Also, mergers and acquisitions with foreign companies in this sector are advocated like "hot cakes" by the Chinese government growing on a yearly basis of 225 per cent since 2010 (Ibid). The biggest dealer with China is the Asia-Pacific region especially in the solar and wind power sector. Given below is the analysis of China's performance in each of the individual clean energy sectors (The section below is based on China Briefing, 2011).

- Solar power: It is dubbed as the government's "poster child" despite having a total share of only 0.01 per cent in China's energy production (Ibid). In fact China is a big player in the international solar power market in terms of both production and consumption and is increasingly looking for newer avenues to explore in this sector. The government is giving increasingly newer sops and tax incentives to push for greater domestic consumption of solar power products, especially solar water heaters. NDRC announced the Golden Sun Programme in July 2009 which catered to investments in the solar power sector (Ibid). These subsidies were fifty per cent of grid connected solar investments and seventy per cent off-grid photovoltaic power investments (300 kilowatt minimum capacity, one year maximum construction period, 20+ years planned operations) (China Briefing, 2011).
- Wind power: The compounded annual growth rate of wind power installed capacity from 2004 to 2009 in China has been 134 per cent (Ibid). As the largest wind energy producer of the world, the installed capacity of wind energy in China has been 44.5 gigawatts, adding 13.8 gigawatts of energy on a yearly basis (Ibid). However, since China is already well developed in the wind sector it does not actively encourage the participation of foreign players in the wind energy market. The foreign players are at the most allowed to invest at the provincial level while national level participation is completely banned and the current policies which are holding agenda until 2015 are in no mood to change from their

present positions. A Boston Consulting Group report cited in the China Briefing post compares the profit margins and revenue generation of the largest turbine manufacturer in China from 2007 to 2011 which shows windfall profits from total revenue of $ 300 million in 2007 to $ 3 billion in 2011. The company was working at a profit margin of 10-15 per cent and this growth shows no signs of abatement, as claimed by the BCG report (Ibid). The government too has been promoting self-manufactured electric power generated from the wind capacity by ranting a VAT rebate of fifty per cent to the producers (Ibid). The NDRC too in 2009 launched the fixed feed-in tariff for wind generated electricity which is pegged at Yuan 0.51, to Yuan 0.61 per kilowatt-hour while the producers generating energy from coal are paid at the rate of Yuan 0.34 per kilowatt-hour (Ibid). Foreign participation in the wind sector is minimal as mergers and acquisitions (M&A) and joint ventures (JV) (Ibid).

- Hydropower: The hydropower industry shares a "love-hate" relationship with the Chinese government. After facing a spate of apathy by the government for more than a decade, China's hydropower industry has got a new lease of life as the government returns from its state of euphoria in economic mirth to an enthusiastic interest in the hydropower industry. Mostly located in the most undeveloped areas of China, i.e., western and southern areas, the industry came into the spotlight after the construction of Three Gorges Dam in 2008 gained worldwide attention (Ibid). However, the government also had to face scathing criticism from leading environment and human rights organisations for the problems of ecological loss and population rehabilitation usually related to large-scale hydropower projects. The Water Resources Ministry of China sees greater prospects in rural hydropower capacity which is expected to increase 26 per cent of the total hydropower capacity (Ibid). The years 2010-2011 saw the approval of ten new major hydropower projects with renewed investment of Yuan 200 billion (Ibid).
- Biogas: It is the natural gas generated from the anaerobic digestion and fermentation of humus and solid waste on the ground. An infant industry in China, the development of biogas digestors is not a matter of choice but of concern requiring immediate attention as it continues to consume and produce corn and pork—both being the perfect raw material for generation of biogas (Ibid). Currently this waste is dumped into the waters turning them into an ecological hazard and contributing to water pollution. While the government has been offering subsidies at all national, provincial and local levels for installation of biogas digestors, this incentive has done little to attract the poultry keepers from installing a digestor in their

vicinity (Ibid). Once used only for the limited purposes of cooking and lighting, biogas now with the help of advanced technology can be a great source of electricity generation and sometimes even be used as a vehicle fuel and for chemical production (China Briefing, 2011).

Given below is the environmental impact of production of various forms of energy both fossil and non-fossil fuels.

Table 5.1: Environmental Impact of Production of Various Energy Resources

Energy type	Energy resource	Production techniques	Main environmental impact
Non- renewable resource	Coal	Exploration, washeries, reserves, processing and transformation	Sinking of ground, destruction of underground water levels, acid rain, solid waste emissions, interior pollution, etc.
Non- renewable resource	Oil and gas	Exploration and exploitation of oil and gas fields. Smelting and establishment of reserves	Air Pollution created by tail exhausts of automobiles, seashore pollution by oil and gas spills, acid rain, greenhouse effect, accidental hazards to workers or public in general
Renewable resource	Hydropower	Naturally occurring or in the form of bio-spherical energy, occurring in physical or chemical forms	Drying up of naturally occurring rivers, loss of natural habitat to marine life causing either emigration or death, extensive destruction to fertility of soil, erosion of sandy soil, problem of people's displacement, ecological and environmental changes in downstream areas, "prolonged illness" of the area due to obstruction and grave changes in naturally occurring areas, effects of constructing large dams and embankments, etc.
Renewable resource	Nuclear power	Radiations	Nuclear accidents and harmful effects of nuclear wastes due to unplanned and ill-treated dumping in ground or water

Renewable resource	Wind power	Area specific wind velocity	Noise pollution, unnatural changes with the landscape, electromagnetic disturbances, disastrous effects on birds
Renewable resource	Solar power	Used in two ways, either through solar heat or solar lights and sometimes both	Harmful effects of sun rays on flora and fauna, birds, and mankind, unnatural changes in ground and landscape
Renewable resource	Bio-energy	Combustion of plants and accumulated humus	Degeneration of ground, soil erosion, ecological destruction and encouragement to agriculture at the cost of forests
Renewable resource	Geothermal energy	Heat pits, emission by solid wastes	Disturbances in ground, sinking of ground, noise pollution, pollution created by heat and chemical discharge
Renewable resource	Oceanic energy	Influence of generating electricity	Negative influence on oceanic environment, marine life and coastline.

Source: Zhao Fang (June 2008:9).

The Coal Industry

Coal always has had and always will have a special mention in the case of China's energy tale. Its Oscar-winning performance right from the time of liberation has earned it the reputation of being the "classic" in the cinema of achieving self-sufficiency. Despite having turned the tables of China from being exported to being imported since 2009 its black armour has not diminished in its sheen or glory even by an inch at the discussion tables of NDRC or the central government (Todd, 2013:5).

Figure 5.1: China's Coal Production and Consumption

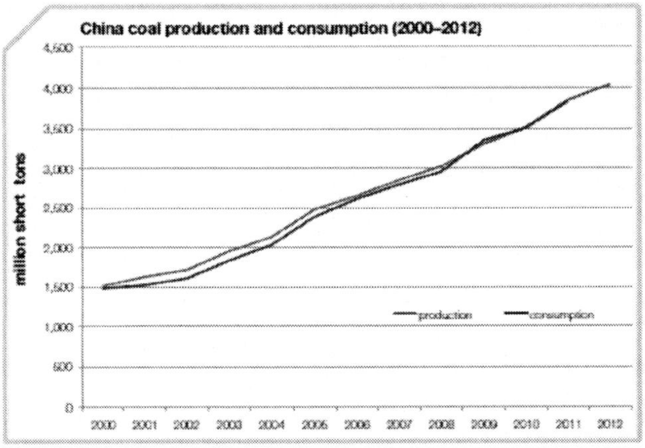

Source: Todd (February 2013:5).

The above figure indicates that China's coal production and consumption have developed hand in hand with consumption being slightly ahead only in the last few years. This rising requirement has boosted the morale of other sagging economies (especially the US) who believe that "China rise" could bring in some tangent foreign exchange at its coffers. However China's investments in coal have not adopted a global mindset as they still stick on to the "dig and deliver" method, believes Woetzel (2003:136). Apart from a few major players, China's coal industry is inherently small-scale and technically deficient which is why it imports metallurgical coal from Australia (Ibid). Most of China's coal production is done from it loss making mines which are not only burdened by overstaff and accumulated losses but are also not able to maintain the safety of their own workers. Adding insult to injury is that good quality coal is buried away far from the coastal areas (areas in and around Shanxi) and transport cost is a burden heavily felt by these mines (Ibid: 127). Railways are a dedicated service provider by bridging the gap by contributing 45 per cent of its total freight capacity (Ibid: 138.). Yet coal has been the "golden goose" a strong and traditional provider giving China two basic requirements of self-sufficiency and large-scale employment.

Figure 5.2: China's Coal Imports

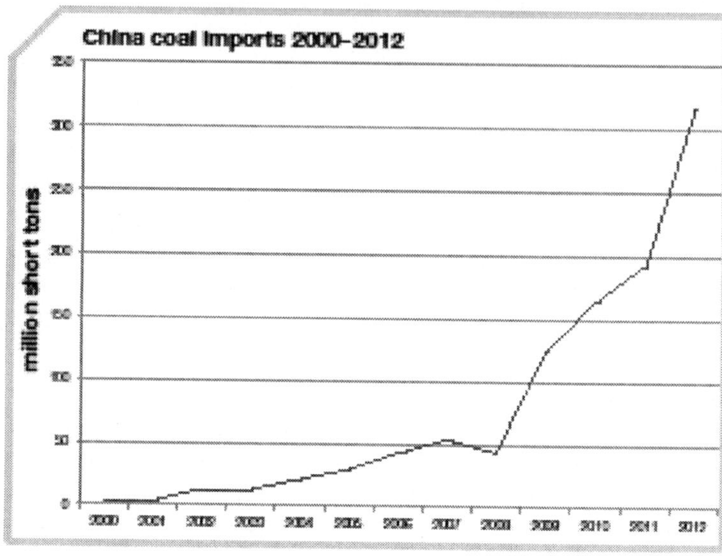

Source: Todd (2013:5).

The above figure indicates that China's coal imports have shown a spectacular rise despite it being more than self-sufficient in its coal production. The spectacular speed at which China's coal imports have risen despite a continuous rise in its production speaks volumes about its voracious appetite for infrastructure and heavy industries. However the coal consumption grew because China's economy grew and with it the demand of electricity which is the biggest consumer of coal. While the 2008 financial crisis and the 2012 Eurozone crisis have hit the Chinese hard in terms of double digit rates, yet it cannot be denied that most of the reasons of slowdown came from outside China on which it had no control, and the domestic economy is still vibrant and going. Chinese premier Li Keqiang had drawn three parameters before the beginning of his tenure to verify the growth engine of China's economy. They were electricity consumption, railway freight volume and the lending rate of banks (Todd, 2013:6). The National Bureau of Statistics has released the data for the first eight months of 2012 which reveal that growth rate for China's electricity consumption, railway freight volume and bank lending have declined continuously in the year 2012 and have shown no signs of abatement (Ibid). Reports from the China Electricity Council have revealed that not only have the production and consumption of coal declined in recent months but there has also been a declining trend in investment too, almost to half (Yuan 227.1 billion in 2005 to Yuan 105.4 billion in 2011) (Ibid). With reports of overheating there is no imperative need for the Chinese investors to take up coal as a priority. The general slowing down of the economy has reduced industrial activity in iron and steel industries and hence the demand for metallurgical coal. The current capacity utilisation of this industry is merely 80 per cent which means that China has begun to stockpile on coal as it continues to import better quality at affordable prices (Ibid). Even major ports like Qinghuangdao port have reported large stockpiles of coal which are continuously rising (Ibid). The cumulative figure in the warehouses of major plants of China was 93.75 million tonnes by 2012 (Ibid). The environment factor too is an add-on to the decline in the coal industry. The reports of the Twelfth Five Year Plan and the latest energy outlook have revealed that the decline in the coal industry is not just market driven but also government induced (Ibid) The government has pegged the overall production capacity to 4.1 billion tonnes and capped the domestic production and consumption to 3.9 billion tonnes by 2015 (Ibid). It has also been reported that the major coal producing provinces have been asked by the government to purposely grow below 4 per cent so that the total production in 2015 does not exceed 63 per cent of the total energy structure (Ibid). In October 2012, Guangzhou, one of the rapidly developing cities of China, announced that it would no longer approve any new coal power capacity in order to contain its coal utilisation level to that of 2010 and abide by the new air quality standards (Ibid:8). Other major cities especially on the developed eastern side like Tianjin, Shanghai, Wuxi, Changzhou and Ningbo have followed suit (Ibid).

China is witnessing a renewable energy revolution and is projected to capture the market like it did in coal by 2020 (Ibid). The State Grid Corporation of China has also announced that they would allow solar PV installation of even less than 6 MW to get grid access in China, which means that rooftop installations of solar plants can become a reality and residents can play a big part in writing the successful renewable energy story (Ibid). .

Figure 5.3: China's Wind and Solar Capacity

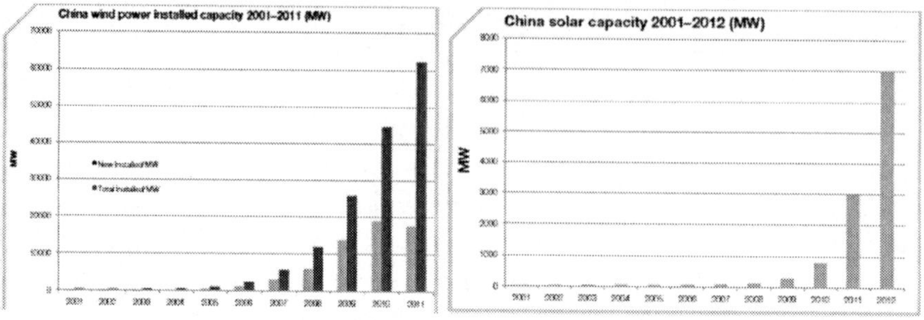

Source: Todd (2013: 10).

Rising wind and solar power capacity are a symbol of growing evidence of the rising awareness of both the government and the public to increasing threats to their health and water bodies. China's Ministry of Environmental Protection has revised its air pollution standards to arrive in tandem with the world standards (Ibid). While the Western economists have always blamed the Chinese statistics for being inflated and for being lenient towards the domestic departments and companies in applying the world ratified environment standards, in a comparative data released by the World Resources Institute it was found that the air pollution standards in China are increasingly turning more stringent than the US and EU standards (Todd, 2013:11). The provincial governments are under increased pressure to maintain and monitor the data about the particulate matter (Ibid). Strangely, for China almost half of its coal abundant regions are also facing acute water scarcity (Ibid). Already China's new coal plants are turning into great water guzzlers and are forcing China into making a tough choice between drinking, agriculture and coal production (Ibid). Particulate matter is the shadow of coal production as no amount of technological breakthroughs like filtering or operating far from populated areas can help reduce the suspended matter from remaining suspended in the air or travelling long distances (Ibid). Pilot carbon trading of the government is seen as the green signal for capping coal production (Ibid). .

> The country is deliberately and quite effectively decoupling its economic growth with coal such that future economic growth may not manifest in increased coal consumption. The results of this decoupling are already present (Todd, 2013: 15).

To support its argument the author cites the "China Power" report of HSBC (Hongkong and Shanghai Banking Corporation of China) which believes that "China will need less new generation capacity by 2015 than planned because of its maturing economy and more efficient use of existing capacity." (Todd, 2013: 15).

The energy companies have always been one of the most instrumental actors in China's energy policies, sometimes providing a tough competition to the government itself. "Energy is a key strategic issue for China's economic development, social stability and national security. As such China sees energy shortages as one of the biggest potential threats." (Lee, 2010) However, what is the road that China follows in its policies in its pursuit for energy security—a liberal institutionalist approach or a realist mercantilist approach to energy security. Aleh Cherp and Jessica Jewel (2011:1) have identified three perspectives related to China's energy security: the "sovereignty" perspective which deals with political science, "robustness" perspective deals with natural science, and the "resilience" perspective having an economic base. Stacey Lee (2010) believes that China's energy strategy is a hedging strategy—i.e., a situation where Beijing deals with all unilateral and multilateral actions to achieve, reliable and cost-effective sources of money supply. Deng Xiaoping in his "24 character strategy" asked China to pursue a strategy "to secure our position, cope with affairs calmly, hide our capacities and bide our time until China can assert its power on the global stage." (Lee, 2010:3) Although this strategy was intended to have geopolitical implications, it can be reasonably argued that China has used this strategy pretty well in unleashing its potential in the domestic energy strategy (Ibid:4). While the development of renewables seem to be an imperative need of the future it cannot be denied that China had hidden its resources well until it had secured its position as the strongest economy ready to capture the world market and to be the market for the world to acquire the best technology and of the best quality. Today most countries look up to China as a bail- out package who would buy their coal during the situation of scarcity in their own domestic sphere. Yet China has played its cards well and is investing only in what it shall require in future rather what it needs at the present.

Regional Differences in Both Energy Production and Consumption

Another glaring mismatch in China is the difference of priority, target and the means adopted for achieving the target between national energy policy and the regional strategies. Perhaps the actual difference lies in the source of goals as national policies formulate policies for each of the different energy resources like coal, oil, etc. While regional strategies confine themselves only to those resources which are copiously available in their own jurisdiction (Wu and Li, 1995: 167), this is not to say that the Chinese government is just a culture of conflicting opinions with contradictory priorities as its initiative of energy conservation did impact indirectly by reducing the rapidity of energy consumption despite a continuous increase in the overall figures.

Since the past two decades fifty per cent of China's energy resources have been derived from five major provinces (Chen Wei et. al., 2011: 39-44). Shanxi leads in coal production providing almost one-fourth of coal supply of China followed by Inner Mongolia which has speedily increased its production to obtain the number 2 slot of China's coal rich provinces (Chen Wei et. al., 2011: 39-44). The northeast of China is its "oil factory" with Heilongjiang and Liaoning as strong bases and concrete contributions by Tianjin and Xinjiang. Gas comes from Sichuan and Chongqing providing almost 30-40 per cent of gas supplies (Chen Wei et. al., 2011: 39-44). Xi'an and Hubei provide hydroelectricity similar to production areas, China's consumption areas also major in consuming different resources (Ibid). Maximum coal is consumed in Shandong, Jiangsu, Neimenggu and Hebei whereas oil is consumed in Shandong, Guangdong, Shanghai and Jiangsu (Ibid). Maximum gas is consumed in Guangdong while maximum hydroelectric consumption happens in Sichuan, Guangdong and Hubei (Ibid). It can be seen that with the exception of hydroelectricity where the biggest producers are also its biggest consumers, none of the fossil fuels have consumption units within their regions which means that not only are these resource rich nations economically deficient but also bring an additional cost of infrastructure build up and transportation costs (Ibid). Perhaps hydroelectricity did not join the norm by the very virtue of its microscopic tendencies to serve the immediate requirements only. Given ahead is the period analysis of energy production and consumption of China's western, central and eastern areas. It is a grave anomaly that while China's energy production from the period of 1995-2008 has been 1.9 per cent, 4 per cent and 10.6 per cent in eastern, central and western China respectively, the consumption charts have been 6.7 per cent, 4.2 per cent and 7.5 per cent respectively (Ibid). It is a strange phenomenon that despite being one of the most under-developed part of China the consumption requirements of the western sector are the maximum exceeding even the highly developed eastern China.

Given below is the production and consumption distribution of coal, oil, gas and hydroelectricity in the eastern part of China.

Table 5.2: Production and Consumption of Various Energy Resources in Eastern, Central and Western China Respectively

Given below are the production and consumption details of eastern part of China.

Year	Production of coal, oil, gas and hydroelectricity in that order (per cent)				Consumption of coal, oil, gas and hydroelectricity in that order (per cent)			
1978	64.7	28.4	3.5	3.4	64.5	28.2	3.7	3.6
1980	62.8	29.5	3.7	4.0	68.3	23.6	5.9	2.2
1985	63.8	31.1	1.8	3.3	72.0	16.9	5.1	6.0
1990	62.2	32.2	2.0	3.6	72.1	16.3	5.7	5.9
1995	63.2	28.9	1.8	6.1	67.7	18.6	7.3	6.4
2000	57.5	32.7	2.9	6.9	68.4	21.8	6.6	3.2
2005	60.8	27.2	2.9	9.1	66.0	21.5	8.2	4.3
2008	57.7	27.6	3.1	11.4	66.2	20.1	8.8	4.9

Source: Chen Wei et. al. (December 2011:43).

Given below are the production and consumption details of central part of China.

Year	Production of coal, oil, gas and hydroelectricity in that order (per cent)				Consumption of coal, oil, gas and hydroelectricity in that order (per cent)			
1978	66.5	30.8	1.7	1.0	86.8	7.5	0.5	5.2
1980	67.6	29.2	1.8	1.4	82.2	9.3	2.9	5.7
1985	73.9	23.1	1.0	2.0	83.2	7.7	2.9	6.2
1990	77.9	18.7	0.9	2.5	82.2	8.0	2.9	6.8
1995	81.3	15.3	0.8	2.6	78.6	11.2	3.0	7.2
2000	76.0	18.9	1.1	4.0	68.1	14.9	7.8	9.3
2005	85.3	8.4	0.7	5.6	75.1	9.4	7.8	7.7
2008	86.5	6.9	0.6	5.9	75.1	7.5	9.1	8.2

Source: Chen Wei et. al. (December 2011:43).

Given below are the production and consumption details of western part of China.

Year	Production of coal, oil, gas and hydroelectricity in that order (per cent)				Consumption of coal, oil, gas and hydroelectricity in that order (per cent)			
1978	86.8	7.5	0.5	5.2	78.9	11.1	2.6	7.4
1980	82.2	9.3	2.9	5.7	75.5	12.0	4.3	8.3
1985	83.2	7.7	2.9	6.2	73.8	11.0	3.3	12.0
1990	82.2	8.0	2.9	6.8	75.0	10.3	2.6	12.1
1995	78.6	11.2	3.0	7.2	75.2	10.6	2.6	11.6
2000	68.1	14.9	7.8	9.3	68.9	11.7	4.7	14.8
2005	75.1	9.4	7.8	7.7	71.5	10.3	5.4	12.8
2008	75.1	7.5	9.1	8.2	71.5	10.0	5.6	12.9

Source: Chen Wei et. al. (December 2011:43).

The above three tables reveal that eastern sector is the least coal producing and consuming sector of China producing merely 57.7 per cent in 2008 against the central provinces which produced 86.5 per cent of total production in 2008. It has also been seen that despite being numerically weaker, the consumption of the developed western areas (66.2 per cent) is far more than its production relying heavily on other supply areas for its economic development. If coal is discussed the production and consumption of the western areas can be placed in the middle of central and eastern areas as the central area is producing 28.8 per cent more and consuming 13.6 per cent more than the eastern area. However the eastern areas far exceed both in production and consumption of oil and gas. In the case of oil and gas we see a reverse trend where central and western areas are consuming far more than their producing rates.

There is a pattern of anomaly almost in the entire China where the production and consumption are not equally distributed. The problem is not just the natural way of distribution but also a realisation that producer states are focusing less in consuming what they are producing and more of what they are importing from other provinces. While oil and gas consumers vouch for its better quality and less pollution, coal consumers advocate its copious availability and cheaper prices. What most forget is that in addition to transportation costs, better technology can eliminate the pollution factor and reduce the cost of production to a large extent.

Energy Investments

It is no news that investment in energy industry is the most lucrative business in today's world, especially in a country which thrives on the growth rates of its economy. According to the World Bank Report, between 2008 and 2012, global trade in new energy would reach new heights, which yet would be just the beginning (Yin and Wu, n.a:28). Global carbon trade has two basic resources: investment in clean energy and energy efficiency both of which aim to reduce carbon emissions. (Yin and Wu, n.a.:28)

Given below are China's major energy investors, its investment programmes and investment quotas.

Table 5.3: Energy Investment in China

Type of Investment	Investor	Investing Sphere	Programme invested in	Invested Volume (Unit: US dollars)
Multilateral funds	World Bank	Renewable energy, energy efficiency	Policy framework for capacity building	800 million to 50 million
Multilateral funds	Energy Foundation	Renewable energy, energy efficiency	Small hydroelectricity, biomass	800 million to 50 million
Multilateral funds	International Finance Corporation	Renewable energy, energy efficiency	Wind electricity, solar energy	800 million to 50 million
Multilateral funds	United Nations Environment Programme	Renewable energy, energy efficiency	Clean production, coal chemical process and energy conservation	800 million to 50 million
Multilateral funds	Asian Development Bank	Renewable energy only	Middle level hydroelectric projects and biomass	800 million to 50 million
Bilateral funds	Denmark Government	Renewable energy and energy efficiency	Wind electricity	45 million Danish Kroner and 20 million Danish Kroner
Bilateral funds	French Government	Renewable energy and energy efficiency	Co-generation	100 million to 50 million Euros
Bilateral funds	Italian Government		–	100 million to 62 million Euros

Bilateral funds	German Government	Renewable energy	–	–
Multinational companies	Shell	Clean energy and renewable energy	Clean coal, co-generation and biomass	–
Multinational companies	BP	Clean energy	LNG, clean fuel vehicles, associated programmes with CASS and research programmes in association with Qinghua University	10 million
Multinational companies	GE	Renewable energy	Wind electricity	–
Multinational companies	Dows	Clean energy	Cogeneration	200 million
Multinational companies	French Electricity Trade company	Carbon trading	Clean Development Mechanism	–
Financial institutions	DFJ	Energy efficiency	Grid energy efficiency improvements	20 million
Financial institutions	KPCB	Renewable energy	Solar photovoltaic films and bio-fuels	2,000 million
Financial institutions	Prax Capital	Renewable energy	Solar photovoltaic films	–
Financial institutions	NEP	Renewable energy	Solar photovoltaic films	–
Financial institutions	KWF	Renewable energy	–	–
Financial institutions	Goldman Sachs	Clean energy	Wind electricity	1,000 million
Financial institutions	J. P. Morgan	Climate change	–	1,000 million

Financial institutions	Morgan Stanley	Carbon trading	–	Investment of five year plan and 3 billion
Financial institutions	HSBC	Climate change	–	100 million
Financial institutions	City Capital	Climate change	–	–
Financial institutions	ABN AMRO	Financial products	ABN AMRO climate change and environmental index	–
Financial institutions	Schroeders	Financial products	Global climate change equity fund	–
Domestic companies	Huaneng Group	Clean energy and energy efficiency	Green coal electricity	Yuan 7,400 million besides several billion dollars for efficiency
Domestic companies	Huadian Group	–	–	–
Domestic companies	China Electricity Investment Corporation	Renewable energy	–	Yuan 2,400 to 3,000 million
Domestic companies	Longyuan Electricity	Renewable energy	Wind electricity	–
Domestic companies	Datang Group	Renewable energy	–	–
Domestic companies	State Electricity Grid	Renewable energy	Wind electricity and biomass power generation	Yuan 1,300 million for biomass and Yuan 4,600 million for wind electricity
Domestic companies	PetroChina	Renewable energy	Bio-fuels and biochemical acetic acid	–
Domestic companies	Sinopec	Renewable energy	–	–
Domestic companies	CNOOC	Renewable energy	–	–
Domestic companies	Shenhua Group	Renewable energy	Coal chemical	Yuan 80,000 million

Domestic companies	Changjiang Power	Renewable energy	Hydroelectricity	–
Domestic companies	Guangdong Nuclear Power Group	Clean energy	Nuclear electricity	–
Domestic companies	COFCO	Renewable energy	Bio-fuels and biochemical acetic acid	Plans to spend several billion Yuan in the forthcoming plan
Domestic companies	National Development Bank	Energy efficiency	–	Yuan 10,000 million
Domestic companies	ICBC	Energy efficiency	–	–
Domestic companies	Bank of Beijing	Energy efficiency	–	–
Private capital	Originating from Guangdong, Zhejiang, Fujian, etc.	–	–	Yuan hundred billion estimate

Source: Yin Yue and Wu Changhua (n.a: 29).

China's energy investment bifurcates into two aspects: investment in energy saving products and technology and clean energy. Energy conservation is required in high consumption areas like construction, infrastructure and lighting as well as metallurgy, iron and steel, chemical industry, etc. NDRC Chief Ma Kai reviews that during the Eleventh Five Year Plan China's energy conservation market expanded from Yuan 1,000 billion to 1,500 billion (Yin and Wu, n.a: 28-29). By 2006, China's renewable energy market had earned an income of 6,900 million dollars, and which is estimated to reach 17,900 million dollars by the first quarter of 2013 (Ibid). There was a time when China's only investor was the government, however in the wake of increasing globalisation and rise of transnational corporations China has a huge lobby of investors to bank upon (See Table 5.3).. The pluralisation of energy investors in China can be judged from the above table where it shows that China is no longer limited to government directed public finance, nationally strategised loan or credit facility, international investment institutions, etc (See Table 5.3). While private capital is fast becoming a force to reckon with, investments from international institutions like World Bank, IFC, etc., also cannot be taken lightly. Currently China's investment can be divided into two categories: hard investment and soft investment. Hard investment involves projects related to exploration of renewable and new energy resources as well as process and technologies related to energy conservation. Soft investment works in capacity building and researching on frameworks of strategy formulation (The above section is based on Yin and Wu, n.a.: 28-29).

Market Risks

The blitzkrieg rise of China's energy market can render anybody speechless (Yin and Wu, n.a.:28-29). They believe that favourable international environment should not be given all credit for stable development of China's energy markets. Domestic policies like those related to macroeconomic adjustment and development of energy industry as well as an exhaustive energy legislative system are also equally responsible for evoking international interest in the country's domestic energy market. Moreover enormous profits earned by domestic companies have also acted as a catalyst to attract global attention. While loosening one's purse strings in China is not extravagance, one cannot insulate energy markets from the vagaries of financial risks even if it is interspersed with socialist ideologies and communist politics. Yin and Wu (n.a.) highlight some of such kind of risks in their paper:

- *Different energies, different territories*: Hydro and nuclear power have always received the benign attention of both the central and the local governments and have almost reached the saturation point of their development. While wind and solar energies are the new buzzwords in China, they have their own natural limitations utilising regional advantages only. Bio-fuels and coal chemicals also do not have a happy audience as they compromise on the air quality, something which they are already reeling under. Thus it neither has the policy backing nor investor confidence (Ibid).
- *Gap between market needs and real investment*: It has been felt that the current investment rate is grossly inadequate to meet the market needs. In fact many Chinese call it the phenomenon of *bei shui che xin* (literally translated as trying to put out a burning cartload of wood with a cup of water) (Yin and Wu, n.a.: 28-29). Despite numerous national and international investment channels market investment in China's domestic energy sector can at best be described a "pittance." The energy market is currently plagued with the questions of how to reduce the gap, how to create effective financial programmes while at the same time protecting and constructing a market with "Chinese Characteristics," how to utilise the investment better, etc. Yet given the complex domestic

conditions and a relatively inexperienced market how well China can address these questions is for time to tell (Ibid).

- *Market misunderstandings*: The headiness of "economic growth" is a smokescreen hiding away the stark realities of the market. A few domestic companies seemed to be too embroiled in the mirth of "making hay while the sun shines," not even attempting to understand the market they are investing in. This is especially true of those investors who are engaging in CDM projects. On the surface the CDM market is an investor's paradise since it has few players and huge profits in its kitty. In such a situation rumours spread fast and are difficult to dissipate. Moreover since it is a relatively new and unexplored field, lack of experience and over-excitement has made its foundations shaky which can not only bring losses to the players involved but also crumble the whole market (Yin and Wu, n.a.: 28-29).

China is currently under a lot of international pressure, especially when news of "overheating of economy" and "depleting reserves" are buzzing in the media. Has the "China bubble" exploded, or is it the founder of a new vibrant Third World, can at best be answered if the government works in consonance with others' experience and its own basic instincts to avoid capsizing its over-endowed ship.

Technology Development and Energy Intensity

The contribution of technology in the energy sector is primarily adjudged by analysing its capacity in reducing energy intensity. However technology does not produce the same result for all industries. The period of the last decade of the twentieth century and early twenty-first century was the golden period for China in terms of its growth of power and prestige in the international arena. While China became a personification for economic prowess, it had also lost its advantage of being an exporter of energy. An ardent supporter of "self-reliance" China now had to travel on "unknown paths" for its "economic food." The table given below analyses the role played by technology in affecting the energy intensity of various industries of China. It was observed that with rapid advancement of technology in the industrial sector, energy intensity of major industries and the industrial sector as a whole declined during the phase of 1994 to 2005 (Wang and He, 2009:157-159). Estimates reveal that advanced technology can be credited with 85 per cent of energy intensity reduction during the period (Ibid). In this context the technological progress and innovation in high energy consuming areas was the biggest contributor of reduction in energy intensity. In contrast the contribution of industries producing residential consumption products was a mere 18.9 per cent (Ibid). Given the backdrop of rising living standards for most Chinese, reasons for reduction in energy intensity of residential consumption industries is less because of declining production but more because of shift from utilisation of coal to other fossil fuels like oil and gas (which are more efficient than coal) as well as using advanced technology in production of consumption goods (Ibid). Technology has helped in greater plurality of consumer products giving the consumer more scope to adopt energy saving products. While all this has had a positive contribution in reducing energy intensity of consumer industries, it has been increasingly felt that sagging innovation has made consumer industries reach their saturation point (Ibid). Also increasing sales of high energy consumption products during the period from 1994 to 2005, such as air conditioners, neutralises the effect of all energy saving done in other consumption products (Ibid).

Table 5.4: Effect of Technology on Energy Intensity

Industry	Energy intensity in 1994	Energy intensity in 2005	Difference in energy intensity from 1994 to 2005	Contribution of technology	Proportion of technological contribution in changing energy intensity
Industry	6.24	2.07	-4.17	-1.501	0.855
Raw chemicals and product manufacturing	21.25	4.84	-16.41	-0.339	0.193
Ferrous metal smelting and rolling processing industry	12.36	5.88	-6.48	-0.201	0.114
Non-metallic mineral products industry	13.86	6.34	-7.52	-0.143	0.082
Steam and hot water production and hot water electricity	7.35	2.61	-4.74	-0.113	0.064
Coal mining	11.35	2.26	-9.09	-0.111	0.063
Oil and gas exploration industry	4.36	0.74	-3.62	-0.075	0.042
Household consumption industry	1.81	0.42	-1.39	-0.331	0.189
Animal husbandry, fisheries, forestry and agriculture	2.06	1.38	-0.68	-0.044	0.025

Trade in wholesale and retail	0.51	0.29	-0.22	-0.042	0.024
Catering industry	0.68	0.42	-0.26	-0.017	0.009
Construction industry	0.48	0.29	-0.19	-0.012	0.007

Source: Wang Junsong and He Canfei (2009:160).

In the above table it has been observed that while technological progress was a positive sign, its contribution in reducing energy intensity has declined steadily since the turn of the century. Moreover while changes in industrial sector decreased energy intensity till 1998, it took a U-turn by contributing to increase in energy intensity since 1998 (Ibid).

> Energy and its consequences for health and the environment are high on the Chinese political agenda. But the hard-headed approach of the country's leaders should give us all pause for thought. China's energy policy will continue to be based around coal, they say, so the question of whether this notoriously filthy fuel can ever be made "clean" is central to the country's development and to the long-term stability of the global climate (Aldhous Peter, 2005: 1152).

Aldhous Peter has practically summed up the general observation of the future of China's energy policies. When coal is discussed it sends reverberations not only as the "fodder for the economy" but also as a poison for ecology and society. Most Chinese whether in government circles or otherwise do not sideline the issues of environment contamination and are serious towards building up the renewable energy sector, yet coal is a "family" product and that too an experienced one and the lure for quadrupling GDP by 2020 is too great to invoke strong measures in restricting coal consumption (Sandklef, 2004:5-9). While the Director General of Energy Research Institute and one of the leading energy analysts to the government, Zhou Dadi considers coal as an issue giving convulsions of paroxysms not only in energy circles but also in terms of human costs, "We understand that coal means not only energy, but also social and environment impacts in the long run," another energy analyst of the same institute, Guo Yuan is unrelenting, "we have to increase coal consumption, it's not a good picture but we have to do it" (Aldhous, 2005). Moreover climbing power demands and frequent blackout cannot go untreated and coal is not just the easiest but also the only option to mitigate if not exterminate the electricity woes of China. Du Minghua, Director of Beijing Research Institute of Coal Chemistry, says that "coal is a solution for all three" satiating China's needs for electricity, liquid fuels and gas (Ibid). Dadi finds a solution in energy efficiency by calling it "technically do-able" as it controls the air quality without mollifying the economic rise (Ibid). Du believes that "technological innovation" could be another way out harping on the importance of coal to liquid technologies to reduce China's demand for crude imports. Experts at Qinghua University Zheng and his team second Du's opinion by exhibiting their experiments of the "syngas city model" which through the process of polygeneration fulfils the task of creating electricity, producing methanol for vehicle fuel and dimethyl ether for domestic cooking and heating (Ibid). Moreover usage of methanol and dimethyl ether also has an ecological value as it helps to reduce the formation of ozone forming compounds which are one of the biggest air pollutants responsible for China's air quality (Ibid). However the application of all these "out of the box innovations" are limited to willingness of market and investment which transcends boundaries and require large-scale effort by domestic government to mobilise both domestic investors and foreign business partners into sincerely contributing towards the harmony of energy, economy and environment (Ibid). The study of efficiency would be incomplete if energy is viewed in terms of only economic viability or environmental tenacity (Ibid).

Green Trade[1]

Since the reform era the economic growth of China has been export driven. "China produces goods for foreign market and pollution for domestic market" has been the common grief of the Chinese. It has been observed that 20 per cent of sulphur dioxide, COD and 30 per cent of carbon emissions of China are produced for export oriented commodities (Pang Jun et. al., 2011: 25-30). This loss in China does not only mean inferior ecology but also causes unmentioned but colossal economic losses to China. Export brings in the vital foreign exchange required in maintaining the national exchequer yet it is quite an irony that the activity which has put China at the pinnacle of economic growth is also responsible for its economic losses because of additional ecological costs. The reasons for this are discussed below. The first and foremost reason is that China's export-import trade structure suffers from the duel plague of "four kinds of poverty" and "four kinds of proserity plenty" (Pang Jun et. al., 2011: 25-30). One is energy consumption which causes either more pollution (if energy consumption is more) or less exports (if energy consumption is less) (Ibid). Another is if traditional exports are high then export of new commodities is low, similarly if the merchandise export is up then the services trade goes down (Ibid). Speaking in concrete terms the bulk of China's exports have traditionally been those commodities

1. The section is adapted from (Pang Jun et. al., 2011: 25-30)

which consume a lot of energy and create a lot of pollution and do not attract a lot of funds like fabric and leather goods, chemicals, food and agricultural products, etc. China's major expertise is in assembling and processing of high-technology products like computers, laptops, etc.(Ibid) On the other hand China imports services or high technology which neither cause pollution nor cause ecological loss both to the countries of production or consumption. China has speedily surpassed the US to become the largest trading partner with major countries. Yet, while it holds the first position in manufacturing items, it holds a dismal fourth position in trade of services (2010 figures) (Ibid). As China proceeds towards macroeconomic adjustments, the trade structure is bound to get affected, yet its EXIM structure requires major basic reforms and not just mere adjustments to support the cause of "green GDP" enunciated in the Twelfth Five Year Plan (Ibid).

Secondly energy efficiency of commodities produced for export is extremely low (Ibid). It has been already highlighted that exports are pollution producing agents (Ibid). Let us take the example of fabric item which is a major export item in the itinerary of China. In order to produce 100 metres of cotton cloth an average of 3.5 tonnes of water and 55 kilograms of coal are consumed. While producing, it releases 3.3 tonnes of water as waste and releases 2,000 grammes of COD and 600 grammes of BOD. Combining even 40 manufacturing units the amount of waste water released becomes 1,530 million tonnes. Interestingly, while China ranks fifth in cotton export it ranks fourth in COD emissions (Ibid).

The third reason is rising quantity of exports. On average China's exports rise by 20-30 per cent every year (Ibid). This means that the related industries too have a meteoric rise as they are earning windfall profits which are mainly high energy consumption industries (Ibid). During the Tenth Five Year Plan it was observed that exports contributed to 20 per cent increase in sulphur dioxide emissions in China during that period (Ibid). When the year 2008 brought reduced demand along with financial crisis, it gave China an opportunity of realisation to shift its export base on non-polluting commodities as well as focus more on stable domestic demand rather than a flimsy international demand (Ibid).

When China became the "manufacturing hub" of the world, it heavily relied on its copious energy resources and cheap labour. However, now the tables have turned. China has already completed twenty years of being an importer of energy whose appetite is growing voraciously and at the same time it has also lost its advantage of being the nation of cheap labour (Ibid). World Bank already places it among middle-income countries pegging per capita GDP to be more than US$ 4,000 in 2011 (Ibid). Perhaps now is the time not just for another macroeconomic adjustment or policy changes but a major revamping of economic structure which accommodates all the grievances of energy and environment. Obviously, turning away from the advantage of traditional exports would not be a major decision yet could reap long-term advantages if practised. Moreover, standing as one of the largest trading partners, China's trade after the financial crisis is repeatedly encountering the limitations of trade through various measures like anti-dumping, anti-subsidy, safeguard mechanisms, special safeguard mechanism, commodity recall, etc. In fact China has been facing the anti-dumping embargo for the last 15 years losing an annual amount of more than 30 billion dollars (Ibid). For example in 2009, China's world trade was approximately 10 per cent while at the same time 40 per cent of anti-dumping cases were also against China alone (Pang Jun et. al., 2011: 25-30). In fact the "double nemesis" of anti-dumping and anti-subsidy duties imposed on China has been a major economic measure made by various countries to contain China's expanding economy (Ibid). It can be observed that China's economic tussles with its other trading partners are getting wider day by day and International Trade Centre of the Commerce Ministry of China has rightly observed that China may not find any takers for its produce by the next international finance crisis. Adding to this problem is the international pressure to appreciate the Yuan due to continuation of surplus foreign exchange and favourable economic trade with most countries (Ibid).

The main aim of adopting a "green trade strategy" has been to dispel the effect of deficit between trade and environment and instal a favourable trading environment. The structure holds strategy spread for twenty years to realise its aim of green trade. It is called the strategy for speedy transformation, normal transformation and slow transformation. However for the sake of this study we shall only discuss the strategy of speedy transformation which is supposed to materialise by the end of the current five year plan. In this strategy it has been targeted that by the end of the Twelfth Five Year Plan, i.e., by 2015, there should be a perfect balance between foreign trade and environment which means that China needs to cut down at least 20 per cent of its emissions every year (Pang Jun et. al., 2011: 25-30). For this it not only needs to achieve its targeted quota of energy conservation measures but also adopt extensive economic measures like imposing carbon duties, sulphur duties, etc. One also needs to stop the active encouragement given to the strategy of universal export duty drawbacks as well as impose a 10 per cent and above environment customs duties on major polluting industries(Pang Jun et. al., 2011: 25-30). Eight major industries have been identified under this strategy, namely, coking industry, metal smelting, metal mining industry, oil and nuclear fuel processing industry, non-metallic mining and production industry, coal exploration and washeries industry, chemical industry and oil exploration industry. It is estimated that if these industries are able to reduce their exports in the range of 18-23 per cent while other industries fill the gap, the government will be able to achieve its targeted reduction of emissions as well as achieve its balance between economy and environment during the Twelfth Plan period (Pang Jun et. al., 2011: 25-30). The below table gives an insight into projected changes in export structure of China's major economic sector before the start (2010) and after the end (2015) of the Twelfth Five Year Plan (2011-2015).

Table 5.5: Changes in Export in Various Sectors of China around the Period of Twelfth Five Year Plan

Sector	Rate of change in export in 2010 (per cent)	Rate of change in export in 2015 (per cent)
Agriculture	-0.086	1.966
Coal exploration and washeries industry	-10.369	-20.914
Oil exploration industry	-7.993	-18.300
Metallic mining industry	-12.454	-19.796
Non-metallic mining industry	0.027	-0.115
Food manufacturing and tobacco processing industry	-0.020	2.246
Textile industry	-0.011	1.444
Manufacturing of garments, leather and woollen industry	-0.038	1.763
Wood processing and furniture industry	-0.068	0.025
Industry related to paper, printing and materials related to culture and education	0.015	1.326
Oil processing and processing of nuclear fuel industry	-12.365	-21.933
Smelting industry	-13.623	-23.134
Chemical industry	-10.352	-20.288
Industry of mining and manufacturing of non-metals	-11.590	-22.086
Metal smelting and mining industry	-12.594	-22.451
Industry of metallic products	-0.019	-2.548
General and special manufacturing	-0.117	0.766
Manufacturing industry of transport and its related equipment	-0.061	1.004

Electrical, machinery and related equipments manufacturing industry	-0.022	0.436
Industry of communications equipment, computers and other electronic equipment	-0.042	0.709
Manufacturing of measuring instruments and other office machinery	-0.033	0.698
Industry related to manufacturing of other products	0.033	0.335
Public administration and social organisation	-0.133	0.222
Industry related to production and supply of heat and electricity	0.091	-0.052
Hydroelectricity	0.321	0.297
Industry related to production and supply of gas	0.143	0.306
Industry related to production and supply of other fuels	0.0000	0.00
Industry of production and supply of water	0	0
Construction industry	-0.083	-0.527
Industry of transportation and warehousing	0.017	-0.467

Source: Pang Jun et. al. (2011:25-30).

From the above table it can be seen that China's export would now contain more of perishable commodities (especially agriculture and textile industry) rather than durable items. Given the condition that perishable items have less cost than durable items, should we then conclude that China is going back to the position of backward economies who import high technologies in exchange of vegetables and fruits? The effect of this strategy was studied on the rate of exchange of various macroeconomic indicators like GDP, overall imports and overall exports. It has been seen that while imports are rising and exports are declining, yet GDP continues to rise (Ibid). This rise in GDP has been attributed to factors like technological progress.[2] On a cursory glance of the given below table one can see that while there is a significant decline in exports, there is less decline in imports. The authors attribute the reasons for this to the short span of time where production sags down due to changes in resource and labour base as they adopt cleaner technologies of production (Ibid). However another reason could also be that the industries begin to focus more on the demand and requirements of the domestic market rather than the foreign markets (Pang Jun et. al., 2011: 25-30).

2. The authors have derived the above calculations based on the CGE model.

Table 5.6: Changes in Economic Indicators of Various Sectors of China around the Period of Twelfth Five Year Plan

Economic indicator	Rate of change in 2010 (per cent)	Rate of change in 2015 (per cent)
GDP	-0.039	0.130
Total imports	-0.010	-0.001
Total exports	-1.371	-1.740

Source: Pang Jun et. al. (2011).

Figure 5.4: The Impact of Conservation Efforts of 1977

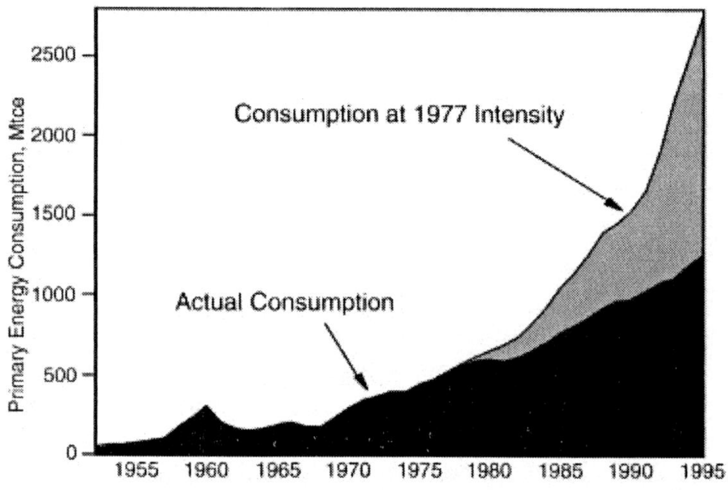

Source: Sinton et. al. (1998).

The above figure reveals that if China had persisted with its energy intensity levels of 1977, then it would have perhaps wolfed down 2.2 times more energy than it actually consumed by 1996 (Sinton et. al., 1998).

However, not always "well begun is half done" and China needs to work extensively but patiently in stabilising its economic growth rates, optimising industrial structure, regulating domestic structure petroleum exploitation and improving transport efficiency to achieve energy security, or if not, then at least deceive the future into delaying the impending loom of an energy catastrophe (Chen and Lin, 2008: 1666-1678).

However it can be an issue of debate that has the economy and environment always been in conflicting positions, especially when energy conservation was introduced as early as 1981. For a country which rode on the back of double-digit growth, market reforms and "opening up" is it really impossible to implement a solution which caters to requirements of both without sacrificing one at the cost of the other. A deeper analysis reveals that for "the manufacturing hub of the world," the market for building solar photovoltaic panels hold a plethora of opportunities and the government has become increasingly interested in boosting this sector by introducing various incentives and subsidies (Andrew, 2013). However, unfortunately the government has maintained the fulcrum of its market only to fuel its coffers for export purposes only. This dichotomy has made the domestic air quality suffer heavily which has paid for the production of such products without enjoying the benefits of any (Ibid). Yet the Clean Technica Director, Zachary Shahan believes that changes are evident in the domestic landscape also (Ibid). This was also driven by economic motives as a huge glut has emerged in the solar cell market and global prices have plummeted (Ibid). This also came at a time when China has expanded its target of solar power capacity from 5 gigawatts to 40 gigawatts by 2015 (Andrew, 2013). In reference to the latest Twelfth Five Year Plan which has been touted as the "greenest plan ever" a consulting firm Solidiance released its own white paper on January 8, 2013 to "demonstrate the challenges and opportunities faced by the renewable energy sector in China." The White Paper titled "China's Renewable Energy Sector: An Overview of Key Growth Sectors" begins by an assumption that the strategies of the Chinese government are solely responsible for the phenomenal industrial growth in China and this is also true for "the continued interest in renewable energy sector in China." (Solidiance Report, 2013) It identifies three main reasons for the government's focus on renewable energy sector:

> The three key drivers behind the continued interest in renewable energy in China are China's increasing demand for electricity, China's need to reduce its reliance on coal for energy production and China's need to reduce its green house its greenhouse gas emissions (Solidiance report, 2013: 4).

Liu Mingliang of China Wind Energy Association also reiterates the same thoughts citing evidence in rising public awareness about changing climate situation and rising greenhouse gas emissions. "More and more people opt for green travel or low-carbon lifestyles and the public media has been increasing its coverage and publicity of the development of low carbon technology and renewable energy" (Andrew, 2013). The report claims that China in order to retain its position as the leader of the manufacturing sector is increasingly getting attracted to technologies of sustainable development and is "investing in moving Chinese manufactures away from low-cost manufacturing and higher up the value chain into greater value-added activities." (Andrew, 2013) The "industrial revolution" of China can now no longer be happy satisfying the growth parameter only but has to get more innovative in gaining brownie points from the sustainable energy sector also (Ibid).

The 2006 Renewable Energy Law has provisions of covering up the cost of renewable energy technologies by forcing the grid operators to buy their product and by taxing the end consumers with an additional surcharge (*Solidiance Report*, 2013: 14). This surcharge has been 100 per cent since December 2011, enhanced from Yuan 0.04 per kilowatt-hour to Yuan 0.08 per kilowatt-hour. This has created a subsidy fund of Yuan 50 billion which, says the *Solidiance Report* (2013:14), "is used to further develop the use of renewable energy in China."

Figure 5.5: China's Installed Wind Power Capacity

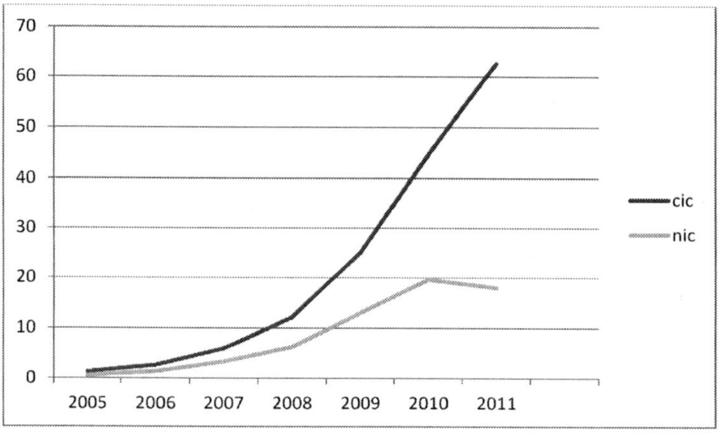

Units: Cumulative Installed Capacity=cic, Newly Installed Capacity=nic
Source: Andrew 2013

Figure 5.6: China's Installed Solar Power Capacity

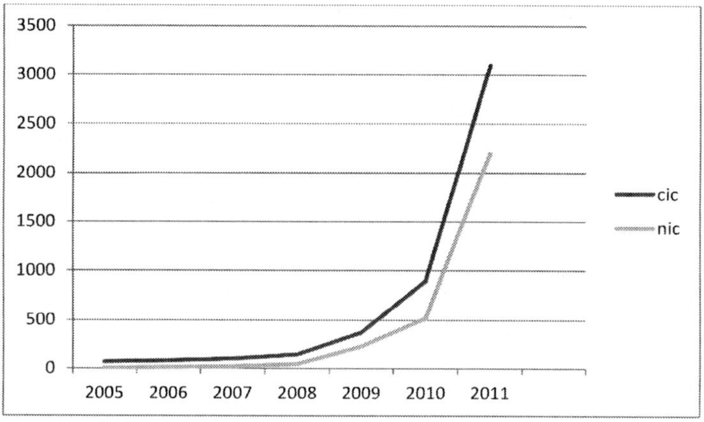

Units: Cumulative Installed Capacity=cic, Newly Installed Capacity=nic
Source: Andrew (January 2013).

The above figures reveal that while investment in the wind sector has seen a gradual increase dipping only in recent years, the solar industry has seen a steep jump in installed capacity especially since 2009. The latest five year plan is testimony to the fact that now even China's economy is showing increasing linkages with the concept of "sustainability." However the analysts at Solidiance believe that the government's exuberance is dimmed by its lack of knowledge and systematic approach towards development of the renewable industry and also the lack of a support structure of industries (Andrew, 2013). Perhaps coordination would have reaped richer dividends than cohesion by the government. After the excessive publicising of aiming for a "green GDP" by the Twelfth Five Year Plan, it has become very natural for organisations focusing on China to lay stress on its renewable sector and the government approach towards each of the cleaner fuels in the recent past decades (Andrew, 2013). Organisations across the globe believe that both the hydro and the wind industry which are already well established in the domestic sphere of China are already past their days of glory as locations of hydropower and distribution channels of wind power are steadily getting fewer and chances of recovery are dim, though not completely extinguished (Ibid). Perhaps the most promising star in the horizon of renewables is the solar industry which is upbeat with receiving the most product innovations and the most generous investments in its industry (Ibid). The bio-fuel industry though at its nascent stage could also be seen carving its own niche in China's economic and technical landscape (Ibid). In fact *China*

Briefing in one of its post dated June 16, 2011 has dubbed China's renewable energy development plan as a "long-term domestic diversification and self-sufficiency strategy." The backing and inspiration of the Twelfth Five Year Plan to maintain the "non-fossil fuel energy production" above 11 per cent and reduction of carbon dioxide emissions by 2015 has been touted as the biggest evidence for accentuation of such a belief (Ibid). Given below is the summation of reduction goals of NDRC across China in accordance with varied capacities and requirements of different provinces (China Briefing, 2011).

Figure and Table 5.7: Reduction Goals of NDRC (province wise)

Reduction goal (per cent)	Targeted province
18	Liaoning, Beijing, Tianjin, Hebei, Shandong, Jiangsu, Shanghai, Zhejiang, Guangdong
17	Heilongjiang, Jilin, Shanxi, Shaanxi, Henan, Anhui, Jiangxi, Fujian, Hunan, Hubei, Henan, Chongqing, Sichuan
16	Guangxi Zhuang Autonomous Region, Yunan, Guizhou, Inner Mongolia Autonomus Region, Ningxia Hui Autonomous Region, Gansu,
15	Hainan, Taiwan, Tibet Autonomous Region, Xinjiang Uyghur Autonomus region, Qinghai

Source: *China Briefing* (June 16, 2011).

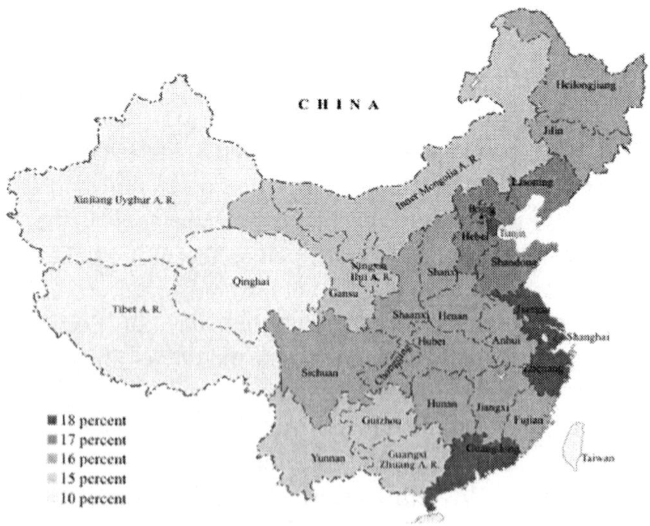

Source: China Briefing 2011

One thought that continues to stay in the backdrop of all the policies, targets and five year plans is that while China is ready to adopt all methods and measures to make itself more energy efficient and sustainable, it is no mood to scale down its consumption levels at any cost (Swartz and Oster, 2010). Obviously, in a country where the biggest consumer of energy is "development" and not merely "utilisation" and where the political system runs and survives on the planks of "rising living standards," it would be suicidal for the government to lower its energy consumption rates which would naturally mean taking a regressive development path (Swartz and Oster, 2010). David Pumphrey, a senior analyst at the Centre for Strategic and Political Studies, opines that "China can now demand a large space inside not just its own but any energy policy tent" (Swartz and Oster, 2010). However it is predicted that like many other developed nations, China's energy requirements would also peak (Ibid). Currently China's investment in energy is in the field of infrastructure and heavy industries whose maturation age is peaking and soon would not require as much of energy as it consumes today (Ibid). While it can be doubted that rising income and living standards could also make the nouveau riche Chinese follow the path of its American brethren in terms of enhanced per capita consumption, it can also be hoped that with an excruciating focus on energy conservation and efficiency by the Chinese government the situation of stabilising the energy needs of China might not be a dream of a distant time but a reality of the immediate future (Ibid).

Table 5.8: Evaluation of Regional Energy Economic Efficiency and Energy Environment Efficiency

Area	Rate of Energy efficiency	Rate of energy economic efficiency	Rate of energy environment efficiency
Beijing	1.000	1.000	0.234
Tianjin	1.000	1.000	0.466
Hebei	0.933	0.933	0.032
Shanxi	0.823	0.823	0.029
Neimenggu	0.879	0.879	0.138
Liaoning	0.796	0.796	0.055
Jilin	0.724	0.722	0.198
Heilongjiang	0.942	0.942	0.129
Shanghai	1.000	1.000	0.191
Jiangsu	0.970	0.970	0.037

Zhejiang	1.000	1.000	0.061
Anhui	0.874	0.874	0.125
Fujian	1.000	1.000	0.130
Jiangxi	1.000	1.000	0.201
Shandong	0.876	0.876	0.025
Henan	1.000	1.000	0.037
Hubei	0.790	0.790	0.081
Hunan	0.868	0.868	0.059
Guangdong	0.999	0.999	0.034
Guangxi	1.000	1.000	0.136
Hainan	1.000	0.940	1.000
Chongqing	0.928	0.894	0.233
Sichuan	0.714	0.714	0.049
Guizhou	0.780	0.705	0.243
Yunnan	0.795	0.755	0.188
Shaanxi	0.746	0.746	0.137
Gansu	0.732	0.667	0.291
Qinghai	1.000	0.648	1.000
Ningxia	0.934	0.642	0.863
Xinjiang	0.922	0.893	0.243

Source: Wu and Wu (2009:108-09).

The above table bifurcates energy efficiency in terms of economic and environmental efficiency. It has been seen that energy economic efficiency is higher in areas of Beijing, Tianjin, Shanghai, Zhejiang, Fujian, Jiangxi, Henan, Guangxi while environmental energy efficiency is higher in areas of Hainan, Ningxia and Qinghai. In fact it has been observed that, with a few exceptions, most provinces have a higher energy economic efficiency than environmental efficiency. This reflects the status of investment as most provinces have strived to extract economic value out of energy resources neglecting their environmental impacts (Wu and Wu, 2009:109). However as the nation begins to calculate the economic costs of environmental atrocities, energy conservation has attracted investors which they view now more as an economic tool than an environmental charity (Ibid). It is widely believed that advancement of technology and adjustments in industrial structure are the major causes of energy efficiency, however analysts have seen that administrative regional patents and the tertiary sector are more influencing aspects in determining energy efficiency of a region in China (Wu and Wu, 2009: 109).

Table 5.9: Evaluation of Regional Energy Efficiency on Technical Terms

Area	Energy efficiency	Pure technical efficiency
Beijing	1.000	1.000
Tianjin	1.000	1.000
Hebei	0.933	0.981
Shanxi	0.823	0.840
Neimenggu	0.879	0.885
Liaoning	0.796	0.855
Jilin	0.724	0.732
Heilongjiang	0.942	0.942
Shanghai	1.000	1.000
Jiangsu	0.970	1.000
Zhejiang	1.000	1.000
Anhui	0.874	0.894
Fujian	1.000	1.000
Jiangxi	1.000	1.000
Shandong	0.876	1.000
Henan	1.000	1.000
Hubei	0.790	0.792
Hunan	0.868	0.870
Guangdong	0.999	1.000
Guangxi	1.000	1.000
Hainan	1.000	1.000
Chongqing	0.928	0.938
Sichuan	0.714	0.717
Guizhou	0.780	0.803
Yunan	0.795	0.799
Shaanxi	0.746	0.749
Gansu	0.732	0.743
Qinghai	1.000	1.000
Ningxia	0.934	0.958
Xinjiang	0.922	0.941

Source: (Wu and Wu, 2009: 108).

The above table has identified energy efficiency based on the variables of income, technology and productive efficiency. It has been seen that economically well-developed areas like Beijing, Tianjin, Shanghai,

Zhejiang, Fujian, Jiangxi, Guangxi, Hainan not only utilise technology to the optimum but have also managed to attain high levels of energy efficiency thanks to a sound economic base. Perhaps the only exception in this case is the region of Qinghai which although economically less developed has managed to attain high levels of energy efficiency due to its focus on the renewable sector (Wu and Wu, 2009). In fact regional differences in energy economics and environmental efficiency has stemmed from differences in energy production and consumption. This has happened because national policies and regional strategies are formulated from completely different viewpoints. For regional strategies energy is not a holistic bundle of resources but only which is in their possession. Hence while for areas like Shanxi and Inner Mongolia coal is energy, Heilongjiang and Liaoning consider oil as energy, gas is energy for Sichuan and Chongqing, etc., while hydroelectricity for Xi'an and Hubei (Wu and Wu, 2009:109). More importantly, fossil fuels carry a unique trend of not being consumed where they are produced which means that they are "the energy" not just for their producing provinces but also consuming provinces (Wu and Wu, 2009:110). Since regional strategies are also the ones which are mostly implemented verbatim, it can also be said that they give a better glimpse of the inside situation of China than the national level policies (Wu and Wu, 2009:110). However this is not to undermine the central policies or elevate the stature of regional policies as regional strategies are derived from the targets and provisions of national policies. When fossil fuels are discussed transportation costs become an alienable factor in the supply spectrum, and this is especially true in provincial analysis where fossil fuels are consumed more in their deficiency area than production areas (Ibid). This happens because of lack of infrastructure and economic development as well as tendency to earn more from intra-regional trade than investing in economic and social infrastructure which carry a long gestation period and which are essentially done at the behest and fund of the central government (Ibid).

Figure 5.8: Renewable Electricity Generation of China

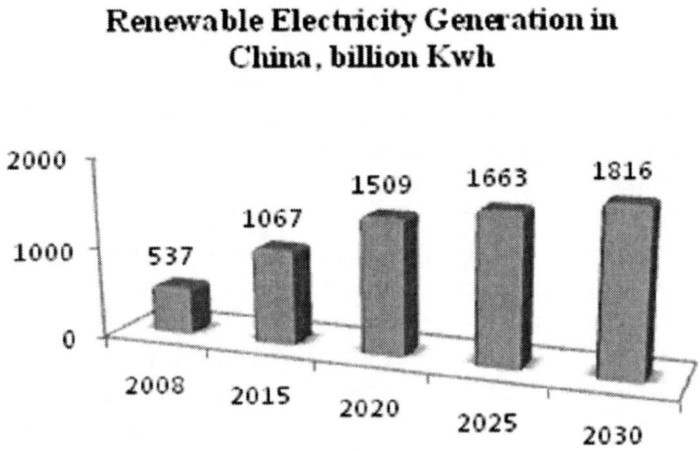

Source: Business Vibes (2012).

The above figure describes the renewable electricity generation of China from the period of 2008 to the projected estimates of 2030. The hopeful projected future forecast by various organisations and institutions is possible only if its seeds are sown now in the present times. Notwithstanding the political or economic pressure, the Energy Research Institute (ERI) working under the aegis of NDRC has time and again highlighted the importance of non-fossil fuels and has recommended the dire need for establishment of an independent energy ministry or granting ministerial status to national energy administration (*China Energy Viewpoint,* 2012a). The latest such suggestion was made was in 2012 when it released a report on "China Energy Policy" (*China Energy Viewpoint*, 2012a). It has also analysed that China's passion for maintaining self-sufficiency in coal is bordering on paranoia as it incurs huge expenditure on transportation costs within the confines of the geographical boundary from coal rich areas of northwest China to the industrialised areas of south-east China (Ibid). The report recommends that in such a case it would be more profitable if China resorts to import substitution rather than harping on self-sufficiency. (Ibid) ERI also believes that import of coal and gas could also be used by the government as a method to force state-owned enterprises to engage in better efficiency and enforcement of cost-effective measures in their enterprises while at the same time helping the government to leverage higher prices on companies and have a bigger share in their profits (Ibid). The report is also vehemently against the transport of electricity using ultra high voltage (UHV) transmission lines which it believes is both expensive and risky (Ibid). Interestingly, the vociferousness of the ERI report (especially about electricity) is in sharp contrast to the state grid strategy where the UHV lines are highlighted as a major contributor to China's development while maintaining its ideal of self-sufficiency (Ibid). Although, while focusing on non-fossil fuels, the ERI has recommendations only for the wind and the solar industries (which are located only in the northern and northwest part of China), it has shown where the political future of China's energy policies lies (Ibid). No wonder, then, while the two biggest economies (U.S and China) are on competing terms with each other on almost every issue, they are very willing to collaborate and help each other in meeting renewable energy goals. Chinese Academy of Sciences (CAS) and Chinese Academy of Engineering (CAE) have conducted joint researches with US National Academies to devise innovations and effective measures in achieving a speedier and a more economical strategy to attain renewable energy goals (National Academy of Engineering et. al., 2010).

In any case China has been topping the charts consecutively for the last four years in being the largest wind market of the world (in terms of annual installed capacity) yet these indicators also have a flip side when it is shown that 20 per cent of the installed capacity is still unconnected to the grid (Bloomberg New Energy Finance, 2013). Moreover, capacity factors (which determine system efficiency) are merely 21.6 per cent and these are just official figures released by the state electricity regulatory commission (Ibid). This is one of the lowest rates in the world, while the capacity factors[3] of wind farms in the US is 30 per cent which means that with every megawatt of wind capacity installed the Chinese productivity of energy is 30 per cent less than that of the USA (Bloomberg New Energy Finance, 2013). However it is also true that all wind turbine suppliers in China are domestic and the prices are also 40 per cent lower than in the USA (Ibid). The largest suppliers are:

Table 5.10: Installed Capacities and Market Share of Various Domestic Renewable Industries

Supplier	Installed capacity (gigawatts)	Market share (per cent)
Goldwind	2.8	19
Guodian United Power	1.9	13
Sinovel	1.5	10

Source: Bloomberg New Energy Finance (February 2013).

3. Capacity factor refers to the total amount of energy produced by a plant in a given amount of time divided by the amount of energy the plant would have produced in full capacity

Similarly the areas which received the most number of wind projects were Inner Mongolia (1.7 gigawatts of new capacity), Shandong (1.4 gigawatts of new capacity) and Hebei (1.1 gigawatts of new capacity) and the top main companies associated with these projects were Longyuan Power Group, Huaneng renewable and Datang renewable sector (Ibid). Demi Zhu, China Wind Analyst of Bloomberg New Energy Finance, argues that China's wind industry is doing exceptionally well despite market bottlenecks created by the grid operators, unpaid subsidies, stringent permitting norms and a general tendency of the local officials to believe that the wind industry of China is "overheating" and needs a "cooling off" period like the general market economy (Ibid). "The fact that China's wind sector overtook nuclear as a generation source even in its most challenging year of recent times is a testament to the massive scale and momentum of the industry in this country," believes Zhu (Ibid). Bloomberg (2013) has predicted that China's wind industry, which has targeted to achieve 100 GW of grid connectivity by 2015, would be able to achieve it much earlier (perhaps even a year). However, how much of the government's interference or cooperation will it receive is still uncertain.

On the other hand the solar industry of China receives the maximum affection of the government and the state-owned financial institutions. The generous loans, received from the China Development Bank has helped the solar manufacturing sector evolve from a random group of companies to a strong institutional organisation (*Big Think*, 2011). The editors of the online website, *Big Think* (2011) contend that "the Chinese strategy is to engage in predatory financing and they are trying to drive everybody else out of the market."

The nuclear energy had its boom during the era of the 1960s when within the period of thirty-two months it had developed nuclear weapons, tested its first atomic bomb, exploded its first hydrogen bomb and launched its first nuclear missile (Gangadar Divya, 2012). Its thirteen functional nuclear reactors produce two per cent of the total power output (Ibid). This figure is expected to rise significantly in the coming years (Gangadar Divya, 2012). The Twelfth Five Year Plan had geared up for "the last lap of adrenalin rush" to embark on forty nuclear projects, which were squashed down by the Fukushima incident (*China Daily*, 2012). Since then China has been cautious in its approach to construction of new nuclear plants and has decided to launch only a small number by 2015 and that too only in coastal areas (Ibid). The government, in its website, made a claim of undergoing the building of nuclear plants in a "steady and orderly way at a reasonable pace." (Ibid) The year 2012, witnessed the screening of two major programmes regarding nuclear energy: the national plan for nuclear power security (2011-20) and the nuclear power development (2011-20) (Ibid). These programmes were passed by the State Council in an executive meeting passed by Premier Wen Jiabao (Ibid). The issue of meeting international safety standards has been a continuous highlighted theme in all plans and approvals undertaken by the Security Council (Ibid). A new national energy development plan has also been approved which deals with energy strategies until 2015 (Ibid). The director of the Institute of Low Carbon Economy at Qinghua University, He Jiankun agrees that "nuclear energy is irreplaceable as it makes the right balance between the compulsion of having increased volume of energy as well as the duty to cut down on greenhouse emissions." (Ibid).

> China's competitiveness will be compromised if it rejects nuclear power or if it fails to use the latest nuclear technology. The choice of a site for a nuclear power station must be based on thorough scientific research. And there must be adequate assurances that under no circumstances would radioactive leakage occur (He Jiankun, director at Qinghua University, adapted from Lan Lan, *China Daily*, 2012).

Shale gas is another renewable energy viewed with greater prospects in China. Many Chinese intellectuals believe that the declining interests of the US in the Middle East is not merely because of its sagging economy but also because of an evident shift in its economic system from an oil base to a gas base structure (*China Energy Viewpoint*, 2012b). The Twelfth Five Year Plan has also laid special emphasis on the development of shale gas in China and has guidelines for pursuing large-scale production and has aimed for producing 100 billion cubic metres a year (*China Energy Viewpoint*, 2012b). Dependency on gas is a natural solution for all of China's problems as it does not carry the stigma of being dependent on imports (oil), of causing pollution (coal) or carrying a delusional fear of living under the threat of an ecological catastrophe (nuclear energy). Moreover the Ministry of Land and Resources has ratified that China is the largest owner of unconventional gas as it has 25 trillion cubic metres of recoverable gas (*China Energy Viewpoint,* 2012). However all good things come with a price tag and shale gas is no exception, a paper in *China Energy Viewpoint (2012)* titled "Shale Gas—Upsides and Downsides" brings forth the problems associated with shale gas manufacturing. Natural gas retrieved from shale rock is done by a process of hydraulic fracturing. This technique involves pumping of liquids under high pressure into a well to fracture the rock and allow gas to escape from its tiny holes. This kind of technique, although extracting large volumes of gas, also carries some environment potholes, which by time can potentially expand into a cause for a major catastrophe. Some of them are listed below (*China Energy Viewpoint*, 2012).

- Fracturing requires huge amounts of water and hence is not a very practical method for countries like China which are already water starved (Ibid).
- Many times, due to the apathy of government officials, hydraulic fracturing fluid is not treated and is let out in public water bodies containing a large number of hazardous chemicals which contaminate both the land and water (Ibid).
- Also the treatment of wastewater released from hydraulic fracturing is a challenge needing meticulous and professional expertise lacked by government officials (Ibid).
- Sometimes hydraulic fracturing causes the occurrence of small earthquakes which push the wastewater into sub-surfaces. This process when repeated causes the wastewater to pile on leading to occurrence of earthquakes which can cause considerable damage (Ibid).

The best aspect in the situation of the shale gas is that the government is not immune to the flipside of shale gas production and has tried to bring this to the notice of the central government. Pan Jiping from the Ministry of Land and Resources, quoted in *China Daily*, said that "survey and evaluation activity related to China's shale gas reserves which is still at the preliminary stage is a key issue before China goes for commercial production"(Ibid). He further adds that to encourage companies in this sector, support policies and technological advancements should be provided by the government rather than leaving the companies to fend for themselves (Ibid).

The White Paper released by China on Energy Policy in October 2012 is clear about its goals regarding the issue of energy development. "China's energy development must follow a path of high technology content, low consumption of resources, light environmental pollution, sound economic returns, as well as energy security." (White Paper on Energy Security, 2012) It also highlights that the contribution of nuclear energy to electricity grid is a mere 1.8 per cent as compared to the world average of 14 per cent for countries rich in nuclear energy (Ibid). However the white paper is confident that China's stringent security checks can guarantee the safety ambit of its nuclear reactors. It has already introduced a quota where a certain percentage of electricity has to be produced from the renewable sector (Ibid).

China Energy Viewpoint (2012c) believes that the biggest problem with many large countries having traditionally relied on fossil fuels is that the energy supplied by the renewable sector, whether wind or solar, is always considered as a supplement to the main sources of energy rather than themselves being focused on as the main sources of energy. This mental set-up is especially true of China as it holds coal in abundance and has imbibed the policy of "self-sufficiency" right from liberation. Obviously for a sector, which is considered as a 'subsidiary existence' (read the renewable sector) is not often accounted for its business operations (Ibid). Many a time this has obscured the problems of the renewable sector, which are not discussed at the central level or acknowledged in the mainstream media. Even the latest Five Year Plan with renewed emphasis on the renewable energy sector highlights only its benefits and not the costs involved to attain it, maintain it and utilise it. (Ibid) Many a time easy solutions to fluctuations in productions are found by restricting the production partially or completely without delving into the reasons for fluctuations of production or market. This is not done because of lack of concern but because the whole country is too preoccupied with the crisis in thermal fuels and has no time or energy left for vagaries in the market of the renewable sector. This is not true in other developed nations where all energy sources receive equal attention and no one's problems receive a stepmotherly treatment (Ibid). The paper highlights the case of Denmark where good governance has boosted the wind energy of even a geographically small country to draw international acclaim. For China apart from the psychological problems its wind farms are also mired in an unsympathetic market where there are no economic incentives, no flexibility for power producers and no encouragement to first use local or regional power transmission lines. The paper believes that for once China should incorporate the European approach to renewable sectors, such as development of smart grids, system flexibility and integration of renewable resources of energy into its ambit of finding solutions with Chinese characteristics (the above paragragh is based on *China Energy Viewpoint,* 2012c).

China-Learning and Unlearning

"When China sneezes the whole world panics," claimed the China director of the Climate Group, Wu Changhua (Jonathan Watts, 2010). He believes that China's rise is met by conflicting opinions; however, unlike the opinion of the Western intellectuals, he has strong confidence in the ability and more importantly the priority of the decision-makers to digress from this volatile model of development into building a low-carbon economy. He cites China's aggressive plans to build nuclear plants which have triggered a global rise in uranium price to unprecedented levels.

Figure 5.9: Comparative Data Analysis of Energy Consumption of Selected Countries

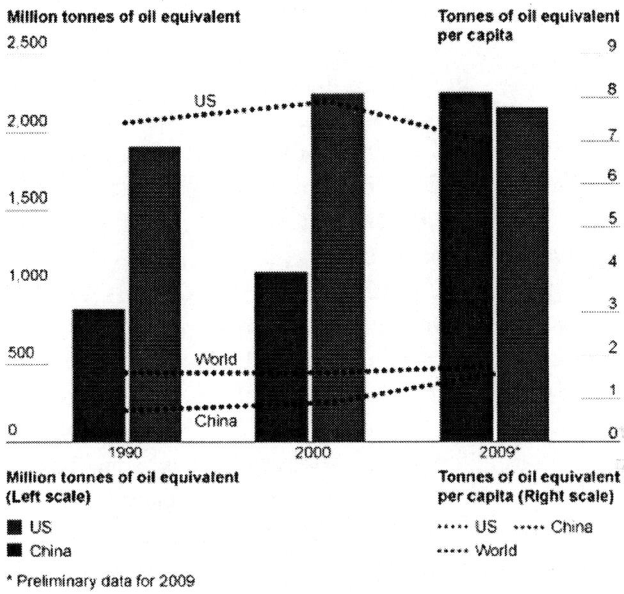

Source: Jonathan Watts (August 2010).

With petrol prices taking a larger than life form and the Middle East going through turbulent political restructuring, China can take a leaf of advice from the experiences of other developed nations. It is said that your enemies can give you the best advice and in a country-wise analysis we shall consider two countries which have historically been China's enemies at worst, and rivals at best (the below section is based on Fan, 2006:80).

- The USA: America was perhaps one of the first nations to acknowledge the issue of an "energy crisis" after its brief stint with the oil shock of the 1970s. Since then it has been vociferously investing in creating one of the largest government crude reserve in the world. This investment has increased manifold especially since the incident of 9/11 and especially around the Mexican coast. America has also slashed down its imports from 25 per cent to 18 per cent (Ibid). Simultaneously the emphasis on conservation and efficiency has also continuously increased. In fact the American government is also exploring the idea of introducing commercialisation of these strategic petroleum reserves to reduce the burden on the government. While China already has a strategic petroleum reserve, its lackadaisical attitude and superfluous investment has just been a fluke and a smokescreen for the government to assuage panic triggers (Ibid).

- Germany: One of the most environment-friendly countries, Germany was the first to find a solution to escalating crude prices and expanding ozone hole. Their investment in renewable energy is a model for other nations. Germany's 10 per cent of electricity is produced from renewable sources and it even exports its wind energy overseas (Ibid). For a country like China, which has a huge potential for wind and solar energy and is eager to embark its future energy structures, taking a cue from the "German model" could be a good guidance (Ibid).
- Japan: Forty years ago Japan imported 99 per cent of its oil supplies (Ibid). However after the oil shocks Japan's GDP reduced its energy consumption to 33 per cent during the period 1973 to 2000 (Ibid). This has happened because Japan's investment in innovation and technological advancement has given it an edge to create the same level of GDP with two-thirds the energy (Ibid). The major advantage of Japan has been that while other countries focused only on energy conservation Japan was perhaps the only nation focusing on pluralistic energy policy. Solar, wind and nuclear energy developed simultaneously though nuclear energy clearly steered the wheel. While the fear of a nuclear disaster looms large it cannot be denied that what Japan achieved during its economic rise did not impose an epidemic on its environment as it did to China (Fan, 2006 : 80).

Conclusion

Energy policies are a reflection of the country's politics, economics and more importantly the ethics of the future energy destiny in China. It is a general perception that China's "growth miracle" has fostered anomalies in its energy and environment paradigms. While this is a substantial cause, it is not the whole story as the regional energy consumption mentioned above reveals that the highest consumption of fossil fuels is made in the western area which is also the most underdeveloped region of China. As the developed east shifts towards the usage of advanced technology and renewable energy, the western sector is still keen on fossil fuel consumption, neutralising the overall progress of renewable consumption. Moreover the provinces of Central China also increase their consumption rates as the "growth miracle" spreads westwards from the east. Hence apart from putting the blame of energy discrepancies totally on the economy one should also consider the effort and will of both the central and the local governments in implementing the provisions of the formulated energy policies. Excessive reliance on a coal directed economy and the subsequent gradual shift into renewable sources does quantify the fact that China invests in that resource in which it sees the future of energy self-sufficiency. While currently the renewable sector is at its nascent stage in China (except the wind sector) due to deficiency of adequate technology, it can also not be denied that China like in other sectors is fast heading towards achieving windfall profits through active capturing of the market.

While it is true that the energy policies have the tall task of synchronising the vested interests of various groups to reflect a holistic development, it also cannot be denied that the interests of the groups are, or can be, altered by the set targets of the energy policies. It has been seen above that with the shifting priority of the energy policies from many financial institutions and fossil fuels, companies have shifted their investment focus to renewable energy. Hence while from a short-term perspective the domestic determinants may seem to be charting the course of energy policies but in a long-term vision the steering is actually in the hands of the government agencies which determine the policies. Moreover the domestic factors, while being at variance with each other due to conflicting laws and duplication of tasks, are also all subtly trying to gain self-sufficiency through their own means. However, whether China can create a shift in its base from a coal driven economy to a renewable based structure and yet retain its well-cherished dream of achieving self-sufficiency is for the future to tell.

> The authoritarian nature of the Chinese state does not mean that the state itself is internally coherent or coordinated. This is all the more true with regard to energy. As a practical matter, the number of actors exercising de facto decision-making power over energy outcomes in China is large, and they are not exclusively confined within China's borders. We should not reflexively invest the actions of even state-owned Chinese energy entities with geostrategic intent. Nor should we assume that China's energy posture at any given time reflects a rational plan or coherent thinking on the part of the political leaders (Lester and Steinfeld, 2007: 39).

Two worlds exist in China: one on paper and one on ground, and each groundwork laid is a different battlefield in itself. Electric power sector in China could be safely termed as the most vibrant one in this aspect. We shall begin with two stories: the government "script" and the "actual truth." On paper, ninety-nine per cent of the local enterprises belong to any of the five main state-owned enterprises (Lester and Steinfeld, 2007:36). An order of hierarchy follows and any decision taken is subject to central authorities at the helm of affairs (Lester and Steinfeld, 2007: 36). This was a smooth journey until now. Now let us come to the pitfalls. Statistics suggest that the power sector in China is much bigger than the figures available in the official register (Ibid). Data reveals that functional (i.e., financed, constructed and operated) "illegal" power plants worth generating capacity of 110 gigawatts (by 2005) exist in China (Lester and Steinfeld, 2007: 36). Herein lies the role of the "director": the local governments. Two motives can be drawn for such actions of the local governments. One is that the metric for efficiency of local governmentrelies almost solely on economic growth; and second, fettered by ideologies of "market reforms" and confusing bureaucratic systems, "entrepreneurial ways" of "getting things done" (including construction and operation of power plants) are soon beginning to be considered as the norm (Lester and Steinfeld, 2007: 36). The "producer" of the movie obviously gets the biggest say—the local officials who dominate the channels of finance: loans from state banks and equity investments from municipal or provincial energy development corporations (Lester and Steinfeld, 2007: 37). Even in the case of state banks the branch officials who extend loans are also dependent on local political support for their career graphs and hence abide by the wishes of local officials more than the orders of the headquarters. Another reason is that comparatively developed provinces like Zhejiang and Guangdong are always power deficit due to their ever burgeoning requirements and hence cannot limit themselves to officially approved power plants (Lester and Steinfeld, 2007: 36). Obviously it is made sure that such plants are not stuck in the rigmarole process of maintaining technical or environmental standards (Ibid). Where does this then place SEPA and its subsidiary local officials, especially at a time when the government is increasingly going in for an exponential green budget every year? With tighter budgets such environmental bureaus are usually left relying on emission fees or charity dole outs from local governments. (Lester and Steinfeld, 2007: 37) In both cases, this means that local environmental bureaus are usually in the hands of big industries who continue to pay and pollute or local governments who shield such industries from environmental bureaus and allow flagrant violations of environmental standards (Ibid). In all this then where does the consumer fit in? Most commercial consumers (read industrial plants) are finding a tailor-made process for this, i.e., turning from energy consumers to energy producers, a kind of self-help, say Lester and Steinfeld (2007). In China a parallel industry of diesel-operated generators runs and is perhaps the biggest contributor to the economy after the fluctuating public power supply (Ibid). China faces a "Catch-22" situation where it is blamed both for increasing the volume of pollution in the global air space and also escalating the prices of cleaner fuels and technology by excessive imports from abroad (Ibid). Such inconsistency of logic exists not just outside but also inside China. Many municipalities are in favour of building speedy coal plants with inferior quality and lack of environmental standards rather than investing in clean coal projects which involve construction of infrastructure on a larger scale, sometimes even beyond the geographical purview (Ibid). Even the developed areas like Shanghai, Guangdong and Zhejiang, who are always struggling with the power deficit, are walking en route to constructing liquefied natural gas (LNG infrastructures) rather than investing in clean coal projects to alleviate their energy needs (Ibid). This is done primarily to accentuate the business of state-owned petroleum companies like CNPC, CNOOC and SinoPec and further their interests in making them an indispensable part of the nation and more importantly the government think tank (Ibid). Moreover, since China is not well fed by natural resources of petroleum, these companies engage in aggressive overseas acquisition process showcasing an image of the drooling dragon on the prowl (Ibid). In fact this pressure of the domestic companies has stemmed from its own pressure of the investors, especially international investors, and the overseas Chinese.

The domestic determinants are the stalwarts of the energy policies of China carrying the potential to break or make its energy structure. However this is not to say that the "duel" between them is against the energy structure itself. In fact they assist in bringing a compromise of sorts between the energy structure and the energy policies so that none feels let down by the other.

6. Conclusion

China's energy recipe comprises three basic ingredients: energy sector, energy policies and domestic determinants of energy. The first chapter discussed the variance in energy policies throughout the chronology of Chinese history. China's energy policies are directed at self-sufficiency of energy resources achieved by optimum utilisation and acquisition. While it is true that China's energy policies have swayed with the prevailing political ideologies, yet it cannot be denied that through all the policies the subtle theme was to maintain self-sufficiency. However the answer to what is self-sufficiency varied with the available natural resources, level of capital and technical know-how to exploit them. The historical baggage of self-sufficiency to the futuristic focus on optimum utilisation constitutes the current energy policy of China. The decision-makers have realised by now that focusing on only one end of the spectrum does not guarantee an ideal energy structure and leaves ample scope for callousness at worst and distortions at least in other areas of the energy sector. Perhaps that is why the call for "environment protection" is supplanted by "development of science and technology," "reliance on domestic supplies" by "promotion of international cooperation" and "economic growth" by "energy conservation." It has been widely contended that the "reform era" gave a new lease of life to the energy sector by granting it the status of mainstream discussion. Although the pre-reform era is replete with examples of setting up of various oilfields and expansion of coal industry, yet it cannot be denied that a holistic approach was adopted only after 1978. Moreover when China speaks about "optimum utilisation" it in no way undermines its aim of "self-sufficiency" which is reflected in its expansion of domestically available renewable resources such as solar and wind energy.

The question that the domestic determinants are at variance with each other holds true in their execution aspect though all try to bring self-sufficiency in their domestic domain. While the CCP and the energy companies struggle for influence over each other, the market and the environment struggle for their existence in the Chinese space. For technology and the consumer it is the matter of utility which stands in front of them. How to contribute to energy conservation is what they have to decipher for themselves. The consumer wants to use technology but is contributing to energy scarcity and environment destruction in this process. What the alternative is, is what they have to find. Another continuous argument plaguing China's domestic energy structure has been that because of the conflict among the interests of different domestic determinants the energy policies have been unable to maintain consistency of priority. To some extent it is true that energy policies have the capacity to influence the domestic determinants through various provisions derived from its historical legitimacy. Yet it is also true that the domestic determinants are not in any way antagonistic to the goal of self-sufficiency and many a time assist the government in doing so. It is not doubted that energy policies of the previous years affect the government psyche and the vested interests of the other determinants yet they cannot dictate them much if the present circumstances are negative. Hence though short term, it is domestic determinants which wield concrete power over the energy policies and whose variance and consonance can determine its future. The below diagram reflects a pattern where the prevailing energy structure determines the interests of the domestic determinants which in turn determine the provisions, aims and targets of energy policies.

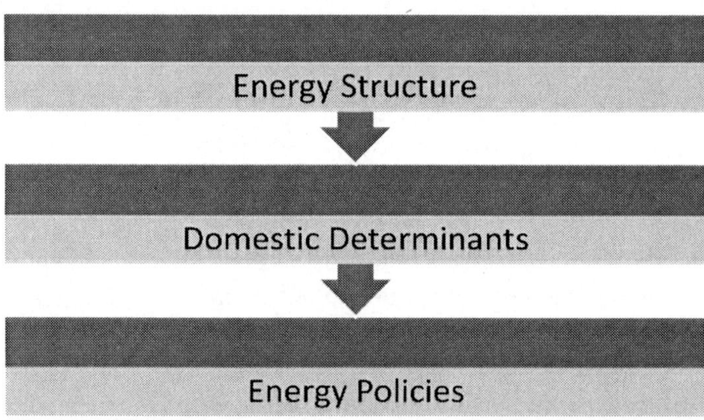

China is making efforts to transcend from a traditional energy structure to a modern energy structure as it maintains its vision of self-sufficiency in energy resources. Ideally a modern energy structure is an amalgamation of high technological content, high quality of resources, low energy consumption, low levels of pollution and a centralised industry with ample space for innovation. It is also a perfect synchronisation of technology, innovation, human resource and information. In short it is an energy mix of sustainable development with economic growth.

From the perspective of China's energy market construction and development of China's energy strategy, it would augur well for China to focus on the following aspects:

- Increase the usage of energy-efficient technology which will reduce the long-term costs of production. This can be done by the government through targeted policies, strict administration and specified standards. There should be a special focus on development of IGCC technology which focuses on clean coal. The development of clean technology industry is a guarantor of both environment protection and economic growth (Fu, 2004:30-31, interviewed by Zhao).
- Renewable energy sector does not develop on the basis of mere laws and policies although large impetus can be given it through such political measures. What it requires is large doses of investment which can be stimulated by the government if it invests from its own treasury attracting both foreign and domestic private investment in the perusal (Fu, 2004:30-31, interviewed by Zhao).
- Nuclear energy has great market potential in China and through environment practicality and disaster management it can provide a big leeway to China's energy woes (Fu, 2004:30-31, interviewed by Zhao).

Even a cursory glance of the first chapter reveals that each plan had a specific target for energy which was based on the existing circumstances and the available resources then. While China did hold a long-term view of energy development, it chose to rely on short-term priorities in determining the direction and pathway of energy development in China. The period from 1949 to 52 which was basking in the glory of liberation was dealing with a politically charged China where communism was not just the answer but also the only available solution for all immediate problems. China's international isolation by Western democracies and a magnanimous Soviet assistance at this point strengthened the faith. The "socialist brethren" of China had begun to believe that centralisation and party hold was an inalienable eligibility criterion to lessen the government's energy and, in turn, economic woes. The importance of the task of energy development in the minds of high-ranking government officials can be deduced from the fact that the Ministry of Petroleum Industry was established on the very day of liberation, i.e., October 1, 1949, an announcement that China's energy structure is not only capable but also powerful enough to fulfil all its domestic demands (*Dangdai Zhongguo de Shiye Gongye*, 2008:629). Despite its other commitments, PLA was given the very important task of not only liberating but also assisting in exploration of oilfields so that no other state could dare to be another Japan for China (Ibid).

As China's political structure mushroomed into a fully functional communist state with the Soviet model of growth as its ideal, the government realised that development means greater demand of energy and China's energy resources would require specific attention rather than clubbing them under one holistic ministry. Thus the Industrial Fuel Department got trifurcated into coal, oil and electricity department during the First Five Year Plan while simultaneously China also adopted the strategy of intensified exploration of various existing and new oilfields (Ibid: 633). By the Second Five Year Plan China had clarified its aims of giving priority to the development of heavy industry which translated into energy terms meant that there would be a tremendous surge in demand for energy products as high consumption industries would be in business for a considerable time (Lee, 2012:97). This was considered good news for the energy sector then because more demand meant more attention and intensified exploration and exploitation of coal mines and oilfields. Daqing had already began to shine as the promising star and the GLF stress on iron and steel meant greater investment and capital for the fossil fuel industry (*Dangdai Zhongguo de Shiye Gongye*, 2008:636). However the agriculture and other economic losses of the GLF period did not allow the five year plan to enjoy its "energy achievements" and annual plans came in from the period 1963 to 1965. It was actually in this period that Zhou Enlai gave the concept of self-reliance the form of a slogan and a target (Ibid: 639). Energy scarcity had begun to show its ambitions through petroleum decline and technology was now given a positive thought as an assistant in exploration and exploitation fields (Ibid).

By the Third Five Year Plan relations with the Soviets were heavily strained and all Soviet technology and expertise which had nurtured China's energy structure for such a long time left it handicapped midway. China already had fought wars with its neighbours within the decade of the 1960s itself and China's political attention was redirected to external security rather than internal development. However energy development did not stop or slow down from these external disturbances but on the contrary intensified as Daqing boosted the morale as well as the self-confidence of the Chinese government, promising to be the answer for all disjuncture between the worker and the farmer and the city and the country (Ibid: 641). The period during 1971 to 1975 (the Fourth Five Year Plan) was the peak period of the Cultural Revolution as well as the fag end of Mao's career. It was a time when China's population began to rice and consumers too began to demand energy apart from industries. Although internationally oil supply had come under severe crisis yet China did not deter from its "intensive exploitation strategy." (Lee, 2012:97). However transportation was becoming a severe headache for the government which not only added to the costs of production but also delayed the time of utility and hence infrastructure build-up became another major target for the government (Lee, 2012:97).

The Fifth Plan was marked by two great political events, the end of the Mao era and the establishment of reforms by Deng Xiaoping. While Mao laid stress on the development of oil, Deng stressed electricity production as his main agenda (Ji, 2011:26). Centralised planning had given way to Household Responsibility System and electricity producers were lured with all sorts of economic incentives to enhance production (Lee, 2012:97). By the Sixth Plan these incentives became the norm while on the other hand voices began to be heard about environment protection and energy conservation (Ibid). Various energy companies like CNOOC and CNPC were established which were actually the remnants of the defunct energy departments and China's foreign ministry shifted its focus from the Soviet Union to Sino-American relations (*Dangdai Zhongguo de Shiye Gongye*, 2008:650-651). The Seventh Plan oversaw the *kaifang* (opening up) strategy not just in economic terms but also in technological exchanges (Lee, 2012:97). While strategies were established for oil and gas build-up, the framework was even laid down for expansion of renewable energy. In the early 1990s China had become a net importer of oil even after achieving population control. China's economy was rising in fast proportions and trade with foreign nations was expanding like never before. Corporate culture had come to stay in the energy market and state councils issued papers for greater integration with foreign countries in the energy trade.

By the year 1993 energy scarcity scare was no more a virtual reality but was reflected in rising prices and expanding inflation in a growing economy. Moreover ecological deterioration due to pollution could no more be ignored and China had to do something concrete and fast to avoid a catastrophe. Hence various legal and political measures took place between the Ninth and the Tenth Five Year Plans like the National Energy Plan (2004-2020), Renewable Energy Law (2005), "863 Plan" by MOST, etc., while, on the other hand, China began to become a world leader in production of almost all the fossil fuels (Wang et. al., 2012:71) and (Lee, 2012:97). The recent two five year plans as well as the various white papers released during this period have shown where the future interests of the government lie in the energy sector. The massive coverage given to wind, solar, nuclear and hydropower industry is a clear indication that China's interest in the renewable sector is here to stay and prosper. There have been recommendations of shifting the attention from heavy to light industries to ease the pressure on the energy sector as well as transform the state-owned companies to strategic emerging enterprises so that energy problems can be dealt in a more professional manner (See Annexure 2).

This work has also identified a few determinants which influence the energy policies, both domestic and international, while residing within the geographical confines of China They constitute both the actors and factors which influence the energy policy. They are: bureaucratic control, energy companies, market mechanism, environment, advanced technology and consumers. What should be the basis of China's energy policy? How should China's energy policy be formed? Can one determinant be given more importance than the other at a particular point of time? If yes, then what would be the implications? If no, then would any objective be fulfilled? These are some of the questions which are answered by evaluating the objectives and circumstances of each determinant separately. Bureaucracy is perhaps the most powerful and the most pressurised group of all as it constitutes the government. Despite the one-party rule the government cannot be oblivious of the needs and concerns of different vested groups nor can it be unwary of the interests of various pressure groups. CCP has been at the mayhem of all Chinese affairs from the start and has the experience of "seen all, done all," which no other determinant has. It created, destroyed and re-created ministries according to varied energy targets and political compulsions. The energy policies have swung between the "leadership cult" and the Politburo dictation and have maintained their strategic importance and interest despite not having a ministry of its own. Why was this decision of abolishing the Energy Ministry in 1993 taken by Premier Zhu Rongji especially at the same time when China had become the net importer of oil and was also facing acute power shortages? Was it the NDRC pressure or had the Ministry become redundant and incompetent, adding burden to the exchequer, are some of the questions which can still be speculated upon. The local governments despite being less talked about and less heard in a centralised administrative structure wield the actual power as they are left with the main task of implementation of policy targets. This institutional framework of the local governments was the outcome of Mao and Deng teachings where Mao taught them to hone their interregional rivalry skills and Deng taught them to seek higher economic targets at all cost. The result was that high energy consumption industries continued to be the government favourites marginalising or even debilitating the interests of all other determinants.

The Deng period had recognised the era of Cultural Revolution as a scourge, and did make vain attempts to restore the fractured past. However it soon abandoned the institutional style of working and took to the "market style" to bring changes in the sagging energy structure, this meant the arrival of national oil companies, coal and power corporations which despite being state-owned enterprises, had more autonomy and influence than various ministries. This "corporate culture" had begun to give results in the form of economic growth and gained the indirect advantage of making a dent in the "ministry coverage" by determining the quantity and quality of ministries so that its own sphere of influence did not get affected.

The CCP and the government do not have an explicit difference in their sphere of influence. The party through Politburo and Leading Group wields enough power to not allow the government to take any step which might conflict with the party manifesto. Yet the working and hierarchy of CCP is itself in transition and as the party shifts from leadership charisma to expansion of Leading Group and Politburo members it can be said that different perspectives and different voices will get a concrete proposal and mainstream position. However it cannot be denied that the Politburo is a strong power holder in China and no corporate, think tank or government institution can dismantle that. As the Politburo gets divided into "populist group" and "elitist coalition" we can expect to see a mixed manifesto especially in the energy context (Lee, 2012:30-31). The National Energy Leading Group, created in 2005, deserves a special mention in this case as its members are not only at the upper echelons of the Party but have also been vociferous in government circles about their current needs and future demands (Lee, 2012:37).. It was this sector which advocated the redirection of investment in renewable energy in which it saw a big market potential (Lee, 2012:30-37).

In the ministry context, NEA, NEC and SASAC hold a special position as they have been instrumental in introducing some major changes in the energy dimension. While the NEA has been dubbed by many as a precursor to the formation of a future energy ministry, the NEC was involved in creating the NELG and has time and again expressed its views about "energy efficiency." (Burke et. al., 2009:8-10) SASAC on the other hand has given kind attention to the environment anguishes by introducing accountability for fossil-fuel companies regarding the environment sustainability (Ibid). When an assortment of ministries, committees and institutions converge, two things happen: good and bad. The bad thing is that it is difficult to draw a consensus between them and proceed towards taking concrete measures to assuage "energy" wounds, and the good thing is that due to identical party affiliations a subtle thought of maintaining unity and drawing to conclusive evidence is existent.

When ministries and their various policies are discussed, it is also necessary to discuss those policies which have been legalised or are enshrined in the constitution. Yet they are not omnipotent and many flaws have been found in their basic provisions and jurisdiction of functions. Many scholars have identified conflict between "government authority" and "political will," market and administration, authority and restraint, price and costs and, perhaps most importantly, politics and professionalism.

It is not an exaggeration to consider energy companies as a resultant property of the process of reform and opening up. *Dangdai Zhongguo de Shiye Gongye* (2008) dubs them as institutes which reconstructed the strength of the party, spiritual civilisation and political thought process. They revitalised the Daqing spirit and the enthusiasm of the "iron man" within the market context bringing forth the true spirit of a "socialist market economy." (*Dangdai Zhongguo de Shiye Gongye*, 2008:391) In terms of SOEs oil completely beats coal, despite the latter being the backbone of China's energy structure. This is expressed not in terms of the number of enterprises but in terms of total annual turnover and spectrum of influence. These companies which are formerly ministries themselves have donned new apparel remaining in synchronisation with the power holders of the country. During the Mao era when centralisation and government administration were omnipresent and omnipotent, these institutions were the energy ministries of the nation and when market and reforms came to rule the roost, they became the corporate of the nation. This is not to say that they are mere power seekers playing trivial politics within the government but are professional conglomerates who seek to expand the country's energy quotient while maintaining their power and prestige in the country.

Table 6.1: Illustrative Examples of Energy Companies with Their Year Of Establishment and Total Assets

Kind of energy resource	Name of the company	Year of establishment	Total assets (hundred million yuan)
Oil and gas	PetroChina or CNPC	1995	19,176
Oil and gas	CNOOC	1982	7,185
Oil and gas	Sinopec	1998	11,301
Coal and power	ChinaCoal	1982	243.9 billion (2012 figure)
Coal and power	China Guodian Corporation	2002	–
Coal and power	Huaneng group	1985	7,531.88

Coal and power	China Datang Power Company Limited	2002	–
Coal and power	Huadian Corporation	2002	–
Coal and power	China Power Investment Corporation		–

Sources: Annual Reports of PetroChina, CNOOC, Sinopec, ChinaCoal, China Guodian Corporation, Huaneng Group, China Datang Power Company Limited, Huadian Corporation, China Power Investment Corporation (2011).

Given above is the list of various energy companies, their year of establishment and their total assets which is a major indicator of their position in front of the government. The above-mentioned figures of the total assets are also coinciding with the initiation of the Twelfth Five Year Plan which had decided to shift its focus from fossil fuel to non-fossil fuel companies. The question of will the fossil fuel companies be able to maintain their turnover rate at the time of shifting government benevolence needs a little more patience and wait for time to reveal the answer.

Energy has two types of market: production market and consumption market. While production has been enhancing in arithmetic progression, consumption, owing to reasons of population and rising living standards, is expanding exponentially in geometric progression. Various economic variables like price, tax, income, demand elasticity, etc., are tested to bring an impact on consumption structure of energy.

When coal is discussed it also brings in an inevitable discussion on electricity. While it is true that raw coal consumption is dwindling with increasing urbanisation among the residential consumers, coal used as a raw material to produce electricity has been increasing on a sustained basis especially when prices of other resources like oil escalate which were once used to produce electricity. Various economic measures like rebate on renewable technology, differential pricing, etc., are used to mitigate the environment losses which many a time offset the economic profits. In fact the power sector has come under severe debate regarding subsidies and marketisation of prices. While coal companies advocate the floating of market price to reveal the actual scarcity situation to the consumers, they are not ready to let go of the subsidies and benefits which they receive from the government by being a state-owned enterprise (Zhao, 2001). A similar kind of oligopolistic market exists in the oil sector where two-three major companies dominate domestic oil supply. Again prices are doctored here and profits do not reflect the actual price or supply conditions. However, here the companies do not demand marketisation of prices which has prompted many international agencies to consider it as a domestic cartel in the making (Zhao, 2001).. In fact in this situation the electricity sector got the better of the two where it not only remained the government's favourite child as it needed the most attention but also because it was never pulled up for its losses or failures, which were redirected to the coal industry. Moreover any improvement in production made it win accolades from the government and showers of gifts, subsidies and rebates under the household responsibility system (Ibid).

The work also explores the reasons why China became the "manufacturing hub of the world" and what implications that imposes on the energy demand and supply pattern. The work also tries to make a distinction between who are the biggest consumers of China's energy, are they the residential consumers who are increasingly splurging in high energy consumption products, or the high end energy consumption industries like iron and steel, paper pulp, etc., which owing to the nature of being basic industries are not only not penalised but in fact appreciated for their "energy extravagance." If the real prices are reflected in the market what implications are created? How does the international rise in price of crude affect the domestic market? What kind of energy investments are done in the country? Who is the investor? Is it only the government and the state owned enterprises? Has infrastructure build up created an economic caveat in the rural areas leaving them to suffer silently the ecological excesses as urban China celebrates the economic mirth are some of the questions which the determinants of market mechanism and environment should answer. China is increasingly seeking towards establishing a low-carbon economic structure with judicious mix of "new energy resources." What is the optimum energy intensity? How can energy efficiency be enhanced? Are all regions in the same level of energy efficiency bracket? Are the developed regions to be blamed for deteriorating air quality? Can economic growth assist in achieving ecological efficiency are a few questions which cannot be analysed with preconceived notions about China's environmental status. For example not many Chinese researchers blame economic growth for environmental deterioration. They cite the case of the 1980s where voices of environment conservation had gained ground, resulting in reduced energy intensity coupled with double-digit economic growth (Sinton et. al., 1998). The developed east is also taken as representative of energy efficiency which means that rising prices and incomes kick-start a market for energy-saving technology and products resulting in overall reduction in energy intensity and enhancement of energy efficiency.

Zhao Suisheng believes that despite the juxtaposition of government and market in the energy sector, the model of "socialist market economy" has not been applied here as freely as in other areas partly because energy was too important to be left as a protégé of the market. al.one. Could energy related environmental concerns be the reasons for this inhibition has not been made clear, though. However the cataclysmic rise of the fossil fuel energy companies seem to defy this opinion as despite being state-owned enterprises they enjoy more autonomy than even private enterprises. While it is true that energy companies cannot do any transaction against the government orders it is also true that the government too cannot afford to live in antagonistic terms with these energy companies and yet dictate their will over them. Similarly the energy market too has been bending with the vagaries of price volatilities despite the state cushion and the many analysts in China who are vociferous about marketisation of prices to reflect the real situation. This is not to say that the government is losing its control in the energy sector as it is still at the helm of affairs and has the support of the entire population. Yet one cannot deny that, like all other sectors, energy too has not been left unaffected by political changes though the impact has been more subtle and long-term.

What domain do energy and environment share, in the nature spectrum as both constitute an important part of it? This has been the scope of much speculation between energy analysts and environmentalists. Do they share an antagonistic relationship or are they complementary to each other. What does the economy have to do with it? Researchers have found that energy efficiency had a better ratio in energy importing provinces than exporting ones. Incidentally energy importing provinces are those where maximum economic development takes place which means that the fault essentially lies with the producer states who, through usage of primitive technology, are creating more harm than good for both the economy and the environment (Chen Wei et. al., 2011).

Environment conservation has now occupied a big space in the government agenda and all including the fossil fuel companies have to compulsorily contribute their share for it. This means either investing in R&D or periodic appraisal and closure of pollution creating plants. At this juncture coal and power companies deserve a special mention as they have been stringently forced to reduce their sulphur dioxide and COD emissions and heavily invest in clean coal technologies. In fact energy companies have utilised their "environment work" as an extension of their corporate social responsibility earning benign attention from the government and the public. Li (2012) aptly puts China as having graduated from self-sufficiency of supplies to self-sufficiency at reasonable price in the energy sector.

The era of the 1990s though does not gather enough support for itself from the environment perspective. It is blamed for putting all the good work in reverse gear by disbanding the balanced approach, focusing only on economic gains (Zhao, 2001). Many favourable price policies and economic measures which could have given some concrete direction to environmental situation and also created a systematic market for companies of renewable energy did not happen thanks to the short-sightedness on the part of the government, business leaders and investors of that time (Zhao, 2001). Li (2012:1) adopts a constructivist perspective towards environmental measures and believes that instead of being cynical towards them one should assiduously promote technical innovation as a necessity for environmental and energy balance. In fact since the Tenth Five Year Plan under the concept of scientific development the issue of carbon reduction and earning carbon credits has gained a lot of popularity among government circles, the media and the public.

Recently China has passed a spate of laws which guarantee a protective coverage (at least on paper) to the environment of China. They have been the Renewable Energy Law (2005), Circular Economy Law (2008), Energy Law (2009), New Building Code (2006), Green Reporting Standards, etc (Chen, Nicholas, 2008). The above-mentioned laws clarify that those sincere efforts for environment protection cannot be achieved without introducing laws in the energy and economy domain to achieve actual results.

Technology plays a two-fold role, assisting economy by enhancing production and assisting environment by enhancing efficiency. Till the twentieth century China focused on developing or importing technology which was related to intensive exploration and exploitation of energy resources. It was only later that it was realised that technology related to developing of renewable energy resources and clean coal should also be employed. Many environment and energy related laws have also stressed the need for expansion of S&T base and investment in R&D. Extended focus has also been made on expansion of renewable energy resources, like wind and solar energy, which employ non-polluting technologies, and greater assistance should be given to expansion of the market dealing with energy efficient products. Also, since the government is aware about the domestic handicap on the technological fronts it actively promotes "international cooperation" encouraging companies to engage in trade or aid in product or process technology. For this purpose it has also made a massive reduction in its import duty rate for the technology sector. Even domestically, tax rebates and reduced VAT rates are a norm in the technology market (Zhao, 2001). Most white papers on energy carry a special column focusing on enhancement of energy technologies in China which means that the government is promising a future for their development. It has even promoted alternative fuels for oil to buy time and cash in the petroleum scarcity situation (*White Paper on China's Energy Policy, 2012*).

The last of the actors in this section are the consumers which is also the most dynamic determinant as it constitutes a wide section of the masses of China ranging from industrial consumers to tertiary sector consumers, residential consumers to the transportation sector. One theme that is continuously underlined in this section is the rising living standards leading to investment by investors and the government in high energy consumption industries and by the consumers in high energy consuming products. Traditionally energy has been subsidised for people to satisfy their basic needs, however when energy becomes a vital product even in luxurious commodities which is proclaimed as "the coming of age of rising China," then the government is caught between the moral dilemma of who should be asked to consume less, the nouveau riche or the ultra poor. At this stage the price factor theory of many economists gets disturbed who feel that rising prices would deter its consumers and ultimately reduce the overall energy consumption. Most residential consumption is made by the nouveau riche who neither feel the pinch of price rise nor any incentive to reduce energy consumption. Another theory was to encourage even small-scale development of renewable energy resources so that many can satisfy their subsistence energy needs. However this requires capital and expertise for sustaining through the long-term gestation period which cannot be done without direct government interference. Electricity in this aspect has been given the largest attention as it is also the maximum consumed commodity among both industrial and residential consumers and many equipments which represent the rich are run by electricity. An energy-intensive lifestyle cannot sustain for long in China and the tech-savvy Chinese who has begun to believe in individual contribution is perhaps in the best position to do something and to do it now.

How do these domestic determinants interact with each other is one final question. Is it an issue of tussle for power and influence? Are they always in contradiction to each other or do they converge to formulate a holistic energy policy, are questions which arise after identifying the domestic determinants of energy policies.

When the first determinant bureaucracy is discussed it is identified that dichotomy exists not just within the ministries but also between the local and central governments. While the central government has moved on from "economic obsession" to "environmental contribution," the same cannot be said about the local governments who treat the economic goal as a tool of their power and their prestige in front of the government, corporations and most importantly the public.

Two models were identified to discuss the interplay of these determinants: One of them being CGE and the other being the PREEST model. Both of them primarily analyse the relationship between energy, economy and environment with oblique reference to the other aspects. The CGE model sums up the relationship as energy creating economy, expanding economy putting pressure on economic resources causing intensive exploration and deteriorating environment. Deteriorating environment eventually deteriorates energy resources which ultimately reduces both the quality and quantity of economic development.

PREEST model on the other hand is a more holistic model which identifies five determinants, namely, the population, resources, economy, environment and science and technology. The PREEST model identifies population and resources to be in an inverse relationship where the quantitative and qualitative expansion of one leads to decline of the other. Quantitative expansion of consumers is population and qualitative expansion is the rising living standards both of which have led to energy scarcity. Quite contrary to popular opinion energy and environment have shared a converging relationship as both are a part of ecology. Hence it is not only the environment which gets affected by "energy" activities but also vice versa. Technology is the "fire" of energy which can cause energy scarcity as well as sustainable development if utilised judiciously. Energy and economy share the donor and giver relationship where economy not only sustains but also determines the level and kind of economic activity.

Almost a similar situation exists not only between the characteristics of these determinants but also between the laws of these determinants. Though they seem unrelated to energy on the surface yet carry a deep analysis of various energy policies as well as hold implications over energy policies through their provisions. The work above also analyses the dichotomy between energy structure and energy policies. China's energy law structure has the following pattern where all energy related laws are invariably linked to each other.

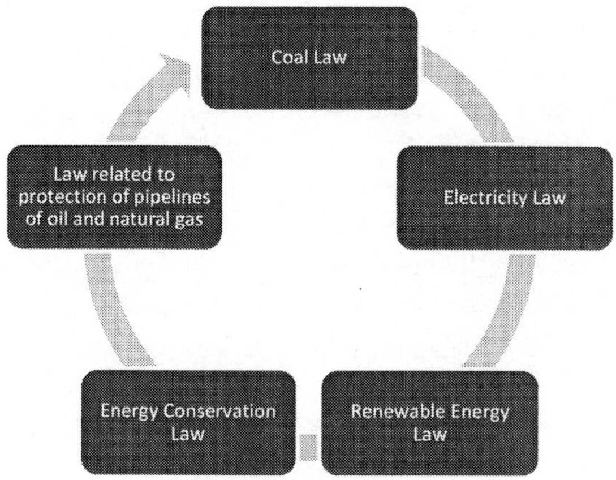

Source: Adopted from Xiao Guoxing (2010).

Energy laws reflect the intermix of political and economic interests, political because law is an administered feature and economic because energy is a state property. The work above reflects energy laws which sometimes get duplicated not only with their own related laws but also various unrelated laws like the company law, competition law, price law, wealth tax law, law for progress of science and technology, safety production law, environment law, circular economy law, foreign trade law and the standardisation law.

When economy is discussed it is imperative to understand industry and its implications for and because of the industry. Coal, power, construction and transport are not just mere industries in China but channelise the direction of its entire economy. On the other hand, it is also true that these industries are high energy guzzling industries and any wastage or over-exploitation on their part holds repercussions not just for the industry itself but also for the entire economy, environment and politics of China.

However it is also true that China's energy industry does not operate within the confines of the geographical territory of China and being the largest economy as well as the largest consumer of energy (though this point is contested), it is unlikely not to compare its energy indicators with other nations and especially with its arch rivals. Also it is not always about competition but also "international cooperation," as former president Hu Jintao has time and again highlighted in his speeches, which means that China not only trades in terms of economy but also gets aid and guidance in terms of technology for energy innovation.

The case of renewable energy resources deserves a detailed analysis as wind, hydro, nuclear and solar energy have a separate market and separate repercussions and circumstances for growth in the domestic sphere. This is especially true for solar and wind energy which is not only available in plenty but also suits Chinese conditions and level of R&D. Recently there has been a spate of investments in the renewable sector not just from domestic sources but also the foreign financial institutions and international organisations who see "huge market potential" is areas of energy efficiency, clean energy, climate change and carbon trading. However the market of any commodity is a volatile phenomenon and so is true even for the renewable sector no matter how much of growth and potential the economy shows. In this conundrum technology plays a very big role as foreign investments not only bring in foreign exchange but also international expertise and advanced technology which can be extremely significant over determining the rates of energy intensity in the country, especially the industrial sector, for both commercial and residential purposes. Many a time the phenomenon of green trade is vouched for as nearness to solution for bringing greater bonhomie between economy and environment. The government of China is increasingly getting interested in this concept as it could be a ticket to achieving the historically cherished dream of achieving self-sufficiency, albeit through the economic route.

However a section of analysts have expressed concern for China's readiness to find alternatives to fossil fuels to alleviate both the energy and environment scare but not to take concrete steps in reducing its overall energy consumption. The consumer is blamed for this, for "rising living standards" which is now no more a desired goal but a practical reality. Also renewable energy, no matter how much of potential it shows, is still taken as a supplementary source to China's regular (read, fossil fuels) energy resources. When this happens it not only hinders the development of the renewable sector but also obscures its dark realities related to its costs and scope of application.

Annexure 1

The below table lists the prominent persons associated with various energy departments and institutes in China

Name	Educational qualifications	Name and post of the organisation currently working in	Service record
Chen Jinen	Master's degree	Secretary of the CPC Committee of the China Energy Conservation Investment Corporation since 2002	1992-98 Engineer, Ministry of Aviation 1998- Director General CPC Working Commission for State-Owned Enterprises
Han Zhi	Senior engineer and research fellow	Vice president of China Energy Conservation Investment Corporation since 2002	1989-91 Engineer at Ministry of Electronics Industry 1991-97 Deputy Engineer at Ministry of Electronics Industry 1991-97 Senior Engineer at Ministry of Electronics Industry 1997-2003 Chief Engineer at Ministry of Electronics Industry
Liu Shunxing	Senior engineer and Master's degree	Vice president of China Energy Conservation Investment Corporation since 1998	1991-94 Official at NDRC, Energy Research Centre, State Planning Commission and Bureau of Energy Conservation 1994-1995 Chief Engineer at China Energy Investment Energy Corporation, Energy Conservation Department 1996-98 General Manager and Director General at China Energy Investment Energy Corporation

Yang Jiayi	Master's degree in economics, Associate Professor and registered accountant	General accountant at China Energy Conservation Investment Corporation since 2003	1991-94 Deputy Director at Central University of Finance and Economics 1994-97 Director at the same university 1997-2003 Deputy General Manager at Beijing International Power Development and Investment Corporation
Yang xincheng	Bachelor's degree with engineering background	Deputy Secretary at China Energy Conservation Investment Corporation since 2002	1979- joined CPC 1986-95 Secretary of CPC , Director General of Economic Commission and Secretary Metallurgy Bureau at Tianjin 1995-2002 Vice Mayor at Tianjin Municipality
Ruan Keqiang	Graduation from Moscow Power Institute	Academician at Chinese Academy for Engineering and Chinese Academy for Sciences since 1995	1950-51 student at Qinghua University 1995 researcher at China National Nuclear Industry Corporation
Wang Dexi	Doctorate degree from Massachusetts Institute of Technology	Academician at Chinese Academy for Sciences, Chief at China National Nuclear Industry Corporation, Dean at Ministry of Nuclear Industry since 1980	1947-???? Professor at Nankai University 1964-75 Deputy at 3rd NPC and Deputy Chief Ministry of Nuclear Industry
Wang Naiyang	Graduated from Physics Department at Beijing University	Academician at Chinese Academy for Sciences	1959-65 worker at Russian Nuclear Research Centre
Lv Bo	Master's degree from China-Europe International School of Business	Deputy general manager of CNOOC since 2010	2002-4 general manager at CNOOC 2004-6 Board of Directors at CNOOC 2006-10 Assistant General Manager at CNOOC 2007 member of CPC leading party group

Li Fanrong	MBA from Cardiff Business School	Deputy General Manager of CNOOC and member of CPC leading party group since 2010	1995-2005 Deputy General Manager at CNOOC Shenzhen branch 2005-9 General Manager at CNOOC, Shenzhen branch 2009-10 Assistant General Manager of CNOOC
Zhao Zhixiang	Master's degree from Institute of Atomic Energy	Editor in Chief of Nuclear Energy Science and Technology, Executive Director, Chinese Academy of Nuclear Sciences	1986 graduated from China Atomic Energy Scientific Research Institute
Chen Qiufa	n.a	Member of 18th CPC central committee since 2012	2005-8 Deputy Director at State Administration for Science, Technology and Industry for National Defense 2008-13 Secretary at State Administration for Science, Technology and Industry for National Defence and Director at China Atomic Energy Authority 2009-13 Director at State Administration for Science, Technology and Industry for National Defence 2010-13 Director of China National Space Administration
Ma Xingrui	Doctorate from Harbin Institute of Technology	Director at State Administration for Science, Technology and Industry for National Defence, Director of China National Space Administration, Director at China Atomic Energy Authority and Vice Minister at Ministry of Industry and Information Technology since 2013	1992-95 Chairman at Harbin Institute of Technology 1996-99 Vice Dean at Chinese Academy of Space Technology 1997-2007 Deputy General Manager at China Aerospace Science and Technology Corporation 2007-13 General Manager at China Aerospace Science and Technology Corporation

Feng Shidong	Senior engineer	Vice president of State Development and Investment Corporation since 2001	1981-86 Deputy and then General Manager at State Development and Investment Corporation, 1986-1996 Secretary at China National Energy Investment Corporation 1996-2001 Secretary of State Coal Industry Bureau
Zhu Jianshi	Graduation from Beijing University	Member of the Engineering and Mining Engineering Department at the Chinese Academy of Engineering	Has had long-term associations with Ministry of Nuclear Industry, China engineering physics research institute 1995- Member of Chinese Academy of Engineering Professor at Beijing University of Science and Engineering
Ma Kai	Graduation from National People's University	Director of State Council Leading Group for promoting medium and small term enterprises, State Council Leading Group for migrant workers, member of State Council, CPC Leading Party Group and Vice Premier of State Council since 2013	Has held various positions in State Council
Ding Xiangyang	n.a.	Deputy Secretary General of State Council since 2013	2003-7 Secretary of Development and Reform Committee and staff member of Ministry of Energy Resources

Jing Tianliang	Graduated from Xi'an College of Mining and Technology	Deputy Secretary and President of China National Coal Industry Import and Export Corporation since 1999	1984-88 Deputy Manager of Ministry of Coal Industry 1988-91 Deputy Director General of Ministry of Energy Resources 1991-93 Deputy Director General of China Corporation of Coal Mines under Central Planning 1993- has held various positions in China National Coal Industry Import and Export Corporation
Shi Dazhen	Graduation from Shandong Engineering Institute	Member of Standing Committee of 9th CPPCC National Committee from 1998-2003	1988-93 Vice Minister of Ministry of Energy Resources 1993-98 Minister at Ministry of Power Industry 1997-98 Member of State Electric Power Corporation
Shi Yubo	Senior Engineer	Deputy Director of National Energy Administration and Vice Chairman of State Electricity Regulatory Commission	1986-88 Engineer at Ministry of Water Resources 1988-93 Deputy Division Head of Ministry of Energy Resources 1993-98 Division Head and Deputy Director Ministry of Power Industry 1998-2002 Deputy Director at State Economic and Trade Power Commission
Wang Shucheng	Attended Qinghua University	Former Minister of Water Resources from 1998 to 2007	n.a-1986 various positions at China Water Conservancy and Hydroelectric Development Corporation, 1986-88 various positions at Ministry of Water Conservancy 1988-93 Director at Ministry of Energy Resources 1993-98 Vice Minister at Ministry of Power Industry 1997-98 Deputy General Manager of State Electric and Power Corporation

Zhu Guangya	Doctorate from Michigan University	Academician at Chinese Academy of Sciences and received medal from CPC Central Committee for work on Nuclear Weapons and Satellites	1982-91- vice president of China Association of Science and Technology 1994-98 President of Chinese Academy of Engineering and Director of SASTIND 1998-2003 Vice Chairman of 9th CPPCC Central Committee
Wu Yin	Graduation from Anhui University in Science and Technology	Deputy Director of National Energy Administration since 2009	1998-2008 Deputy Director of NDRC Energy Bureau
Zhao Xiaoping	Graduation from Northeast China University of Finance and Economics and Law Department, Beijing University	Vice Chairman of Ningxia Hui Autonomous Region since 2009	2006-8 Director of NDRC Energy Bureau 2008-9 Deputy Director of NEA and member of NEA, CPC Leading Party Group
Li Junfeng	n.a	Deputy Director of NDRC Energy Research Institute , Beijing since 1994	1982-92 senior research fellow at ERI
Liu Qi	n.a	Deputy director of NEA since 2013	n.a
Liu Tienan	n.a.	Director of NEA from 2011 to 2013	1999-2003 Director at NDRC, Industrial Development Department and Deputy Director at NDRC, general office 2003-6 Director at NDRC, Industry Department 2006-8 Deputy Director at the Office of the Leading Group for revitalising North East China and other old industrial bases of the State Council 2008-11 Deputy Director at NDRC and member of NDRC, CPC Leading Party Group

Wang Yumin	n.a	Deputy Director of NEA since 2013	n.a
Wu Xinxiong	Senior economist	Vice Minister at NDRC and Director of NEA since 2013	Political career throughout working in Jiangxi province 2011-13 Chairman of SERC
Xu Yongsheng	n.a	Deputy Director at NEA since 2012	20038 Deputy Director at NDRC, Electric Power Department 2008-12 Director at NEA Electric Power Department
Zhang Guobao	Graduation from Xi'an Jiatong University in mechanical engineering	2008-11 Director at NEA	1991-2003 Secretary General at NDRC, Economic Research Centre, State Planning Commission 2003- till date Vice Minister of NDRC 2008- till date member of NEA CPC Leading Group
Zhang Yuqing	n.a	Member of NEA CPC Leading Party Group and Deputy Director at NEA since 2012	1988-2003 member at NDRC, Economic Research Centre, State Planning Commission 2003-05 Deputy Director at NEA, Petroleum and Natural Gas Department 2005-7 Deputy Director of State Petroleum Reserve Office 2007-8 Deputy Director at NEA and Director of State Petroleum Reserve Office 2008-12 director at NEA, Petroleum and Natural Gas Department
Li Keqiang	Degree in economics	Premier of the State Council, Director of the State Energy Commission and Director of National Leading Group for Climate Change and for Energy Conservation and Reduction of Pollution Discharge since 2013	2008-13 Executive Vice Premier of the State Council

Yang Jiechi	Studied at Bath University and London School of Economics	Deputy Director of National Leading Group for Climate Change and for Energy Conservation and Reduction of Pollution Discharge since 2013	Has been associated with the MEA at various ministerial positions
Zhang Gaoli	Graduated from Xiamen University	Vice Premier of the State Council, Deputy Director of State Energy Commission and Deputy Director of National Leading Group for Climate Change and for Energy Conservation and Reduction of Pollution Discharge since 2013	n.a
Shi Hongxiang	Senior engineer	Vice President of State Development and Investment Corporation since 2002	1983-86 Acting General Manager, SDIC, Financial Investment Department 1986-93 Deputy Director, SDIC Research and Development Department and Director at SDIC, Strategic Development Department 1993-95 Director at SDIC, Comprehensive Planning Department and Power Industry Department 1995-99 Director at SDIC, Hydropower Department 1999-2002 Deputy Director at State Energy Commission Comprehensive Planning Department
Wen Jiabao	Graduation from Beijing Institute of Geology	Former Premier of the State Council	2003-13 Director of State Energy Commission
Zeng Qinghong	Engineer	Secretary general of the 17th Party Congress from 2007 to 2012	High ranking political career in CPC
Fan Mingwu	Graduation from Huazhong Institute of Technology	President of Huazhong Institute Of Science and Technology since 2001	1996-???? Held various posts at China Atomic Energy Scientific Research Institute

Kang Rixin	Senior engineer	Deputy General Manager of China National Nuclear Corporation from 1999 to 2010	1978-96 Held various posts at China Atomic Energy Scientific Research Institute 1996-99 General Manager at 3rd Qinshan Nuclear Power Company Ltd.
Wang Fangding	Graduation from Sichuan Chemistry Institute	Academician at Chinese Academy of Sciences since 1999	Researcher at China Atomic Energy Scientific Research
Zhan Yong	Doctorate from China Atomic Energy Institute	Vice President of Hebei Institute of Technology since 2001	1995-96 Deputy Chief at Hebei Institute of Technology
Xie Jialin	Doctorate from Stanford University	Academician at Chinese Academy of Sciences since 1980	Researcher at Chinese Academy of Sciences since 1980
Fang Shouxian	Graduated from Fudan University	Academician at Chinese Academy of Sciences since 1991	Researcher at Chinese Academy of Sciences since 1991
Guo Shuyan	Graduated from Nankai University	Vice Chairman of the Three Gorges Construction Committee from 1993 to 2003	1978-82 Deputy Chief at Chinese Academy of Sciences, High Energy Physics Research Institute
Zhang Zongye	Physicist	Academician at Chinese Academy of Sciences since 1999	Researcher at Chinese Academy of Sciences since 1999
Lu Zhicheng	Graduated from Qinghua University	Vice President and Director General at Qinghua Tongfang Company since 1997	1977-96 Professor at Qinghua University

Source: www.chinavitae.com

Annexure 2

The below table outlines the focus of each Five Year Plan on various energy dimensions of China.

Plan and Its Period	Energy Focus
Pre-Plan Era (1949-52)	China establishes Ministry of Petroleum Industry, exploration in Yumen and Shanxi oilfields, PLA commissioned for exploration, heavy Soviet assistance
First Five Year lan (1953-57)	Soviet model adopted for economic growth, Industrial fuel department gets bifurcated into petroleum, coal and electricity department, rapid exploration in various other oilfields, energy seen as a major supplementary source for industrial growth
Second Five Year Plan (1958-62)	Focus on heavy industry, dignitaries visit Daqing, newer oilfields discovered in Shengli, Huabei, Liaohe, etc. GLF highlights reliance on iron and steel.
Annual Plans (1963-65)	Zhou Enlai issues the concept of self-reliance, petrol recognised as a problem, fillip given to refining technology, gas exploration and oil production, Mao and Zhou give the call of "learn from Daqing" and "growth of kerosene era" respectively
Third Five Year Plan (1966-70)	Focus on agriculture and defence, strained relations with Soviet, China feels handicapped on technology and expertise front, "iron man" gets felicitated, Daqing production as a one-stop solution for integration of worker with farmer and city with country, industrial chemical fuel department established
Fourth Five Year Plan (1971-75)	Economy turns favourable, infrastructure becomes the focus, ministry of petroleum and chemical industry established, international oil crisis, yet China continues with "intensive resource exploration strategy," transportation bottlenecks, population and energy consumption escalate to high proportions
Fifth Five Year Plan (1976-80)	GPCR ends and reform era arrives, after oil electricity becomes the new obsession, work begins at Dalian and Shengli, voices of energy conservation and environment conservation begin to be heard, PetroChina begins exploration in Bohai and gas reserve established in Daqing

Sixth Five Year Plan (1981-85)	Environment protection mentioned by government, plan outlays need for strong socio-economic development, CNOOC established as focus begins on technology and conservation, Sino-American relations "thaw" through energy, rise in production as China allows excess production to be used for personal consumption after fulfilling certain amount of quota
Seventh Five Year Plan (1986-90)	"opening up" for economic efficiency and technological exchanges, CNPC established, framework and laid for renewable energy through economic incentives, exploration begins in Tarim basin, 9 days fire in Shengli oilfields, National Energy Department *guojia nengyuan bu* was formally established, State Council releases Protective Administrative Measures for Oil and Gas, *shiyou tianranqi guandao baohu tiaolie, kang shi* and releases ninety years strategy for development of oil industry
Eighth Five Year Plan (1991-95)	Double-digit economic growth, population control achieved, foreign trade expanded, China turns net importer of oil, CNOOC floats three subsidiaries directed to east China, south China and Bohai, State Council issues paper on international cooperation on oil resources
Ninth Five Year Plan (1996-2000)	Moves to establish a "modern enterprise system," China stood first in production of crude coal, third in power capacity and fifth in oil industry, Zhou Yongkang leads the department of land resources
Tenth Five Year Plan (2001-05)	Conservation of natural resources and reduction of pollutants was stressed upon, renewable energy established, national energy plan was drafted from 2004 to 2020, NOC's get listed in New York Stock Exchange, largest gas field discovered in inner Mongolia, MOST launches "863 plan," well-off society by 2020 declared as an aim
Eleventh Five Year Plan (2006-10)	Environment gains more headway, energy conservation law introduced, National Energy Commission established with the then premier as its head, focus intensifies on wind and solar energy
Twelfth Five Year Plan (2011-15)	Suggests a shift from heavy to light industry, renewed focus on nuclear and hydropower, white paper on energy policy released suggesting transition of state-owned enterprises to strategic emerging enterprises

Sources: Lee (2012) and *Dangdai Zhongguo* (1988, 2008).

Annexure 3

The composition of energy production in 2013

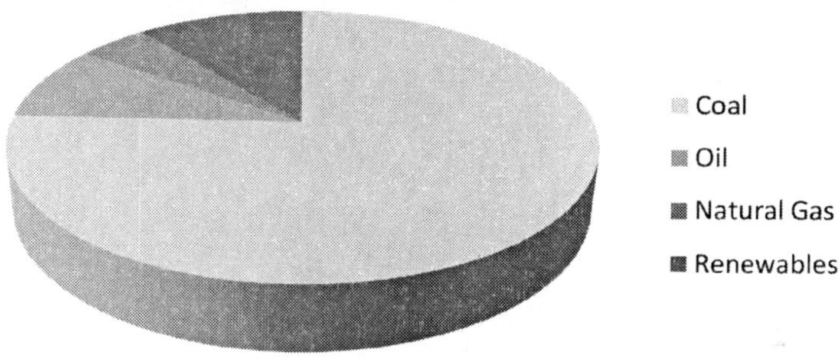

Coal: 75.6 %, Oil: 8.9%, Natural Gas: 4.6%, Renewables (Hydro, Wind and Nuclear): 10.9%

The composition of energy production in 1978

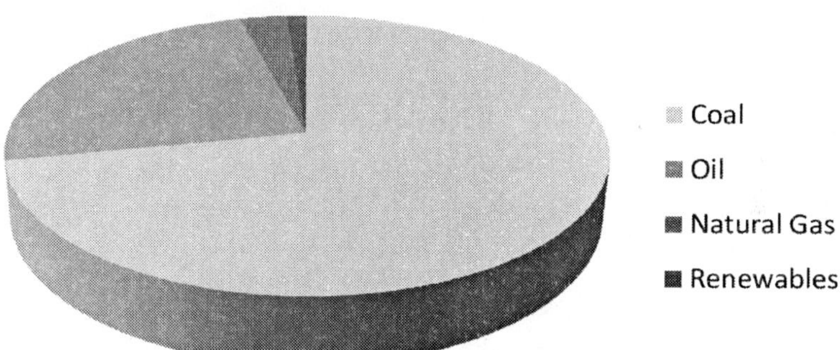

Coal: 70.3 %, Oil: 23.7%, Natural Gas: 2.9%, Renewables (Hydro, Wind and Nuclear): 3.1%
Source: China Statistical Yearbook (2014)

Annexure 4

The composition of energy consumption in 2013

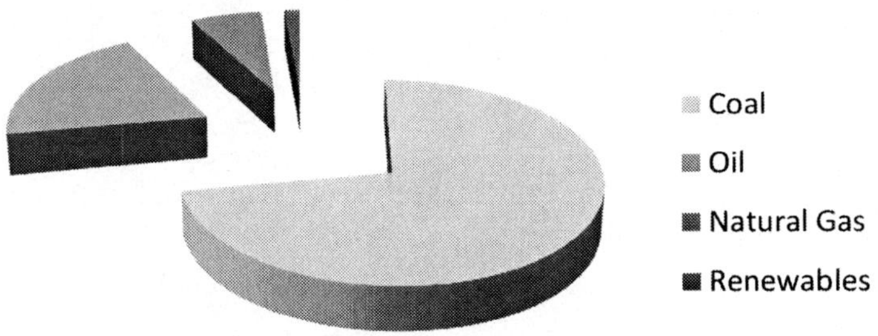

Coal: 66 %, Oil: 18.4%, Natural Gas: 5.8%, Renewables (Hydro, Wind and Nuclear): 9.8%

The composition of energy consumption in 1978

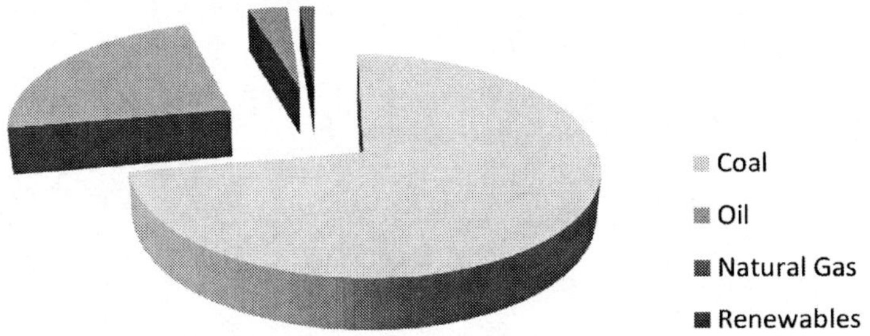

Coal: 70.7 %, Oil: 22.7%, Natural Gas: 3.2%, Renewables (Hydro, Wind and Nuclear): 3.4%

Source: China Statistical Yearbook (2014)

Bibliography

(* indicates primary source)

Aldhous, Peter. June 2005. "China's Burning Ambition." *Nature* 435 (30): 1152-1154.

Andrews, James. January 2013. "China and Renewable Energy: The Outlook for Growth." *Clean Technica.*

Andrews-Speed, Philip. Trans. by Wang Yanyan August 2005. "Zhongguo Nengyuan Zhengce de Chengxiao Yu Tiaozhan 中国能源政策的承销与挑战 [Energy Policy and Regulation in the People's Republic of China] *Zhongwai Lilun Dongtai* 中外理论动态 [*Sino–Global Theoretical Trends*] 8: 32-36.

Anthony Wanjohi. 2011. "State's Foreign Policy: Determinants and Constraints." [Online: web.] Accessed: May 14, 2013. http://www.kenpro.org/papers/foreign-policy-determinants-constraints.htm

APCO Worldwide. 2011. "China's 2011 National People's Congress: Fine Tuning the Economy with an Eye on Social Stability." [Online: web.] Accessed: December 20, 2012. http://www.apcoworldwide.com/content/PDFs/npc_briefing_2011.pdf

Austin Angie. 2005. *Energy and Power in China: Domestic Regulation and Foreign Policy.* United Kingdom: Foreign Policy Centre.

*Annual Report of ChinaCoal 2013. [Online: web] Accessed January 2, 2015 http://www.chinacoalenergy.com/n43830/n43840/n43841/n43842/c582275/attr/582276.pdf

*Annual Report China Petroleum and Chemical Corporations 2011. [Online: web.] Accessed: February 22, 2013 http://www.petrochina.com.cn/ptr/ndbg/201404/582f6995e74c4d508e826e16dca639e9/files/044582e18969434caa525f0374f5f839.pdf

*Annual Report Sinopec Corporation 2011 [Online: web.] Accessed: February 22, 2013 http://english.sinopec.com/download_center/reports/2011/20130110/download/2011AnnualReport.pdf

*Annual Report Sinopec Corporation 2013 [Online: web.] Accessed: February 22, 2015 http://english.sinopec.com/download_center/reports/2013/20140323/download/2013_Annual_Report.pdf

*Annual Report Sinopec Corporation 2012 [Online: web.] Accessed: February 22, 2015 http://english.sinopec.com/download_center/reports/2012/20130324/download/2012AnnualReport.pdf

*Annual Report Sinopec Corporation 2010 [Online: web.] Accessed: February 22, 2013 http://english.sinopec.com/download_center/reports/2010/20110328/download/2010AnnualReport.pdf

*Annual Report Sinopec Corporation 2009 [Online: web.] Accessed: February 22, 2013 http://english.sinopec.com/download_center/reports/2009/20100329/download/AnnualReport2009.pdf

*Annual Report China Petroleum and Chemical Corporations 2010. [Online: web.] Accessed: February 22, 2013. http://www.cnpc.com.cn/resource/english/images1/

pdf/10AnnualReportEn/CNPC_Annual_Report_2010.pdf

*Annual Report PetroChina Company Limited 2013. [Online: web.] Accessed: December 22, 2014. http://www.petrochina.com.cn/Resource/Petrochina/img/2012bg/2011ndbg_en.pdf?COLLCC=2181621560&

*Annual Report PetroChina Company Limited 2012. [Online: web.] Accessed: December 22, 2014. http://www.petrochina.com.cn/ptr/ndbg/201404/0ae3cf19ea8b449ea7a272d60a6a920b/files/08acbaad0b634b529305620e053e35b1.pdf

*Annual Report PetroChina Company Limited 2010. [Online: web.] Accessed: February 22, 2014. http://www.petrochina.com.cn/Resource/pdf/xwygg/2010ANNUALREPORT%28e%29.pdf

*Annual Report PetroChina Company Limited 2011. [Online: web.] Accessed: February 22, 2013 http://www.petrochina.com.cn/ptr/ndbg/201404/582f6995e74c4d508e826e16dca639e9/files/044582e18969434caa525f0374f5f839.pdf .

*Annual Report PetroChina Company Limited 2009. [Online: web.] Accessed: February 22, 2013 http://www.petrochina.com.cn/ptr/ndbg/201404/c28ed92780ce4bf29dcdf56fb328f4e8/files/04481d826fc842dba8a46a9ba25cbb1c.pdf

*Annual Report China National Offshore Oil Corporation 2012. [Online: web.] Accessed: December 22, 2014 http://www.cnoocltd.com/upload/encnoocltd/tzzgx/dqbd/nianbao/images/2013481075.pdf

*Annual Report China National Offshore Oil Corporation 2013. [Online: web.] Accessed: December 22, 2014 http://www.cnoocltd.com/upload/Attach/mrfj/2014/04/2395984295.pdf

*Annual Report China National Offshore Oil Corporation 2011. [Online: web.] Accessed: December 22, 2014 http://www.cnoocltd.com/upload/encnoocltd/tzzgx/dqbd/nianbao/images/2012412936.pdf

*Annual Report China National Offshore Oil Corporation 2010. [Online: web.] Accessed: December 22, 2014 http://www.cnoocltd.com/upload/encnoocltd/tzzgx/dqbd/nianbao/images/201147767.pdf

*Annual Report China National Offshore Oil Corporation 2009. [Online: web.] Accessed: December 22, 2014 http://www.cnoocltd.com/upload/encnoocltd/tzzgx/dqbd/nianbao/images/201049660.pdf

*Annual Report China National Offshore Oil Corporation 2010. [Online: web.] Accessed: December 22, 2014 http://www.cnoocltd.com/upload/encnoocltd/tzzgx/dqbd/nianbao/images/201147767.pdf

*Annual and Sustainability Report China National Offshore Oil Corporation 2011. [Online: web.] Accessed: July 22, 2015 http://www.cnooc.com.cn/data/upload/2011reporten.pdf

*Annual Report China Shenhua Energy Company Limited 2010 [Online: web.] Accessed: February 22, 2013. http://www.shenhuagroup.com.cn/english/images/the0listed0company/periodic0reports/2010/annual/2011/03/28/C0BF742B7D64CF59AC62F6870BF6AD97.pdf

*Annual Report of China Guodian Corporation 2011. [Online: web.] Accessed: February 22, 2013. http://www.guodiantech.com/en/news/details.aspx?id=940

*Annual Report of China Huadian Corporation 2011. [Online: web.] Accessed: February 22, 2013. http://m.todayir.com/todayirattachment_hk/huadian/attachment/20120423165001001412434_en.pdf

*Annual Report of China Power Investment Corporation 2011. [Online: web.] Accessed: February 22, 2013. http://202.66.146.82/listco/hk/chinapower/annual/2011/ar2011.pdf

*Annual Report of China Huaneng Power International Inc. 2005. [Online: web.] Accessed: February 22, 2013. http://pg.jrj.com.cn/acc/HK_DISC/stock_time/2011/04/20/001192669-0.PDF

*Annual Report of China Huaneng Power International Inc. 2013. [Online: web.] Accessed: August 22, 2015 http://www.hpi.com.cn/sites/english/reportYH/e009022013.pdf

*BP Statistical Review of World Energy 2014 [Online: web] Accessed January 2, 2015 http://www.bp.com/content/dam/bp/pdf/Energy-economics/statistical-review-2014/BP-statistical-review-of-world-energy-2014-full-report.pdf

*BP Statistical Review of World Energy 2013 [Online: web] Accessed January 2, 2015 http://www.bp.com/content/dam/bp/pdf/statisticalreview/statistical_review_of_world_energy_2013.pdf

Byrne, John., Bo Shen and Xiaoguo Li 1996. "The Challenge of Sustainability: Balancing China's Energy, Economic and Environmental Goals." *Energy Policy,* 24 (5): 455-62

Beijing Review (2008) "Reviewing China's Energy Policies" Xinhua News Agency

Buijs Bram (2012). "China and the Future of New Energy Technologies: Trends in Global Competetion and Innovation" *Clingendael International Energy Programme* 3-120

Burke Christopher, Johanna Jansson and Wenran Jiang 2009. "Formulation in Energy Policy in China: Key Actors and Recent Developments." *Centre for Chinese Studies University of Stellenbosch.*1-28

Bloomberg New Energy Finance. 2013. "China Was World's Largest Wind Market in 2012." February 4, 2013. [Online: web.] Accessed: March 5, 2013. http://about.bnef.com/press-releases/china-was-worlds-largest-wind-market-in-2012/

Business Vibes. 2012. "Renewable Energy Industry in China." [Online: Web.] Accessed: December 8, 2012. http://www.businessvibes.com/blog/renewable-energy-industry-china

Big Think (2011) "China Dominating Solar Energy Market" [Online: web] Accessed January 22, 2015 http://bbs.wenxuecity.com/currentevent/423890.html

Bradsher Keith (2013) "Chinese Solar Panel Giant is Tainted by Bankruptcy" *The NewYork Times* [Online: web] Accessed January 22, 2015 http://www.nytimes.com/2013/03/21/business/energy-environment/chinese-solar-companys-operating-unit-declares-bankruptcy.html?_r=0

*Beijing City Environmental Bureau (2013) " Beijing Shi Renmin Zhengfu Bangongding Guanyu Yinfa Beijing Shi 2013-2017 Nian Qinjie Kongqi Xingdong Jihua Zhongdian Renwu Fenjie De Tongzhi 北京市人民政府办公厅关于印发北京市2013-2017年清洁空气行动计划重点任务分解的通知 [Notification of Beijing Municipal People's Government on the issuance of Beijing 2013 - 2017 Clean Air Action Plan] [Online: web] Accessed January 22, 2015 http://zhengwu.beijing.gov.cn/gzdt/gggs/t1322955.htm

*China Academy of Social Sciences 2008 *The China Economy Yearbook Volume 1* CASS Beijing ISSN 1872-7220

*China Statistical Yearbook 2014 [Online: web] Accessed January 22, 2015 http://www.stats.gov.cn/tjsj/ndsj/2014/indexee.htm

China Energy Viewpoint. 2012a. "ERI: Make NEA an Energy Ministry Focusing on Demand Side and Fossil Fuels." [Online: web.] Accessed: December 8, 2012. http://www.sandholts.dk/?p=256

China Energy Viewpoint 2012b. "Shale gas in China-Upsides and Downsides" [Online:web] Accessed: May 15, 2015 Url http://www.chinaenergyviewpoint.com/?p=76

China Energy Viewpoint. 2012c. "Denmark 2012: 30% Wind power and no Curtailment at all—How is it Possible?" [Online: web.] Accessed: December 8, 2012. Url. http://www.sandholts.dk/?p=321

*China Vitae [Online: web] Accessed: May 15, 2013 http://www.chinavitae.com/search/main.php

Churchill, Anthony. 1993. "The Developing World: The New Energy Consumer." [Online: web.] Accessed: March 3, 2013. http://archive.unu.edu/unupress/unupbooks/uu17ee/uu17ee0j.htm

Chen, Chengzhong and Lin Zhenshan. 2008. "Multiple Timescale Analysis and Factor Analysis of Energy Ecological Footprint Growth in China 1953-2006." *Energy Policy* 36 (5):.1666-1678.

Cai, Weiying. May 2007. *Kechixu Yueshu Xia De Jingji Fazhan Yu Nengyuan Xietiaoxing Fenxi- Yi Jilin Sheng Weili* 可持续约束下的经济发展与能源协调性分析-以吉林省为例 *[The Coordination Analysis of Economy Development and Energy Consumption under Sustainable Restriction: A case study in Jilin Province]*, Master's Dissertation, Dongbei Shifan Daxue [Northeast Normal University].

Chen, Nicholas. 2008. "China's Energy Market: Overview and Opportunities." *Terralex Energy Practice Group.*

"China's Electricity Production by Source." [Online: web.] Accessed: February 25, 2013. The EIA. http://www.eia.doe.gov/emeu/international/electricitygeneration.html

China Briefing. 2011. *An Overview of China's Renewable Energy Market.* [Online: Web.] Accessed: February 22, 2013. http://www.china-briefing.com/news/2011/06/16/an-overview-of-chinas-renewable-energy-market.html

Cherp, Aleh and Jessica Jewel. 2011. "The Three Perspectives on Energy Security: Intellectual History, Disciplinary Roots and Potential for Integration." [Online: web.] Accessed: October 5, 2012. www.sciencedirect.com

Chen Wei, Gao He, Bai Jianhua and Wang Di December 2011. "Gaige Kaifang Yilai Wo Guo Nengyuan Gongxu Qingkuang De Yanbian Licheng Fenxi 改革开放以来我国 能源供需情况的演变历程分析[Evolution Course of China's Energy Supply and Demand since Reform and Opening Up]" *Nengyuan Jishu Jingji* 能源技术经济 *Energy Technology and Economics* 23(12):.39-44.

China Climate Change Info-Net. [Online: web.] Accessed: December 20, 2012 http://en.ccchina.gov.cn/

Conserve Energy Future. n.a. "Who Uses Energy." [Online: web.] Accessed: March 3, 2013. http://www.conserve-energy-future.com/EnergyConsumption.php

China FAQ's World Resources Institute (2011) "China's Energy Conservation Accomplishments of the 11th Five Year Plan" *China FAQ's The Network for Climate and Energy Information* 1-3

Correspondent Report. February 2012. "Bei da Huang Jituan Yao Jinkuai Shixian Zhuanxing—Hu Angang Jiaoshu Fangtan lu 北大荒集团要尽快实现转型-胡鞍钢教授访谈录 [Beida Huang Group Needs a Real and Rapid Transformation—An Interview with Professor Hu Angang] *Nongchang Jingji Guanli* 农场经济管

理 ： 16-23.

*Corporate Social Responsibility Report 2013 China Datang Corporation [Online: web.] Accessed: March 3, 2015. http://www.china-cdt.com/dtwz/UserFiles/File/201411/20141114085751867.pdf

*Corporate Social Responsibility Report 2008 China Datang Corporation [Online: web.] Accessed: March 3, 2015. http://www.china-cdt.com/dtwz/UserFiles/Flash/201409/2008socialresponsibility-e.pdf

Crompton, Paul and Yanrui Wu. January 2005. "Energy Consumption in China: Past Trends and Future Directions." *Energy Economics* 27(1)-1-20.

Cui, Herui and Di Wang. April 2010. "Jiyu Huise Guanlian Lilun de Zhongguo Nengyuan Xuqiu Yingxiang Yinsu Yanjiu 基于灰色的 关联理论的中国能源需求影响因素研究 [The Study on China's Energy Demand Factors Based on Grey Relational Theory]" *Dianli Xuebao*电力学报 *Journal of Electric Power* 25(2): 107-10.

China Daily (2012) "China Aware of Energy Challenges" [Online: Web.] Accessed: December 8, 2012 http://nsa.chinadaily.com.cn/business/2012-10/24/content-15840930.htm

*CNPC Website (2012) "CNPC and China Guodian Corporation Sign Strategic Cooperation" [Online: web.] Accessed: March 3, 2013. http://www.cnpc.com.cn/en/nr2012/201211/cd52e9300aa8472dabc7eb62846ffe23.shtml

China Energy Report. 2012.Enerdata Energy Research Estore . [Online: web.] Accessed: February 22, 2013. https://estore.enerdata.net/energy-market/china-energy-report-and-data.html

*China Energy Fund Committee (2015) "CEFC China Energy Focus 2014: Towards Clean Coal" Online: Web] Accessed: June 2, 2015 www.cefc.org.hk

**Database of China's Laws and Regulations* (Year Unavailable) Law of the People's Republic of China on Energy Conservation: Section on Economic Laws . [Online: web.] Accessed: March 3, 2015 http://www.npc.gov.cn/englishnpc/Law/Frameset-index.html

Downs, Erica. December 2006. *Grappling with Rapid Energy Demand Growth.* The Brookings Foreign Policy Studies Energy Security Series: China. 1-69[Online: web.] Accessed: May 31, 2012 http://www.brookings.edu/~/media/research/files/reports/2006/12/china/12china.pdf

Downs, Erica. 2008. "China's New Energy Administration." The Brookings Institution: 42-45. Online: web.] Accessed: March 3, 2013 www.chinabusinessreview.com

Downs Erica 2004 "China's Energy Security" *Princeton University*

*Eds. Dangdai Zhongguo当代中国[Contemporary China]. 1988. *Dangdai Zhongguo De Shiyou Gongye* 当代中国的石油工业*[Contemporary China's Oil Industry],* Beijing: Dangdai Shehui Kexue 当代社会科学 [Contemporary Scientific Society].

*Eds. Dangdai Zhongguo当代中国 [Contemporary China]. 2008. *Dangdai Zhongguo De Shiyou Gongye* 当代中国的石油工业 *[Contemporary China's Oil Industry].* Beijing: Dangdai Shehui Kexue 当代社会科学 [Contemporary Scientific Society].

*Eighth National Congress of the Communist Party of China (CPC), 1956. [Online: Web.] Accessed: December 8, 2012. http://www.chinatoday.com/org/cpc/cpc_8th_congress_standing_polibureau.htm

*Energy Information Administration 2014. [Online: Web] Accessed December 22, 2014. http://www.eia.gov/beta/international/analysis.cfm?iso=CHN

Fan, Yunfang. August 2006. "Youjia Shangzhang Dui Shijie Jingji De Yingxiang Ji Zhongguo Nengyuan Zhengce Xuanze 油价上涨对世界经济及中国能源政策选择 [The World Economy Affected by Rising of Oil Price and China Energy Source Policy Choice]. *Xi'an Caijing Xueyuan Xuebao* 西安财经学院学报 [Journal of Xi'an Institute of Finance and Economics] 19(4): 77-82.

Fang, Lifeng. February 2013. *The Myth of China's Endless Coal Demand—A Missing Market for US Exports*. USA: Greenpeace.

Fu, Rongde. Interviewed by Zhao Anying. December 2004. "Zhongguo Nengyuan: Tiaozhan Yu Jiyu Bingcun" 中国能源挑战与机遇并存 [An Analysis of China's Energy Policies: Opportunities and Challenges] *Caijing Jie* 财经界 *[Money China]*: 30-31.

Gangadar, Divya. December 2012. "China's Energy Insecurity: Challenges in the Twenty-first Century." *Mainstream* L (51).

Guo Sizhi (2007) "The Business Development of China's NOC's : The Government to Business Relationship in China" *James Baker III Institute for Public Policy Rice University*

Hongpo Shen. October 25, 2012. "China Issues White Paper on Energy Policy." [Online: web.] Accessed: December 20, 2012. http://proedgewire.com/green energyintel/china-issues-white-paper-on-energy-policy//

Hu, Junchao and Liu Xue December 2012. "Zhongguo Nengyuan Zhengce Zhanxian Si Da Liangdian 中国能源政策展现四大亮点 [The Four Main Points of Development of China's Energy Policies]. *Xin Shidian* 新视点 *New Viewpoint*: 16-19.

Hyung Kwon Jeon and Seong-Suk Yoon. 2006. "From International Linkages to Internal Divisions in China: The Political Response to Climate Change Negotiations." *Asian Survey* 46 (6): 846-66.

*Information Office of the State Council. February 1995. "China's White Paper on Energy Conservation and Energy Utilisation."1995:3-4

*Information Office of the State Council. October 2012 " China's Energy Policy 2012" *Embassy of People's Republic of China in the United States of America*

*Interim Report of China Datang Corporation 2011. [Online: web.] Accessed: February 22, 2013. http://www.dtxny.com.cn/en/UploadFiles_9185/201109/2011090717132463.pdf

*Interim Report of Petrochina Company Limited 2012. [Online: web.] Accessed: February 22, 2013. http://www.petrochina.com.cn/Resource/pdf/xwygg/2012interimreportEn.pdf?COLLCC=2181621560&

*International Energy Agency 2014 [Online: web] Accessed February 20, 2014 http://www.iea.org/

IEA Key World Energy Statistics 2014[Online: web] Accessed February 20, 2014 https://en.wikipedia.org/wiki/Electricity_sector_in_China

IHS EIATrack (2004) "Summary of China's Energy Regulations Governing Energy Efficiency Labeling" *Environmental Intelligence Analysis*

International Rivers (year unavailable) [Online: web] Accessed February 20, 2014 "China Guodian Corporation http://www.internationalrivers.org/campaigns/china-guodian-corporation

Jiang, Yejun. March 2008. *Kechixu Fazhan Shiyu Xia De Nengyuanshui Lifa Yanjiu* 可

持续发视域下的能源税 立法研究 *[A Research on China's Energy Tax Laws from the Perspective of Sustainable Development]*. Phd Thesis, Chongqing：Xi'nan Zhengfa Daxue 西南政法大学 [Southwest University of Political Science].

Ji, Jianjun. 2011. *Jinrong Weiji Xia Zhongguo Nengyuan Zhengce Xuanze Yanjiu* 金融危机下中国能源政策选择研究 *[A Research on Choices of China's Energy Policies during the Financial Crisis]*. Specialised Master's Dissertati Joanna on, Xi'an: Xibei Daxue [Northwest University].

Lewis Joanna March 2011. "Energy and Climate Goals of China's Twelfth Five Year Plan." *Center for Climate and Energy Solutions* [Online: web.] Accessed: December 21, 2012 http://www.c2es.org/international/key-country-policies/china/energy-climate-goals-twelfth-five-year-plan

Lan, Lan. 2012. "China to Resume Construction of Nuclear Plants." *China Daily*. USA: October 25, 2012. [Online: web.] Accessed: December 8, 2012. http://www.chinadaily.com.cn/china/2012-10/25/content_15844353.htm

Lee, Michelle Hung Wai. 2012. *Analysing the Influence of Major Actors in China's Renewable Energy Policy Processes as a Means of Predicting Future Renewable Energy Policy Trends*. Master's Thesis, Michigan: Michigan University.

Lester, Richard and Edward Steinfeld. 2007. "China's Real Energy Crisis." *Harvard Asia Pacific Review*: 35-38.

Leung, Guy. March 2011. "China's Energy Security: Perceptions and Reality." *Energy Policy* 39(3): 1330-1337.

Lewis, Steven. March 2007. "Chinese NOC's and World Energy Markets: CNPC, Sinopec and CNOOC." *James A Baker III Institute for Public Policy Rice University.*:1-79

Li, Chunmei. December 2003. "Ruhe Yingdui Zhongguo Nengyuan Zhengce Yuelaiyue Da De Guoji Yingxiang—Fang BP—Zhongguo Youxian Gongsi Chen Xinhua Boshi 如何应对中国能源政策越来越大的国际影响-访BP – 中国有限公司陈新华博士 [How to handle the increasing international influence on China's Energy Policies—An Interview of Dr. Chen Xinhua from BP- China Limited Company.

Li, Rugan. 'Qi Wu 'Qijian Beijing Shi Jieneng Gongzuo Chengji Xianzhu七五期间北京市节能工作成绩显著[The Remarkable Results of Conservation Efforts in Beijing During the Seventh Five Year Plan], 11-12.

Li, Xinlei. 2012. "Green Evidence for Energy Security Transformation in China: Reconceptualisation of China's Energy Policy and its Implications to China's Renewable Energy Policy Change." Paper Presented at Berlin Conference 2012, *Berlin Conference on the Human Dimensions of Global Environmental Change—Evidence for Sustainable Development.*

Lieberthal, K. and M. Oksenberg. 1988. *Policy Making in China Leaders, Structures, and Processes* Princeton. NJ: Princeton University Press.

Lin, Jenny. 2012. "China's Energy Security Dilemma." *Project 2049*: 1-12.

Ling Haoshu, Xie Jingchao, Yangwei, Wang Jieteng and Zhueryu 2010. "Beijing Shicheng Zhen Shenghuo Fangshi De Huanjing Yu Nengyuan Diaocha Fenxi 北京市城镇生活方式的环境与能源调查分析 [Investigation and Analysis into the Indoor Environment and Energy Concerning Beijing Lifestyle]." *Zhongguo Renkou Ziyuan yu Huanjing* 中国人口资源与环境 *[China Population, Resources and Environment]* 20 (12): 35-39.

Lin Shi. 2005. "Electricity Agency Lacks Power." *China Daily*. [Online: web.] Accessed: March 23, 2013. http://www.chinadaily.com.cn/english/doc/2005-03/06/content_422145.htm

Liu Yixin February 2007. "Ke Zaisheng Nengyuan Liyong Qianjing Guangkuo 可再生能源利用前景广阔 [The Expanding Future of Utilisation of Renewable Energy Resources]. *Zhongguo Tongji* 中国统计 *China Statistics*: 47-48.

Liu, Jiejiao. June 2003. "Cong Zhanlue Shijiao Bawo Zhongguo De Nengyuan Jiegou Tiaozheng 从战略视角把握中国的能源结构调整 [Analysing Adjustments in China's Energy Structure from a Strategic Perspective]." *Zhongguo Nengyuan*中国能源 *China Energy* 25(6): 17-23.

Liu Zhiyan, San Feng and Long Xiaobai 2008. *Chinese Perspectives on Energy and Climate Security: A Study Commissioned by Chinese Academy of Social Sciences Urban Development and Environment Research Centre.* London: Chatham House.

Lu Yinzhong. "Cong Wo Guo Nengyuan Xuqiu Yuce Kan Nengyuan Zhanlue Shang De Ji Ge Wenti."从我国能源需求预测看能源战略上的几个问题 [A Few Questions About China's Energy Strategy From The Estimates of China's Energy Needs]." 30-34.

*Ma Kai (2006) "The 11th Five Year Plan: Targets, Paths and Policy Orientation" *National Development and Reforms Commission (NDRC) People's Republic of China*

Mathews, John and Tan Hao. 2012. "China's Industrial Energy Revolution: Renewable Targets Become Even More Demanding." *The Asia Pacific Journal* 10 (52).

Men, Kepei. January 1996. "'Jiu Wu' Zhongguo Nengyuan Xingshi Fenxi Yu Yuci 九五中国能源形势分析与预测[Analysis and Predictions Concerning China's Energy Situation During the Ninth Five Year Plan]." *Guoji Shiyou Jingji* 国际石油经济 *(International Petroleum Economics)* 4 (1): 16-18.

M. Diana. 2011. "5 Strategies to Make Sure Your Energy Related Organisation gets Taken Seriously." *Energy in Asia.* [Online: web.] Accessed: March 10, 2013. http://energyinasiablog.com/2011/11/16/5-strategies-to-make-sure-your-energy-related-organization-gets-taken-seriously/

Modern Chinese Dictionary. Xiandai Hanyu Cidian 现代汉语词典 1992. *Beijing: Commercial Press.*

Major Lee, Stacey. 2010. *China's Energy Security: The Grand Hedging Strategy.* KS: School of Advanced Military Studies.

Mao, Yaqing. "China Issues White Paper on Energy Conservation." [Online: web.] Accessed: December 20, 2012. http://english.cri.cn/7146/2012/10/25/2702s728964.htm

Mo, Bei. "Ju Guo Tizhi" Zhangxian Nengyuan Zhi Zhong 举国体制彰显能源之中, *Shiyou Fengxiang Biao* 石油风向标 *[Petroleum Vane].*

National Academy of Engineering, National Research Council and Chinese Academy of Sciences 2010 *The Power of Renewables:Opportunities and Challenges for China and the United States* National Academic Press ISBN- 13-978-0-309-16000-1

Oxford Dictionary. 1992. London: Oxford University Press.

Pang Jun, Hu Tao, Guo Hongyan and Cao Chunmiao March 2011. "'Shi er Wu' Wo Guo Luse Maoyi Zhuanxing Fang'an Yanjiu 十二五我国绿色贸易转型方案研究 [Study on China's Green Trade Transformation Scenarios for Twelfth Five Year Plan]. *Huanjing Yu Kechixu Fazhan* 环境与可持续发展*[Environment and Sustainable Development]* 3: 25-30.

*People's Republic of China, Information Office of the State Council. November 2011.

China's Policies and Actions for Addressing Climate Change. [Online: web.] Accessed: December 29, 2012. http://www.gov.cn/english/official/2011-11/22/content_2000272.htm

*People's Republic of China, Information Office of the State Council. October 2012. *China's Energy Policy 2012.* [Online: web.] Accessed: December 28, 2012: http://www.gov.cn/english/official/2012-10/24/content_2250497.htm

Qiu, Xin and Honglin Li. 2012. "Energy Regulation and Legislation in China." Environmental Law Institute. 42: 10678-10691.

Rosen, Daniel and Trevor Houser. 2007a. *China Energy—A Guide for the Perplexed.* Peterson Institute for International Economics.

Rosen, Daniel and Trevor Houser. 2007b *What Drives China's Demand for Energy*-25:54 [Online: web.] Accessed: December 28, 2012 http://csis.org/files/media/csis/pubs/090212_02what_drives_china_demand.pdf

Sandklef Kirstina 2004. *Energy in China : Coping with Increasing Demand* 2-44 [Online: web.] Accessed: August 27, 2015 http://www.iaea.org/inis/collection/NCLCollectionStore/_Public/36/045/36045273.pdf

Sascha Muller-Kraenner. 2008. "China and India's Emerging Energy Foreign Policy." German Development Institute.

Shao, Yankathy. March 2011. *Variance in Environmental Policy Implementation in China: A Study of Energy Efficiency and Air Pollution Policies across China's Provinces from 2001-2008.* Senior Honours Thesis. San Diego: University of California.

Sinton J E, M.D. Levine and Q.Y.Wang 1998. "Energy Efficiency in China: Accomplishments and Challenges." *Energy Policy* 26(11): 813-29.

Shi Dan. 2000. "Zhongguo Nengyuan Zhengce Huigu Yu Weilai De Zhengce Quxiang 中国能源政策回顾与未来的政策取向 [The Past and Future Directions of China's Energy Policies] *Jingji Yanjiu Cankao* 经济研究参考 *[Journal on Economic Research]* 20: 20-26.

Shi Dinghuan (n.a) "China's Tenth Five Year Plan on the Renewable Energy Research and Development" *Department of High and New Technology and Industrialization Ministry of Science and Technology China*[Online: web] Accessed February 22, 2013 http://frankhaugwitz.com/doks/general/2000_08_06_China_RE_10_Five_Year_Plan_MOST.pdf

Solidiance Report. January 2013. *China's Renewable Energy Sector: An Overview of Key Growth Sectors*. [Online: web] Accessed February 22, 2013 www.solidiance.com/whitepaper/chins.renewable pdf

Song, Feng and Xinye Zheng. 2012. "What Drives the Change in China's Energy Intensity: Combining Decomposition Analysis and Econometric Analysis at the Provincial Level." *Energy Policy* 51: 445-53.

*Sustainable Development Report Sinopec (2011) [Online: web] Accessed February 22, 2013 www.english.sinopec.com/environment_society/4en.pdf

*Sustainability Report PetroChina Company Limited (2013) [Online: web] Accessed April 22, 2014 http://www.petrochina.com.cn/petrochina/2013kcxfz/201404/846156ac266f438484e5b99851fa371f/files/cfff8238a42a45b5aaf03a3a4025c442.pdf

*Sustainability Report China National Offshore Oil Corporation (2013) [Online: web] Accessed April 22, 2014 http://www.cnooc.com.cn/data/upload/2013qzls_en.pdf

*Sustainability Report China National Offshore Oil Corporation. 2011 [Online: web.] Accessed: February 22, 2013. http://en.cnooc.com.cn/data/upload/2011reporten.pdf

*Sustainability Report PetroChina Company Limited 2010. [Online: web.] Accessed: February 22, 2013. http://www.petrochina.com.cn/Resource/pdf/xwygg/PetroChina2010SustainabilityReport.pdf

*Sustainability Report PetroChina Company Limited 2011 [Online: web.] Accessed: February 22, 2013. http://www.petrochina.com.cn/Resource/pdf/kcxbg-en/PetroChina2011SustainabilityReport.pdf

Swartz, Spencer and Shai Oster. 2010. "China Tops US in Energy Use." *The Wall Street Journal,* July 18, 2010. [Online: web.] Accessed: March 5, 2013. http://online.wsj.com/article/SB10001424052748703720504575376712353150310.html?mod=googlenews_wsj

Tao, Ye and Huifeng Xue. December 2008. "Bianji Chengben Yueshu Xia De Nengyuan Caishui Jui'ce Moxing 边际成本约束下的能源财税决策模型 [The Energy Tax Policy Decision Making Model Based on Marginal Cost Constraint]." *Xitong Gongcheng* 系统工程 *Systems Engineering* 26 (12): 14-19.

Tan, Baiping and Zhenzhong Huang. August 2010. "Lun Wo Guo de Nengyuanfa de Si xiang Jiben Yuanze 论我国的能源法的四项基本原则 [A Discussion About The Four Principles of China's Energy Law]." *Zhongwai Nengyuan* 中外能源 *[Sino-Global Energy]* 15 (8): 1-6.

The Free Dictionary n.a "Policy" [Online: web.] Accessed: March 5, 2013. http://www.thefreedictionary.com/policy

The National Development and Reform Commission 2012 "China's Policies and Actions for Addressing Climate Change" [Online: web.] Accessed: March 5, 2015. http://www.ccchina.gov.cn/WebSite/CCChina/UpFile/File1324.pdf

Tian, Haijun and Liying Wu. March 2005. "Shijie Ziyuan Zhanlue Dui Zhongguo Nengyuan Chanye Jiegou Tiaozheng Qishi 世界资源战略对中国能源产业结构调整其实 [The Enlightenment of International Energy Strategy towards the Adjustment of China's Energy Production Structure]."*Yinshan Xue Kan* 银山学刊 *Yinshan Academic Journal,* 19 (1): 59-61.

Tong, Yuanchun. 2008. "Neng Yuan Fa Jian Yan 能源法检验[A Preface to China's Energy Law]."*Jinri Zhongguo Luntan* 今日中国论坛 [China Today Forum] : 100.

Wang Yanxing, Wang Heibo and Fan Liuyan September 2012. "Zhongguo Nengyuan Zhengce de Yanbian Ji Qushi 中国能源政策的演变及趋势 [The Evolution and Trends of China's Energy Policies]." *Lilun Xuekan* 理论学刊 *[Theory Journal]* 9 (223): 70-73.

Wang, Jian. 2012. "China's Energy Consumption and the Idea of an Energy Efficient Society." *Chinascope.* [Online: web.] Accessed: May 23, 2012. http://chinascope.org/main/content/view/388/148/

Wang, Zhengxu and Yongnian Zheng. November 2007. "Key Policy Outcomes of the 17th National Congress of the Chinese Communist Party." China Policy Institute, the University of Nottingham Briefing Series 31:1-10.

Wang Xiaozong.(2011) "Zhongguo Zhanlue Shiyou Chubei 中国战略石油储备[China's Strategic Petroleum Reserves]." *Zhongguo Jingji Baokan* 中国经济报刊 *China Economic Weekly.40-42*

Wang, Junsong and Canfei He. 2009. "Jishu Jinbu, Jiegou Biandong Yu Zhongguo Nengyuan Liyong Xiaolue 技术进步结构变动与中国能源利用效率 [Technological Change, Structural Change and Chinese Energy Consumption

Efficiency].” *Zhongguo Renkou, Ziyuan Yu Huanjing*中国人口资源与环境 *[China Population, Resources and Environment]* 19 (2):157-61.

Wang, Qingyi. “Zhongguo Xuyao Changqi Wending de Nengyuan Zhengce 中国需要长期稳定的能源政策 [China Needs a Long-term Stable Energy Policy].” 25-29.

Warshaw Todd (2013) “The Myth of China’s Endless Coal Demand: A Missing Market for U.S Exports” *Greenpeace Report*

Watts, Jonathan. 2010. “China Overtakes US as World’s Biggest Energy Consumer.” *The Guardian.* August 3, 2010. [Online: web.] Accessed: March 13, 2013. http://www.guardian.co.uk/environment/2010/aug/03/china-overtakes-us-energy-consumer

Wee, Keanfong. November 5, 2012. “China’s Latest Energy Consumption Data Reveals New Challenges and Opportunities.” *China FAQs the Network for Climate and Energy Information* [Online: web.] Accessed: December 21, 2012. http://www/Chinafaqs.org/..../chinas-latest-energy-consumption-data-reveals-new-opportunities-and-challenges-0

Wei, Weixian. July 2009. “Jiyu CGE Moxing De Zhongguo Nengyuan Huanjing Zhengce Fenxi 基于CGE 模型的中国能源环境政策分析 [An Analysis of China’s Energy and Environment Policies Based on CGE Model].” *Tongji Yanjiu* 统计研究 *[Stastical Research]* 26 (7): 3-12.

Wei, Zhihong. 2004. “Economic Development and Energy Issues in China.” Working Paper prepared for 1st KEIO-UNU-JFIR Panel Meeting on February 13-14, 2004 at The 21st Century Centre of Excellence Program Economics Development and Human Security, Tokyo.

*Website of SASAC (2003) State Owned Assets Supervision and Administration Commission of State Council (2003) www.en.sasac.gov.cn/n1461859/c1463753/content.html

*Website of China Shenhua *Business Overview* [Online: web.] Accessed: March 13, 2013. http://www.shenhuachina.com/cs/sh_china_en/index.html

*Website of China Datang Corporation [Online: web.] Accessed: March 13, 2013 http://www.cccme.org.cn/shop/cccme8991/index.aspx

*Website of China Huadian Corporation [Online: web.] Accessed: March 13, 2013 http://eng.chd.com.cn/channel.do?cmd=show&id=500

*Website of China Power Investment Corporation [Online: web.] Accessed: March 14, 2013 http://eng.cpicorp.com.cn/AboutUs/cp/201406/t20140609_233973.htm

*Website of China Huaneng Company Overview [Online: web.] Accessed: March 14, 2013 http://www.chng.com.cn/eng/n75861/n75925/index.html

*Website of China Guodian Corporation [Online: web.] Accessed: August 14, 2015 http://www.cgdc.com.cn/corporate.jhtml

*White Paper on Energy (2007) “China’s Energy Conditions and Policies” [Online: web.] Accessed: March 13, 2013. www.china.org.cn/english/environment/236955.htm#5

Woetzel, Jonathan. 2003. *Capitalist China: Strategies for a Revolutionized Economy.* McKinsey & Company. ISBN-13: 978-0470821084.

Wu, Yanrui. 2011. “Energy Intensity and Its Determinants in China’s Regional Economies” forthcoming in *Energy Policy:* 1-32.

Wu, Qi and Wu Chunyou. February 2009. “Jiyu DEA de Nengyuan Xiaolue Pingjia Moxing Yanjiu 基于DEA 的能源效率评价模型研究 [Research on Evaluation Model of Energy Efficiency Based on DEA].” *Guanli Kexue* 管理科学 *[Journal of Management Sciences]* 22 (1):103-12.

Wu, Kang and Binsheng Li. 1995. “Energy Development in China: National Policies and Regional Strategies.” *Energy Policy* 23(2):167-78.

Xiao, Guoxing. November 2010. "(Nengyuan fa) yu Nengyuan Falue Zhidu Jiegou 能源法 与能源法律制度结构 [Energy Laws and the Legal Structure of the Energy Laws]." *Zhongzhou Xuekan* sim

[Academic Journal of Zhongzhou] 6 (180): 78-84.

Xia, Lihong. November 2012. "Duo Yuanhua De Nengyuan Gongying Baozhang Guojia Nengyuan Anquan—Nengyuan Zhuanjia Ceng Xingqiu Tan Zhongguo Nengyuan Zhengce 2012 Baipi Shu 多元 的能源供应保障国家能源安全---- 能源专家曾兴球 谈中国能源政策2012 白皮书 [Diversify Energy Supply to Ensure National Energy Security—An Interview of Energy Expert Ceng Xingqiu on the White Paper on China's Energy Policy 2012]." *Shidian* 视点 *Viewpoint* :.1-5.

Xie, Xina. 2010. "Chinese Oil Companies Taking Advantage of Energy Consumers." *Energy Tribune.* May 25, 2010.

*Xinhua Network. October 24, 2012. "China Issues White Paper on Energy Policy." [Online: web.] Accessed: December 21, 2012. http://news.xinhuanet.com/english/china/2012-10/24/c_131927587.htm

*Xinhua Network. October 25, 2012. "China's Aware of Domestic Energy Challenges, Tackles Them: Official." [Online: web.] Accessed: December 21, 2012. http://www.fmcoprc.gov.hk/eng/xwdt/jzzh/t982043.htm

*Xinhua. 2012. "China Emphasizes Energy Conservation: White Paper." *China Daily.* Beijing: October 24, 2012. [Online: Web.] Accessed: December 8, 2012. http://www.chinadaily.com.cn/bizchina/2012-10/24/content_15843577.htm

*Xinhua. 2012. "China Strives to Develop New Renewable Energy: White Paper." *China Daily.* Beijing: October 24, 2012. [Online: Web.] Accessed: December 8, 2012. http://www.chinadaily.com.cn/business/2012-10/24/content_15843598.htm

*Xinhua 2007 "China Sets Up Oil Reserve Center" December 18, 2007 [Online: Web.] Accessed: December 8, 2012 http://lr.chineseembassy.org/eng/majorevents/t391173.htm

Xu, Shoubo. July 2008. "Gaige Kaifang 30 Nian Zhongguo Nengyuan Fazhan Zhanlue De Biange 改革开放30年中国能源发展占率的变革 [On The Transformation of China's Energy Development Strategy in the Past 30 Years of Reform and Opening Up]." *Beijing Jiaotong Daxue Xuebao (Shehui Kexue Ban)*北京交通大学学报（社会科学版） *[Journal of Beijing Jiaotong University (Social Sciences Edition)* 7(3) : 8-14.

Xu Shaofeng and Chen Wenying (2005) "The Reform of Electricity Power Sector in the People's Republic of China *Energy Policy* 34 (2455-2465)

Yan Wenjuan, Guoju E and Gong Li 2009. "Cidai Weiji Yingxiang Xia Wo Guo Nengyuan Shengchan Taishi Yuce 次贷 危机影响下我国能源生产态势预测 [Chinese Energy Production Situation Forecasting Based On Sub- Prime Mortgage Loan Crisis]." *Zhongguo Renkou Ziyuan Yu Huanjing* 中国人口资源与环境 *[China Population, Resources and Environment]* 19(2): 7-12.

Yang, Yuanhua. 2005. "Gao youjia Dui Shijie He Zhongguo Jingji Yingxiang You Duo Da 高油价对世界和中国经济影响有多大 [How Much is the Effect of Petrol Price Rise on the World and the Chinese Economy]." *Quanju* 全局 *Outlook*: 26-28.

Yang, Zhanshou and Qu Weiguo. 2009. "Youhua Zhongguo Nengyuan Jiegou de Zhengce Yanjiu 优化中国能源结构的政策研究 [Policy Research on Energy Mix Optimisation in China] *Zhongguo Fazhan* 中国发展 *China Development* 9(2): 24-27.

Yi Mingwei, Hua Liao and Ying Fan . 2007. "Shi yi Wu Qijian Wo Guo Nengyuan Xuqiu ji Jieneng Qianli Yuce 十一五期间我国能源需求及节能潜力预测 [China's Energy Demand and Conservation Potential Forecast During the 11th Five Year Plan Period] *Zhanlue Yu Juece Yanjiu* 战略与决策研究 *Strategy and Policy Decision Research* 22(1): 20-25.

Yin, Yue and Wu Changhua. (Year unavailable). "Zhongguo Nengyuan Zhengce Ji Touzi Shichang Fenxi 中国能源 政策及投资市场分析 [Energy Strategy and Investment Market in China]." *World Environment* : 26-29.

Yu, Bao and Gordon Houlden. February 2013. "The Evolution of China's Energy Institutions: Centralisation versus Decentralisation." *China Institute Ocassional Paper Series* 1(1): 3-19.

Yu, Xiaojiang. 2010. "An Overview of Legislative and Institutional Approaches to China's Energy Development." *Energy Policy* 38: 2161-2167.

Zhang Guofeng. 2009. " Low Carbon Economy 低碳经济" 聚焦决策者*[Jujiao Juece zhe Focus]* 8:01-4

Zemin, Jiang. March 2008. "Dui Zhongguo Nengyuan Wenti De Sikao 对中国能源问题的思考 [Reflections On Energy Issues In China]." *Shanghai Jiaotong Daxue Xuebao* 上海交通大学学报 *[Journal of Shanghai Jiaotong University]* 42(3): 345-59.

Zhao, Fang. 2008. *Jiyu 3E Xietiao de Nengyuan Fazhan Zhengce Yanjiu* 基于 *3E* 协调的能源发展政策研究 *[Research on Energy Development Policies on the Basis of 3E Harmony]*. Phd Thesis, Haiyang: Zhongnan Haiyang Daxue.

Zhao, Jimin. 2001. "Reform of China's Energy Institutions and Policies: Historical Evolution and Current Challenges." BCSIA Discussion Paper 2001-20, Energy Technology Innovation Project, Kennedy School of Government, Harvard University.

Zhao, Nan. 2009. "Beijing Deng Si Zhixiashi Nengyuan Liyong Xiaoguo De Duibi Fenxi 北京等四直辖市能源利用效果的对比分析 [Comparative Analysis on Energy Efficiency of China's Four Main Municipalities]." *Chengshi Fazhan Yanjiu* 城市发展研究 *[Urban Studies]* 16 (1):114-19.

Zhao, Suisheng. "China's Global Search for Energy Security: Cooperation and Conflict." [Online: web.] Accessed: March 3, 2013. www.japanfocus.org/-Suisheng-Zhao/2978

Zhongguo Shehui Kexueyuan Shuliang Jingji yu Jishu Jingji Yanjiusuo Ketizu Guojia Nengyuan Zhengce De Xingcheng Gongcheng 中国社会科学院数量经济与技术经济研究所课题组国家能源政策的形成工程 [Economics Department of China's Academy of Social Sciences] (2006) *Jingji Yanjiu Cankao* 经济研究参考 *[Journal on Economic Research]*: 36.

Zhongguo Kechixu Nengyuan Xiangmu 中国可愁绪能源项目[The China Sustainable Energy Programme] [Online: web.] Accessed: Decemeber 21, 2012 http://www.efchina.org/Front-Page-zh

Zhou, Li. June 2009. "*Kaifang Jingji Yu Jieneng Jianpai De Xietiao Jizhi* 开放经济与节能减排的协调机制 *[Coordinated Path of Open Economy, Energy Saving and Pollution Reduction]*. Phd Thesis, Nanjing: Nanjing Agricultural University.

Zhou, Hongchun. 2012. "Dui Ditan Beijing Xia Zhongguo Nengyuan Zhanlue de Ruogan Sikao 对低碳背景下中国能源战略的若干思考 [Analysing China's Energy Strategy against the Backdrop of Low Carbon Economy]." *Zhuanjia Luntan* 专家论坛 *Expert Forum* 34(5): 5-12.